Citroen GS Owners Workshop Manual

by J H Haynes
Member of the Guild of Motoring Writers
and B. Gilmour

Models covered:
All models fitted with the 1015 cc or
1222 cc engine from 1971 to 1976

ISBN 0 85696 290 2

© Haynes Publishing Group 1977

ABCDE 290
FGHIJ
KLMNO
PQRS

Printed in England

HAYNES PUBLISHING GROUP
SPARKFORD YEOVIL SOMERSET ENGLAND
distributed in the USA by
HAYNES PUBLICATIONS INC
861 LAWRENCE DRIVE
NEWBURY PARK
CALIFORNIA 91320
USA

Acknowledgements

Thanks are due to the Societe Anonyme Automobiles Citroen of France for the supply of technical information and certain illustrations. Castrol Limited provided lubrication data.

Car Mechanics magazine supplied many of the photographs used in the bodywork repair sequence of Chapter 12.

Lastly, thanks to all those people at Sparkford who helped in the production of this manual. Particularly, Brian Horsfall and Les Brazier who carried out the mechanical work and took the photographs respectively; Ted Frenchum who planned the layout of each page and the editor Rod Grainger.

Introduction to the Citroen GS

The Citroen GS was first introduced in the UK in 1971 with the GS Confort, powered by a 1055 cc engine. Since then additional models, with a larger 1220 cc engine, have been added to the range.

The design gives maximum space and safety in conjunction with good appearance and smooth aerodynamics, always a feature of Citroen design.

From the outside it has the looks of a medium sized (rather than small) car.

A feature of the car is the use of the well established Citroen self-levelling, hydro-pneumatic independant suspension previously only available on the larger Citroen models. The suspension height can be adjusted manually to increase the ground clearance when driving over rough ground. A 4-speed manual transmission is fitted as standard with a 3-speed semi-automatic transmission as optional equipment.

About this manual

The aim of this manual is to assist those owners of a GS Citroen who are the do-it-yourself type of motorist interested in carrying out the servicing and repairs necessary to get the best out of their car. By doing the work themselves they will have the satisfaction of knowing the servicing has been properly carried out, thus saving in running costs, and at the same time be able to spot minor faults and correct them before they develop into serious defects necessitating major repairs of an expensive nature.

Throughout the manual there are photographs and illustrations showing the layout and functions of the various systems and components accompanied by a description of the step-by-step sequence of the operations. These should enable the amateur mechanic to cope with tasks which he would otherwise consider too complicated to undertake.

The operations described assume that a good basic toolkit is available. The Manufacturers call up a large number of special tools, but in most cases the work can be done without them by improvising suitable equipment, in these instances the method is described. Where special tools are essential to carry out the job their use is detailed, and the Citroen part number quoted. Because of the cost and limited use of special tools you may find it more economic to let your Citroen agent carry out the tasks requiring special equipment.

Using the manual

The manual is divided into 12 Chapters. Each Chapter is divided into numbered Sections which are headed in **bold type** between horizontal lines. Each Section consists of serially numbered paragraphs. There are two types of illustrations, figures and photographs. The figures are numbered in sequence with decimal numbers, according to their position in the Chapter; eg, Fig. 1.3. is the third illustration in Chapter 1. All photographs apply to the Chapter in which they occur, so that the reference number in their caption indicates the Section and paragraph number to which they relate.

Use of cross-reference is made so that procedures, once described in the text, need not be repeated. Where cross-reference is made between Chapters the reference is given in Chapter number, Section number and, if necessary, paragraph number. Cross-references given without the word Chapter relate to a Section within the same Chapter.

When the left or right side of the car is mentioned it is as if one is seated in the driving seat, looking forward.

Whilst every care is taken to ensure that the information in this manual is correct, no liability can be accepted by the authors or publishers for loss, damage or injury caused by any errors in, or omissions from, the information given.

Contents

Note: *Specifications and general descriptions are given in each Chapter immediately after list of contents. When applicable 'Fault diagnosis' is given at the end of each appropriate Chapter.*

Citroen GS Saloon

Citroen GS Estate

Buying spare parts and vehicle identification numbers

Buying spare parts

Spare parts are available from many sources, for example: Citroen garages, other garages and accessory shops, and motor factors. Our advice regarding spare parts is as follows:

Officially appointed Citroen garages - This is the best source of parts which are peculiar to your car and otherwise not generally available (eg, complete cylinder heads, internal gearbox components, badges, interior trim etc). It is also the only place at which you should buy parts if your car is still under warranty; non-Citroen parts may invalidate the warranty. To be sure of obtaining the correct parts it will always be necessary to give the storeman your car's engine and chassis number, and if possible, to take the old part along for positive identification. Many parts are available under a factory exchange scheme - and parts returned should always be clean. It obviously makes good sense to go straight to the specialists on your car for this type of part for they are best equipped to supply you.

Other garages and accessory shops These are often very good places to buy material and components needed for the maintenance of your car (eg, oil filters, spark plugs, bulbs, fan belts, oils and grease, touch-up paint, filler paste etc). They also sell general accessories, usually have convenient opening hours, charge lower prices and can often be found not far from home.

Motor factors - Good factors stock all of the more important components which wear out relatively quickly (eg, clutch components, pistons and cylinders, valves, exhaust systems, brake pipes/seals and pads,

etc). Motor factors will often provide new or reconditioned components on a part exchange basis - this can save a considerable amount of money.

Vehicle identification numbers

Modifications are a continuing and unpublished process in vehicle manufacture quite apart from major model changes. Spare parts manuals and lists are compiled upon a numerical basis, the individual vehicle numbers being essential to correct indentification of the component required.

There are considerable specification differences between the models covered by this manual. Always use the correct Citroen model number when describing your car to a storeman.

The *vehicle manufacturer's plate* is located under the bonnet, on the right-hand side behind the L.H.M fluid reservoir. This plate has the following information on it:

Type of vehicle
Series
Chassis number
Gross vehicle weight (PTC)
Gross train weight (with trailer) (PTR)

The *engine plate* carries the make, engine type and engine number.

Manufacturer's plate

Engine plate location

Routine maintenance

Maintenance is essential for ensuring safety and desirable for the purpose of getting the best in terms of performance and economy from the car. Over the years the need for periodic lubrication has been greatly reduced if not totally eliminated. This has unfortunately tended to lead some owners to think that because no such action is required the items either no longer exist or will last forever. This is certainly not the case, it is essential to carry out regular visual examination as comprehensively as possible in order to spot any possible defects at an early stage before they develop into major and expensive repairs.

The maintenance information given in this Section is not of a detailed nature as the information required to carry out the necessary task is to be found in the appropriate Chapters throughout this manual.

Every 250 miles (400 km) or weekly - whichever comes first

Steering
Check the tyre pressures
Examine the tyres for wear or damage

Hydraulic system
Check the fluid level in the reservoir

Lights, wipers and horns
Do all the lights work at the front and rear?
Are the headlamp beams aligned properly?
Check the windscreen washer fluid level

Engine
Check the level of the oil, top-up if necessary
Check the level of the electrolyte in the battery and top-up the level as necessary

Every 3,000 miles (4,800 km)

Engine
Change the oil

Gearbox
Check the oil level and top-up if necessary

Doors, bonnet and boot lid
Lubricate hinges and locks

Handbrake
Check the operation and efficiency

Every 6,000 miles (10,000 km)

Engine
Clean the spark plugs and check the gap. Renew if necessary
Renew the oil filter cartridge
Air filter cartridge - clean and oil dip
Check operation of carburettor choke

Alternator
Check belt tension
Check terminals for tightness

Clutch
Check free-movement, adjust if necessary.

Hydraulic system
Clean the filter. Check the system visually for leaks.

Car height

Check the operation of the manual control

Brakes
Check the pad thickness of the front and rear brakes
Adjust the handbrake

Roadwheels
Tighten the wheel nuts

Every 12,000 miles (20,000 km)

Engine
Tighten the cylinder heads
Adjust the rocker clearances (cold)
Clean and adjust the carburettor
Renew the in-line fuel filter
Contact breaker - renew
Check the static timing of the distributor
Check tightness of inlet manifold clamp (early G10 engines)
Adjust the tension of the timing belts

Suspension
Lubricate the front and rear suspension ball joints
Check and adjust the car heights

Steering
Examine steering linkage for wear
Check wheel alignment

Gearbox
Change the oil
Renew the filter (torque converter only)

Every 24,000 miles (40,000 km)

Hydraulic system
Drain and refill with L.H.M fluid
Check all unions for tightness
Main accumulator - check the pressure rise

Engine
Renew the timing belts

Other aspects of Routine Maintenance

1 *Cleaning:* The best way to examine a car and know its general condition, is to clean it thoroughly, inside and out. One of the main results of this, not covered by other maintenance operations, is the finding of any traces of rust in the body panels. If rust is allowed to go unchecked it could affect some panels which may make the car unsafe and keep it off the road.

2 *Exhaust systems:* Although no periodic maintenance is prescribed for the exhaust system it must be checked regularly. The system must be secure and leakproof to keep the noise level to the minimum. Leaks can result in dangerous fumes entering the car interior and affecting the driver and passengers with disastrous consequences. Faults in the exhaust system can result in the vehicle being declared unfit for use.

3 *Safety;* When jacking-up the car always select a suitable strong point, chock a wheel on the opposite side, in front and behind. Never work under a car supported by the jack only, use axle stands or other reliable supports.

When towing the car use the two holes provided in the ends of the front frame crossmember. From the rear, do not attach hooks to the axle, but to the two holes provided on the bumper support, after opening the boot door.

Quick reference data

Capacities and settings

Engine crankcase	4 litre (7 Imp pints) engine dry
Gearbox (manual)	1, 4 litre (2.5 Imp pints)
Gearbox (semi-automatic):	
Dry	4 litre (7 Imp pints) converter included,
Oil change	1, 4 litre (2.5 Imp pints)
Hydraulic reservoir	3, 3 litre (5.8 Imp pints)
Spark plug gap	0, 65 to 0, 80 mm (0.026 to 0.032 in)
Contact breaker gap	0, 35 to 0, 45 mm (0.014 to 0.018 in)
Rocker clearance (cold)	0, 20 mm (0.008 in)
Petrol tank	43 litres (9.75 Imp gall)
Tyre pressures:	
Front	1.8 kg/sq cm (26 psi)
Rear	1.9 kg/sq cm (28 psi)

Wheel alignment

Front	0 to 2 mm (0 to 0.08 in)
Rear:	
To September 1973	4 mm (0.16 in) toe-in to 4 mm toe-out
From September 1973	0 to 2 mm (0 to 0.08 in) toe-in

Car height (normal road position)

Front	189 ± 10 mm (7.44 ± 0.4 in)
Rear	272 ± 10 mm (10.71 ± 0.4 in)

Voltage ... ...   12 volts

Lubrication chart

Component		Lubricant
1	Engine	Castrol GTX
2	Gearbox - without torque converter	Castrol Hypoy 80
	with torque converter	See Handbook
3	Hydraulic system	Green 'LHM' Fluid
4	Wheel bearings	Castrol LM Grease

The above are general recommendations only. Different territories require different lubricants. If in doubt consult your nearest Citroen dealer or the Driver's Handbook supplied with the car.

Torque wrench settings

Engine

	kg f m	lb f ft
Camshaft wheel stud	2,5 - 3	18 - 22
Camshaft bearings housing nuts	1,5 - 8	11 - 13
Oil strainer bolts	1,4	10
Oil cooler by-pass valve plug	4,5 - 5	32 - 36
Lubrication system plugs	3,5 - 4	25 - 29
Crankcase assembly nuts	3,4 - 4,5	24 - 32
	1,2 - 1,5	9 - 11
Oil pump retaining bolts	1,5 - 1,8	11 - 13
Cylinder head nuts	1,6 - 1,8	12 - 13
	2 - 2,5	15 - 17
Camshaft wheel nut	8,2	59
Tensioner roller nut	1,8	13
Rocker cover nut	0,8 - 1	6 - 7
Cylinder head oil pipe union	1,8 - 2	13 - 14
Oil pressure switch	6,4 - 6,9	46 - 50
Oil temperature switch	2,5	18
Oil cooler bolts	1,8	13
Hydraulic pump retaining nuts	1,3 - 1,4	9.5 - 10
Starter dog-nut	18	130
Spark plugs	2 - 2,5	14 - 18
Engine mounting bolts :		
Front	4 - 4,5	29 - 32
Rear	2,3 - 4	16 - 29

Transmission

	kg f m	lb f ft
Clutch cover retaining bolts	1,8	13
Bevel pinion shaft nut	10 - 12	72 - 86
Primary shaft nut	7 - 8,5	50 - 62
Reverse gearlever spindle	2,7 - 3,3	21 - 25
Crownwheel bolts	4,8 - 5,5	35 - 38
Half-casing assembly bolts	1,4 - 1,5	10 - 11
Clutch housing nuts	1,3 - 1,5	10 - 11
Differential shaft ring nut	6 - 10	43 - 72
Reverse light switch	1,2 - 1,5	9 - 10
Converter oil pump bolts	1,9	13
Converter distributor/electro valve bolts	1,2 - 1,7	9 - 12
Converter oil strainer	1 - 1,5	7 - 11

Hydraulic system

	kg f m	lb f ft
Hydraulic pressure switch	1,1 - 1,2	8 - 9
Automatic control rod clamps	0,8 - 0,9	6 - 6.5
Pressure regulator retaining bolts	1,8	13
Connector control rod clamp	0,8 - 0,9	6 - 6.5

Front axle and suspension

	kg f m	lb f ft
Upper arm pivot pin nut	5,9 - 6,5	43 - 47
Upper ball joint nut	2,7 - 3	20 - 22
Lower arm pivot pin nut	8 - 9	58 - 64
Lower ball joint nut	2,7 - 3	20 - 22
Anti-roll bar bearing nuts	1 - 2,1	13 - 15
Drive shaft to hub, nuts	35 - 40	250 - 290
Drive shaft to output shaft, nuts	5	36
Hub bearing retaining ring nut	40 - 50	290 - 360
Hub retaining nut	35 - 40	250 - 290
Axle unit mounting bolts	4,5 - 5	33 - 36

Braking system

	kg f m	lb f ft
Front caliper bolts:		
Old type	4,5 - 5	33 - 36
New type	6	43
Rear caliper bolts	3,6 - 4	26 - 29
Control valve retaining bolts	1.7 - 1.8	

Steering

	kg f m	lb f ft
Steering box receiving bolts	3,6 - 4	26 - 29
Gordon shaft clamp bolt	1,3 - 1,4	9.5 - 10
Tie-rod to rack ball joint	3,6 - 4	26 - 29
Tie-rod to steering arm nut	1,8 - 2	13 - 14

Rear axle and suspension

	kg f m	lb f ft
Arm to anti-roll bar bolt	1,8 - 2	13 - 14
Brake disc securing bolt	4,5 - 5	33 - 36
Hub nut	35 - 40	250 - 290
Hub bearing ring nut	35 - 40	250 - 290
Axle unit mounting bolts	3 , 4	25

Tools and working facilities

Introduction

A selection of good tools is a fundamental requirement for anyone contemplating the maintenance and repair of a motor vehicle. For the owner who does not possess any, their purchase will prove a considerable expense, offsetting some of the savings made by doing-it-yourself. However, provided that the tools purchased are of good quality, they will last for many years and prove an extremely worthwhile investment.

To help the average owner to decide which tools are needed to carry out the various tasks detailed in this manual, we have compiled three lists of tools under the following headings: Maintenance and minor repair, Repair and overhaul, and Special. The newcomer to practical mechanics should start off with the 'Maintenance and minor repair' tool kit and confine himself to the simpler jobs around the vehicle. Then, as his confidence and experience grows, he can undertake more difficult tasks, buying extra tools as, and when, they are needed. In this way, a 'Maintenance and minor repair' tool kit can be built-up into a 'Repair and overhaul' tool kit over a considerable period of time without any major cash outlays. The experienced do-it-yourselfer will have a tool kit good enough for most repair and overhaul procedures and will add tools from the 'Special' category when he feels the expense is justified by the amount of use these tools will be put to.

It is obviously not possible to cover the subject of tools fully here. For those who wish to learn more about tools and their use there is a book entitled 'How to Choose and Use Car Tools' available from the publishers of this manual.

Maintenance and minor repair tool kit

The tools given in this list should be considered as a minimum requirement if routine maintenance, servicing and minor repair operations are to be undertaken. We recommend the purchase of combination spanners (ring one end, open-ended the other); although more expensive than open-ended ones, they do give the advantages of both types of spanner.

Combination spanners - 10, 11, 13, 14, 17 mm
Adjustable spanner - 9 inch
Engine sump/gearbox/rear axle drain plug key (where applicable)
Spark plug spanner (with rubber insert)
Spark plug gap adjustment tool
Set of feeler gauges
Brake adjuster spanner (where applicable)
Brake bleed nipple spanner
Screwdriver - 4 in. long x ¼ in. dia. (plain)
Screwdriver - 4 in. long x ¼ in. dia. (crosshead)
Combination pliers - 6 inch
Hacksaw, junior

Tyre pump
Tyre pressure gauge
Grease gun (where applicable)
Oil can
Fine emery cloth (1 sheet)
Wire brush (small)
Funnel (medium size)

Repair and overhaul tool kit

These tools are virtually essential for anyone undertaking any major repairs to a motor vehicle, and are additional to those given in the Basic list. Included in this list is a comprehensive set of sockets. Although these are expensive they will be found invaluable as they are so versatile - particularly if various drives are included in the set. We recommend the ½in. square-drive type, as this can be used with most proprietary torque wrenches. If you cannot afford a socket set, even bought piecemeal, then inexpensive tubular box spanners are a useful alternative.

The tools in this list will occasionally need to be supplemented by tools from the Special list.

Sockets (or box spanners) to cover range 6 to 27 mm
Reversible ratchet drive (for use with sockets)
Extension piece, 10 inch (for use with sockets)
Universal joint (for use with sockets)
Torque wrench (for use with sockets)
'Mole' wrench - 8 inch
Ball pein hammer
Soft-faced hammer, plastic or rubber
Screwdriver - 6 in. long x 5/16 in. dia. (plain)
Screwdriver - 2 in. long x 5/16 in. square (plain)
Screwdriver - 1½ in. long x ¼ in. dia. (crosshead)
Screwdriver - 3 in. long x 1/8 in. dia. (electricians)
Pliers - electricians side cutters
Pliers - needle nosed
Pliers - circlip (internal and external)
Cold chisel - ½ inch
Scriber (this can be made by grinding the end of a broken hacksaw blade)
Scraper (this can be made by flattening and sharpening one end of a piece of copper pipe)
Centre punch
Pin punch
Hacksaw
Valve grinding tool
Steel rule/straight edge
Allen keys
Selection of files

Wire brush (large)
Axle stands
Jack (strong scissor or hydraulic type)

Special tools

The tools in this list are those which are not used regularly, are expensive to buy, or which need to be used in accordance with their manufacturers instructions. Unless relatively difficult mechanical jobs are undertaken frequently, it will not be economic to buy many of these tools. Where this is the case, you could consider clubbing together with friends (or a motorists club) to make a joint purchase, or borrowing the tools against a deposit from a local garage or tool hire specialist.

The following list contains only those tools and instruments freely available to the public, and not those special tools produced by the vehicle manufacturer specifically for its dealer network. You will find occasional references to these manufacturers special tools in the text of this manual. Generally, an alternative method of doing the job without the vehicle manufacturers special is given. However, sometimes, there is no alternative to using them. Where this is the case and the relevant tool cannot be bought or borrowed you will have to entrust the work to a franchised garage.

Valve spring compressor
Piston ring compressor
Ball joint separator
Universal hub/bearing puller
Impact screwdriver
Micrometer and/or vernier gauge
Carburettor flow balancing device (where applicable)
Dial gauge
Stroboscopic timing light
Dwell angle meter/tachometer
Universal electrical multi-meter
Cylinder compression gauge
Lifting tackle
Trolley jack
Light with extension lead

Buying tools

For practically all tools, a tool factor is the best source since he will have a very comprehensive range compared with the average garage or accessory shop. Having said that, accessory shops often offer excellent quality tools at discount prices, so it pays to shop around.

Remember, you don't have to buy the most expensive items on the shelf, but it is always advisable to steer clear of the very cheap tools. There are plenty of good tools around, at reasonable prices, so ask the proprietor or manager of the shop for advice before making a purchase.

Care and maintenance of tools

Having purchased a reasonable tool kit, it is necessary to keep the tools in a clean and serviceable condition. After use, always wipe off any dirt, grease and metal particles using a clean, dry cloth, before putting the tools away. Never leave them lying around after they have been used. A simple tool rack on the garage or workshop wall, for items such as screwdrivers and pliers is a good idea. Store all normal spanners and sockets in a metal box. Any measuring instruments, gauges, meters, etc., must be carefully stored where they cannot be damaged or become rusty.

Take a little care when the tools are used. Hammer heads inevitably become marked and screwdrivers lose the keen edge on their blades from time-to-time. A little attention with emery cloth or a file will soon restore items like this to a good serviceable finish.

Working facilities

Not to be forgotten when discussing tools, is the workshop itself. If anything more than routine maintenance is to be carried out, some form of suitable working area becomes essential.

It is appreciated that many an owner mechanic is forced by circumstances to remove an engine or similar item, without the benefit of garage or workshop. Having done this, any repairs should always be done under the cover of a roof.

Wherever possible, any dismantling should be done on a clean flat workbench or table at a suitable working height.

Any workbench needs a vice: one with a jaw opening of 4 in. (100 mm) is suitable for most jobs. As mentioned previously, some clean dry storage space is also required for tools, as well as the lubricants, cleaning fluids, touch-up paints and so on which soon become necessary.

Another item which may be required, and which has a much more general usage, is an electric drill with a chuck capacity of at least 5/16 in. (8 mm). This, together with a good range of twist drills, is virtually essential for fitting accessories such as wing mirrors and reversing lights.

Last, but not least, always keep a supply of old newspapers and clean, lint-free rags available, and try to keep any working area as clean as possible.

Spanner jaw gap comparison table

Jaw gap (in.)	Spanner size
0.250	1/4 in. AF
0.275	7 mm AF
0.312	5/16 in. AF
0.315	8 mm AF
0.340	11/32 in. AF/1/8 in. Whitworth
0.354	9 mm AF
0.375	3/8 in. AF
0.393	10 mm AF
0.433	11 mm AF
0.437	7/16 in. AF
0.445	3/16 in. Whitworth/1/4 in. BSF
0.472	12 mm AF
0.500	1/2 in. AF
0.512	13 mm AF
0.525	1/4 in. Whitworth/5/16 in. BSF
0.551	14 mm AF
0.562	9/16 in. AF
0.590	15 mm AF
0.600	5/16 in. Whitworth/3/8 in. BSF
0.625	5/8 in. AF
0.629	16 mm AF
0.669	17 mm AF
0.687	11/16 in. AF
0.708	18 mm AF
0.710	3/8 in. Whitworth/7/16 in. BSF
0.748	19 mm AF
0.750	3/4 in. AF
0.812	13/16 in. AF
0.820	7/16 in. Whitworth/1/2 in. BSF
0.866	22 mm AF
0.875	7/8 in. AF
0.920	1/2 in. Whitworth/9/16 in. BSF
0.937	15/16 in. AF
0.944	24 mm AF
1.000	1 in. AF
1.010	9/16 in. Whitworth/5/8 in. BSF
1.023	26 mm AF
1.062	1 1/16 in. AF/27 mm AF
1.100	5/8 in. Whitworth/11/16 in. BSF
1.125	1 1/8 in. AF
1.181	30 mm AF
1.200	11/16 in. Whitworth/3/4 in. BSF
1.250	1 1/4 in. AF
1.259	32 mm AF
1.300	3/4 in. Whitworth/7/8 in. BSF
1.312	1 5/16 in. AF
1.390	13/16 in. Whitworth/15/16 in. BSF
1.417	36 mm AF
1.437	1 7/16 in. AF
1.480	7/8 in. Whitworth/1 in. BSF
1.500	1 1/2 in. AF
1.574	40 mm AF/15/16 in. Whitworth
1.614	41 mm AF
1.625	1 5/8 in. AF
1.670	1 in. Whitworth/1 1/8 in. BSF
1.687	1 11/16 in. AF
1.811	46 mm AF
1.812	1 13/16 in. AF
1.860	1 1/8 in. Whitworth/1 1/4 in. BSF
1.875	1 7/8 in. AF
1.968	50 mm AF
2.000	2 in. AF
2.050	1 1/4 in. Whitworth/1 3/8 in. BSF
2.165	55 mm AF
2.362	60 mm AF

Chapter 1 Engine

Contents

Specifications

Engine (general)

	1015cc	1220cc
Type	**1015cc**	**1220cc**
Number of cylinders	4 (flat)	
Bore	74 mm	77 mm
Stroke	59 mm	65.6 mm
Cubic capacity	1015cc	1220cc
Maximum power (DIN)	55.5 hp at 6500 rpm	60 hp at 5750 rpm
Maximum torque	7.2 mkg (52 lb f ft)	8.9 mkg (64.4 lb f ft)
	at 3500 rpm	at 3250 rpm
Maximum engine speed	6500 rpm	6250 rpm
Location of No. 1 cylinder	Left-hand - rear	
Firing order	1 - 4 - 3 - 2	

Camshafts

	1015cc	1220cc
Drive	Toothed belt	
Number of belt teeth:		
RH belt	91 teeth	93 teeth
LH belt	103 teeth	105 teeth
Endfloat	0.05 to 0.15 mm (not adjustable)	

Crankshaft and connecting rod assembly

	1015cc	1220cc
Endfloat of connecting rods	0.13 to 0.18 mm	
Bore of small-end bushes	$20.005 \, {}^{+0.011}_{-0.006}$ mm	$22.005 \, {}^{+0.011}_{-0.006}$ mm
Endfloat of crankshaft	0.09 to 0.20 mm (not adjustable)	
Number of crankshaft bearings	3	
Type of bearings	Split shell	
Diameter of bearings:		
No mark	57.5 mm	
Red mark	57.4 mm	

Crankcase

Type	Light alloy, split in two halves

Cylinder heads

Type	Light alloy, 1 to each pair of cylinders

Cylinders

	1015cc	1220cc
Type	Single barrel - finned	
Height:		
Red mark	75.78 to 75.80 mm	86.88 to 86.90 mm
Green mark	75.80 to 75.82 mm	86.89 to 86.92 mm

Pistons

Type	Light alloy
Width of ring groove:	
Compression ring	1.5 mm
Scraper ring	2 mm
Oil control ring	4 mm

Piston rings

Gap	0.30 to 0.45 mm

Gudgeon pins

Type	Fully-floating
Length	69.9 mm
Diameter	20 mm

Rockers

Rocker shaft diameter	$16.975 \, {}^{+0.01}_{-.0}$ mm
Rocker arm bore diameter	$17.02 \, {}^{+0.25}_{-.0}$ mm

Valves

Inlet:	
Head diameter	39 mm
Stem diameter	8 mm
Face angle	120°
Length	97.4 mm
Exhaust:	
Head diameter	34 mm
Stem diameter	8.5 mm
Face angle	90°
Length	96.3 mm

Valve springs

Length under load	32 mm at 25.4 kg ± 2.5 kg
	24 mm at 59.6 kg ± 2 kg

Rocker clearance (cold)

Inlet	0.20 mm
Exhaust	0.20 mm

Note: Rocker clearance is set at 1 mm (0.040 in) for checking valve timing only.

Valve timing

Inlet valve opens (BTDC)	2° ± 1° 30'	4° 10' ± 1° 30'
Inlet valve closes (ABDC)	34° ± 1° 30'	31° 50' ± 1° 30'
Exhaust valve opens (BBDC)	34° ± 1° 30'	36° 10' ± 1° 30'
Exhaust valve closes (ATDC)	2° 30' ± 1° 30'	0° 20' ± 1° 30'

Fan

External diameter	290 mm
Number of blades	9 (offset)
Drive	Direct from crankshaft

Lubrication system

Type	Pressure feed
Oil pump type	Twin gear
Oil pressure at 80°C:	
2000 rpm	4.7 bar (68 psi) minimum
6000 rpm	6.2 to 7 bar (90 to 102 psi)
Pressure switch setting	0.5 to 0.8 bar (7 to 11.6 psi)
Thermal switch setting	135 ± 3°C
Relief valve spring:	
Free-length	58.5 mm
Length under load	33 mm
Bypass valves setting:	
Filter (white marking)	0.9 to 1.15 bar (13 to 16.6 psi)
Cooler (green marking)	1.8 to 2.5 bar (26 to 36 psi)
Oil cooler	Pressure fed tube type
Oil capacity:	
Engine dry	4 litre (7 Imp. pints)
Oil change (without new filter)	3.5 litre (6.25 Imp. pints)

1 General description

Two engines of different capacity are fitted in Citroen GS models: 1015cc and a 1220cc.

Both engines are very similar in design although quite different in terms of parts used. The operations described in this Chapter apply to both engines unless special mention is made to the contrary.

The engine is of an air-cooled, horizontally opposed flat four cylinder design. In both engines the bore diameter is greater than the stroke. The crankcase and cylinder heads are of light alloy. The crankshaft and connecting rod assembly runs in three split shell bearings between the two halves of the crankcase. The crankshaft and connecting rod assembly is a factory assembled part and cannot be dismantled. Crankshaft or big-end bearing failure necessitates renewal of the complete assembly. Oil seals are fitted at the front and rear ends of the crankshaft. There is no separate sump, the crankcase acts as an oil reservoir.

The four, finned cylinder barrels are separately mounted and each pair has a common cylinder head. The two camshafts, one in each cylinder head are driven by toothed-belts from the driving pinions on the front of the crankshaft. The right-hand camshaft operates the fuel pump and the distributor is driven by the left-hand shaft. The overhead valve mechanism has two rocker shafts to each cylinder head and the rockers are operated directly by the camshafts. The valves are fitted with single coil springs and split collets retain the valve caps. (On early G10 engines two springs were fitted to each valve).

The lubrication system is pressurized by an oil pump driven at half crankshaft speed by the left-hand toothed-belt. A connecting rod, operated by an eccentric on the oil pump shaft, drives the hydraulic high pressure pump. Incorporated in the lubrication system is a light alloy cooler, relief valve, bypass valves and filter. The cooler bypass valve allows the oil, when cold, to pass directly to the filter. The filter bypass valve allows the oil to bypass the filter in the event of the filter becoming blocked (due to lack of maintenance) and the relief valve passes oil back to the sump when the pressure is in excess of 7 bar (102 psi).

The cooling fan is fitted directly on the front of the crankshaft and is secured with the hand starting dog. Ducting directs air from the fan shroud round the cylinders and cylinder heads, and over the oil cooler. The alternator, which is belt driven from the fan, is mounted on top of the engine at the front.

A conventional flywheel, having a ring gear with which the starter motor pinion engages, is bolted to the rear end of the crankshaft. On engines with a semi-automatic transmission the torque converter drive-plate is bolted to the crankshaft.

The engine and gearbox assembly is mounted at three points in the car, two flexible mountings at the rear of the crankcase and one at the rear of the gearbox.

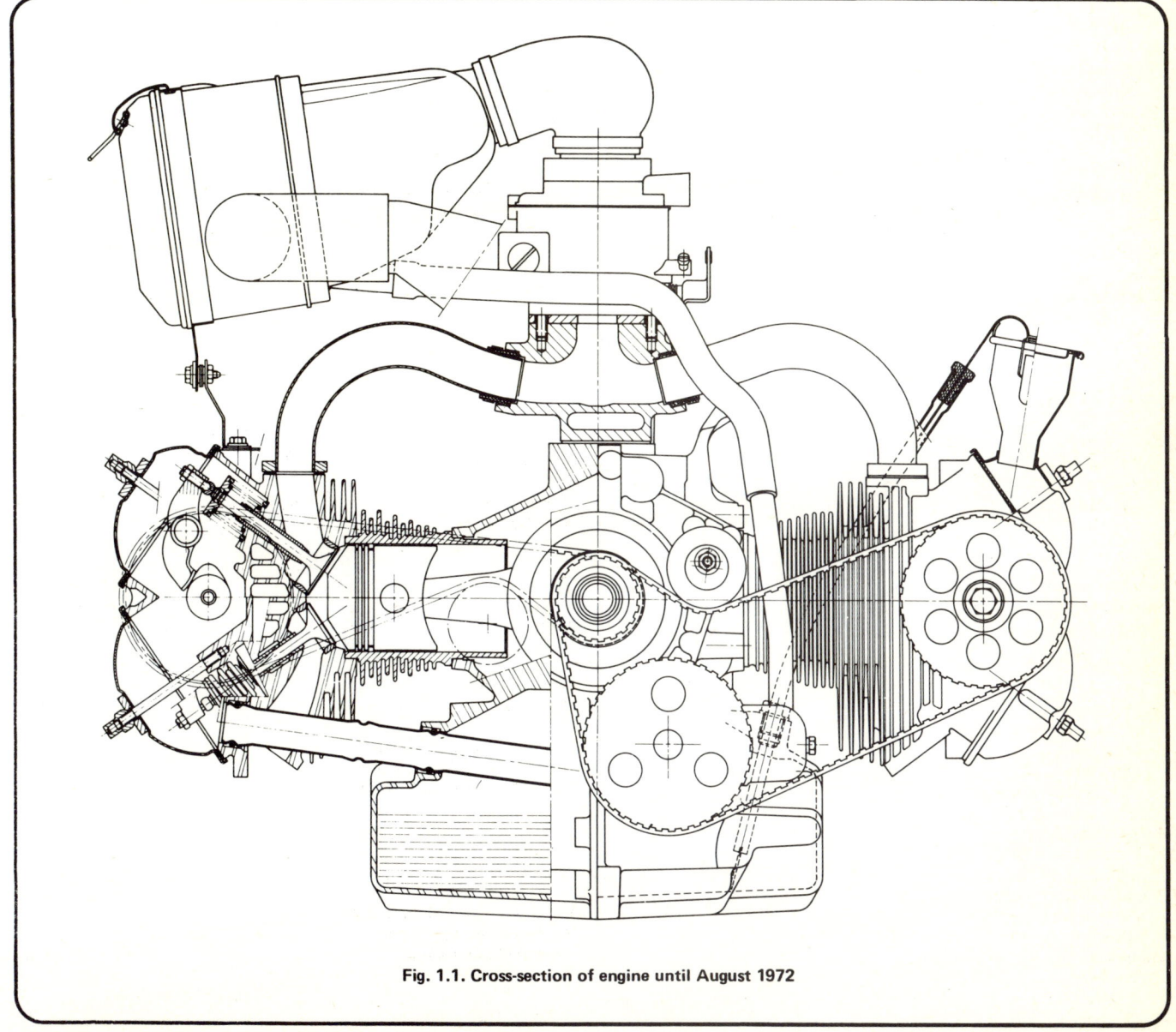

Fig. 1.1. Cross-section of engine until August 1972

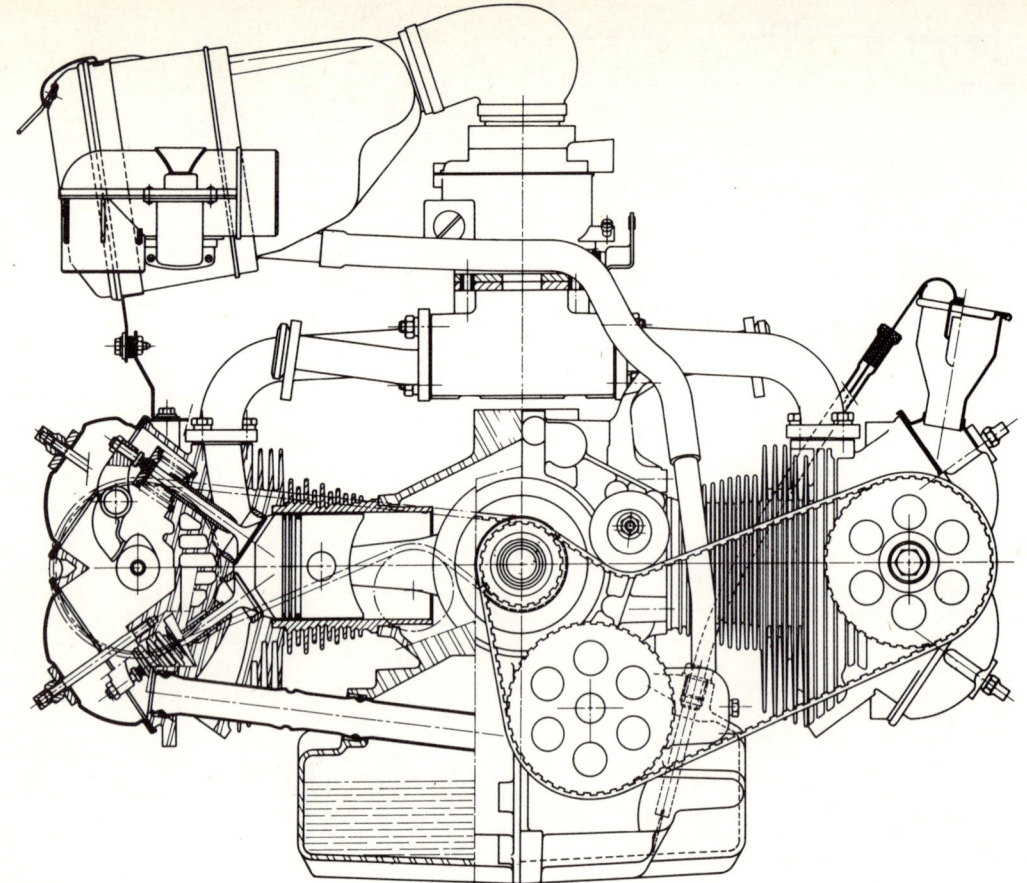

Fig. 1.2. Cross-section of engine until August 1972

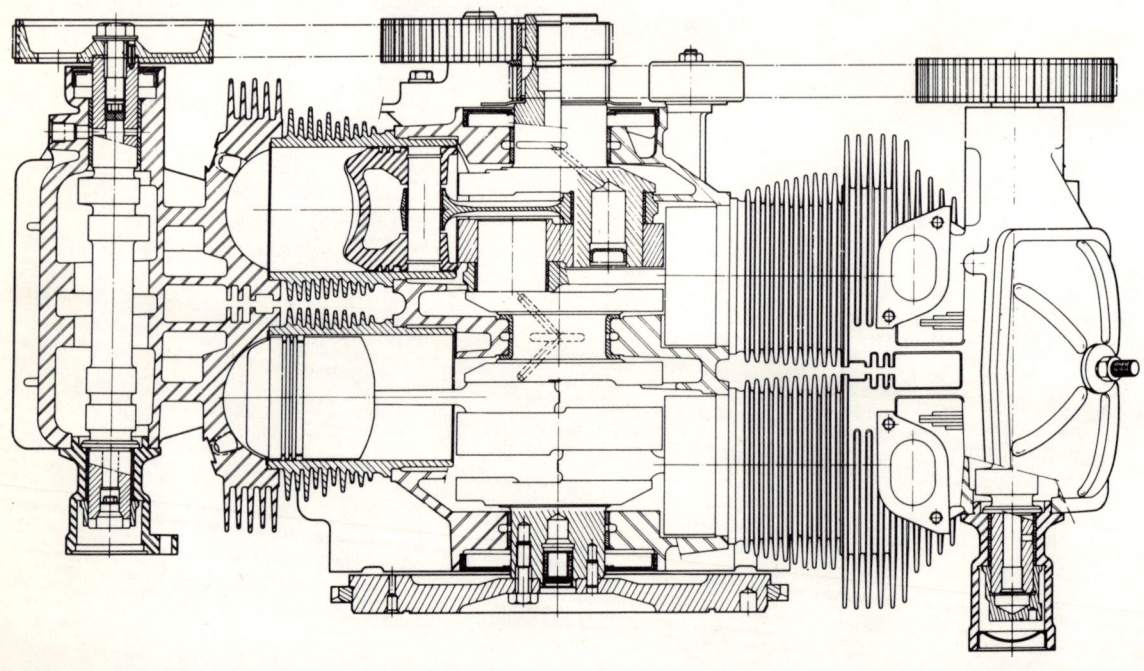

Fig. 1.3. Horizontal cross-section of engine

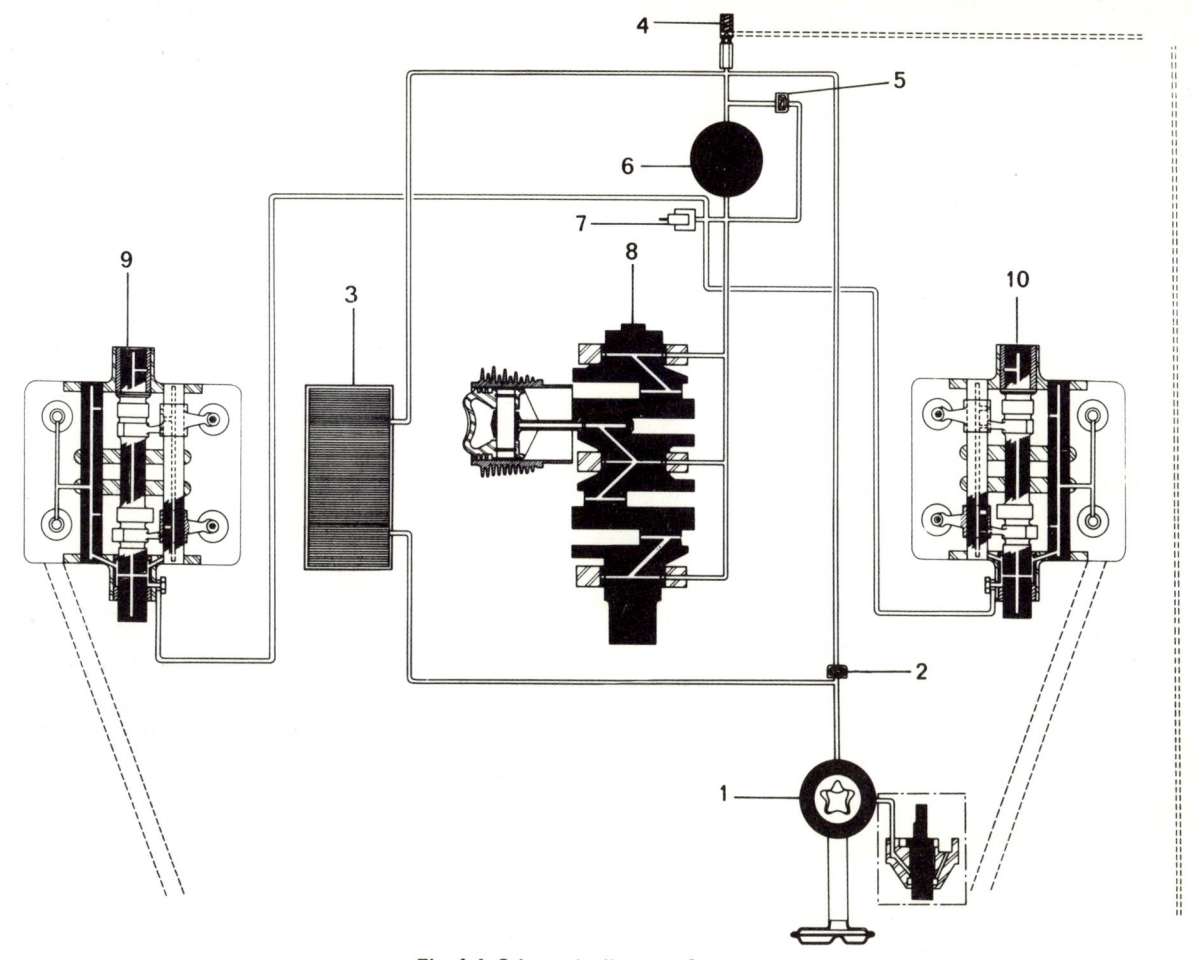

Fig. 1.4. Schematic diagram of lubrication system

1	Oil pump	3 Oil cooler	5 Bypass for oil filter	8 Crankshaft
2	Bypass for cooler	4 Oil pressure control valve	6 Oil filter	9 RH cylinder head
			7 Oil pressure switch	10 LH cylinder head

Fig. 1.5. Lubrication system

2 Major operations possible with the engine in the car

1 Removal and replacement of a rocker shaft or rocker arm.
Note: When removing the exhaust valve rocker shaft it is necessary to remove the bolts from the front flexible engine mountings and raise the engine gearbox assembly.
2 Removal and replacement of a driving belt, tensioner or timing gear. **Note:** Always set the engine to the timing marks as shown in Fig. 1.39 before removing the belts and ensure that the engine is not turned until the belts are replaced.
3 Removal and replacement of a camshaft.
4 Removal and replacement of a pump drive (or seal) or an oil pump.
5 Removal and replacement of a hydraulic high pressure pump.

3 Major operations requiring removal of the engine

Before the following work can be carried out it is necessary to remove the engine from the car.
1 Removal and replacement of main bearings.
2 Removal and replacement of crankshaft and connecting rod assembly.
3 Removal and replacement of crankshaft front and rear seals.
4 Removal and replacement of flywheel or torque converter.
5 Removal and replacement of cylinder heads, cylinders and pistons.

4 Engine removal - method (general)

There are two methods of engine removal: as an engine and gearbox assembly or the engine only, as a separate unit (if removal of the gearbox is not required). Both methods are described in this Chapter.

5 Engine and gearbox assembly - removal procedure

1 For removal of the engine and gearbox assembly, a hoist, engine sling or strong rope and four axle stands or solid wooden blocks are required.
2 Jack-up and support the front of the car with the wheels off the ground.
3 Slacken the pressure regulator bleed screw to release the pressure in the suspension circuits.
4 Place the height control lever in the 'high' position and wait until the rear suspension has completely settled. Check that there is no pressure in the front suspension system (cylinders free), if not, operate the front height corrector. Jack-up and support the rear of the car.
5 Prop up the bonnet on its stay and mark the position of the hinges, this will help when replacing the bonnet. Remove the nut holding the stay on the bonnet and the four bolts securing the bonnet to the hinges. Lift away the bonnet, it helps to have an assistant for this, and place it safely out of the immediate work area.
6 Disconnect the battery leads, negative terminal first.
7 Remove the spare wheel and front wheels.
8 Slacken the securing bolts and remove the grille by pulling it upwards.
9 Remove the indicator lights, pull out the connectors from the headlights and free the electrical harness from its brackets on the fan panel. Disconnect the leads from the alternator (or generator) and the horn. Remove the rubber collar from the inlet tube to the air filter.
10 Rotate the locks while holding the headlights. Release the spring clip holding the sidelights, and remove the head and sidelights.
11 Disconnect the control cable from the bonnet lock. Remove the bolts holding the fan panel on each side. Remove the horn with its bracket and the fan panel.
12 From each side of the lower finishing panel remove the nut and bolts holding the lateral parts of the bumper, the bolts holding the front of the plates protecting the anti-roll bar bearings and the bolts holding the panel. Remove the finishing panel.
13 Uncouple the driveshafts by removing the two nuts and four bolts securing the driveshafts to the differential shafts and the two bolts holding the ball joints of the lower suspension arms. Drop the lower suspension arm and pull the driveshafts from the studs on the differential shafts.

14 Disconnect the leads from the:

> *Distributor*
> *Engine oil pressure warning lamp*
> *Coil to distributor (HT lead)*
> *Starter motor*
> *Engine oil thermal switch*
> *Reversing light contactor*

and for cars fitted with a torque converter disconnect the following additional leads:

> *The leads from the electro-valve (on the clutch housing)*
> *The leads from the starter inhibitor switch (on the rear cover of the gearbox).*

15 Remove the spare wheel support.
16 Remove the fixing bolts from the heater distribution box, uncouple the control cable and remove the box with its hose.
17 Remove the speedometer flexible drive by removing the spring clip and withdrawing the drive.
18 Uncouple the handbrake cable by removing the locknuts, and the adjusting nuts and releasing the cable ends from the brake units.
19 Slacken the clutch cable adjusting nuts and release the cable from the clutch fork. If an assistant is available have him depress the clutch pedal whilst, from underneath the car, you chock the clutch fork. Have the assistant release the pedal and the cable end can easily be released from the clutch fork.
20 Remove the retainer from the gearlever link pin. Remove the pin and uncouple the gearlever.
21 Disconnect the accelerator and choke cables from the carburettor. Remove the bolts holding the cable sheath bracket on the clutch housing.
22 Disconnect the flexible feed pipe from the fuel pump (blank the orifice with a 7mm diameter bolt).
23 On cars fitted with a torque converter disconnect the flexible pipes from the converter oil cooler.
24 Disconnect the hydraulic pipes:

> a) *Disconnect the main feed pipe from the two way union.*
> b) *Remove the bolt holding the pipe bracket.*
> c) *Unscrew the feed pipe for the front brakes and release it from the left-hand brake unit.*
> d) *Remove the bleed screw, fitted on early models only, to avoid it being damaged when the engine-gearbox assembly is being removed (blank off the orifice).*
> e) *Disconnect the return pipe from the pressure regulator and remove the rubber collar which holds the pipe.*
> f) *Disconnect the intake pipe from the high pressure pump. Release the pipe from the bracket on the right-hand wheel arch.*

25 Fit a sling around the engine, positioned so that it will not damage any accessories when taking the weight of the engine and gearbox assembly. Place the hoist in position and take up the tension on the sling until the weight of the engine and gearbox assembly is supported without lifting it.
26 Remove the clamps from the exhaust pipe, the bolt holding the central exhaust pipe support on the gearbox housing and the 'Y' shaped connecting pipe. Remove the bolt holding the rear flexible mounting at the rear of the gearbox and the bolts from the flexible mountings at the rear of the engine crankcase, from underneath the car.
27 Pull the engine and gearbox assembly carefully forward and remove the collar holding the dust cover on top of the gearbox. Pull up the dust cover and, using a pin punch, remove the split pin holding the fork operating lever to the ball joint. Remove the operating lever.
28 Make a final check that there are no more items to disconnect and that there is nothing likely to get caught-up when the engine and gearbox assembly is removed.
29 Pull the engine and gearbox assembly forward, clear of the car, taking care that the distributor does not foul the left-hand wheel arch and that the pipe linking the brake units does not come in contact with the crossmember of the axle unit.
30 Remove the crankcase drain plug, drain the oil into a container and replace the drain plug. Place the engine on a bench or wooden platform.
31 Remove the left and right-hand exhaust connecting pipes.

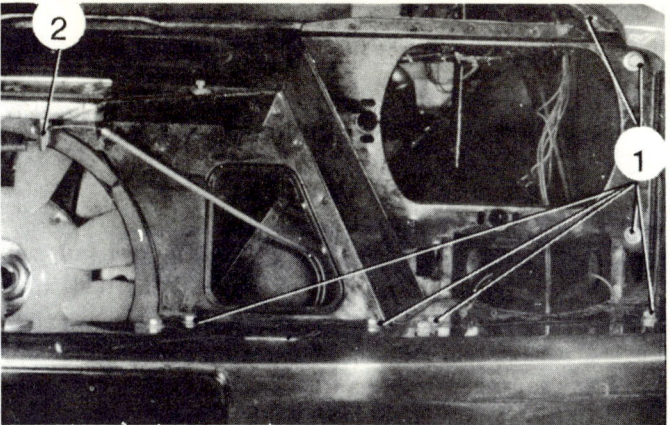

Fig. 1.6. Removing the fan panel

1 Securing bolts   2 Bonnet catch

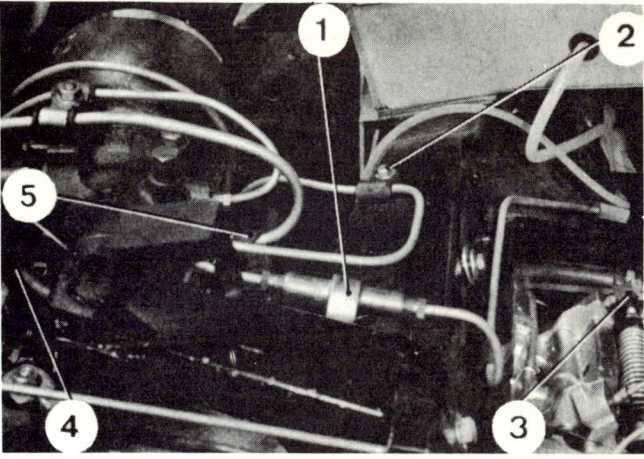

Fig. 1.9. Hydraulic piping

1 Two-way union	4 Pressure regulator return
2 Bolt	pipe
3 Bleed screw	5 Collar

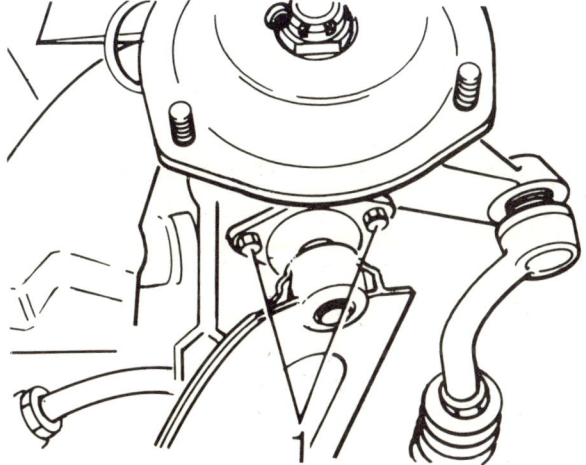

Fig. 1.7. Uncoupling the driveshafts

1 Lower suspension arm ball joint bolts

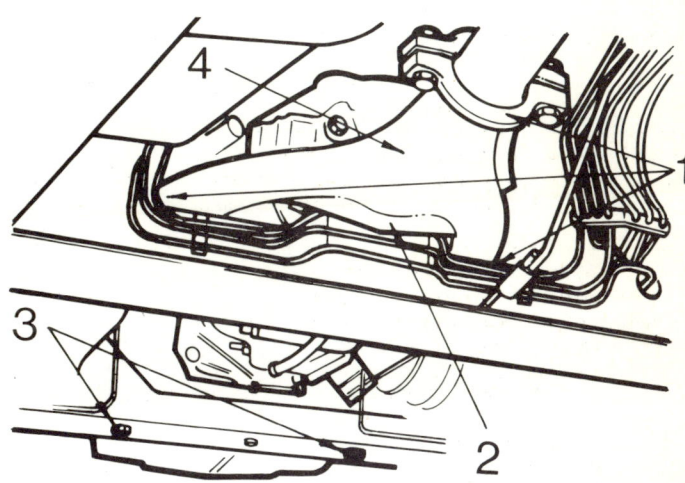

Fig. 1.10. Front engine mountings and exhaust pipe support

1 Exhaust pipe clamps	3 Front mounting bolts
2 Bolt	4 Exhaust pipe

Fig. 1.8. Removing the heater distribution box

1 Distribution box	2 Hose
	3 Bolts

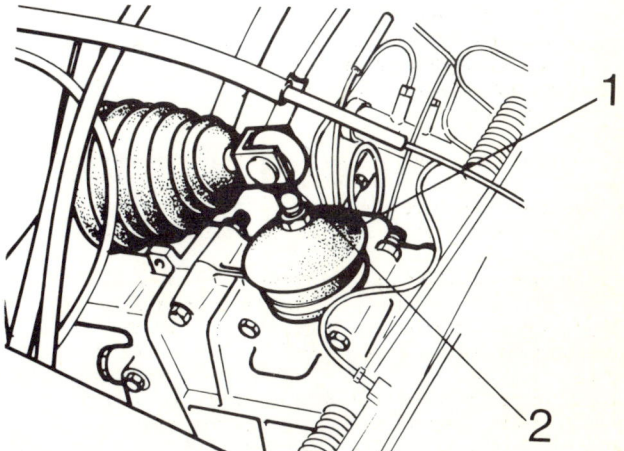

Fig. 1.11. Gearchange linkage

1 Dust cover   2 Fork operating lever

Fig. 1.12. Removing the fork operating lever

1 Pin punch

5.3 Slackening the pressure regulator bleed screw to release the pressure from the hydraulic system

5.5 The bonnet hinge bolts

5.8a Front grille securing bolt

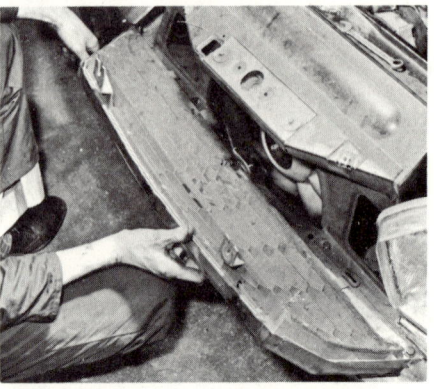

5.8b Removing the front grille

5.10 Removing the side and headlights

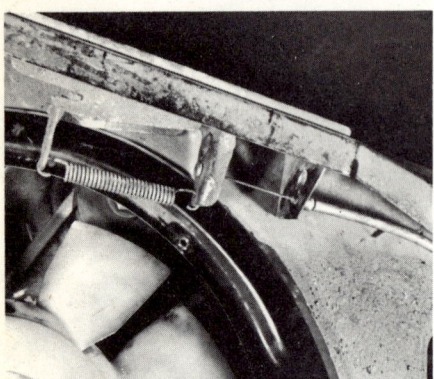

5.11a Bonnet lock and control cable

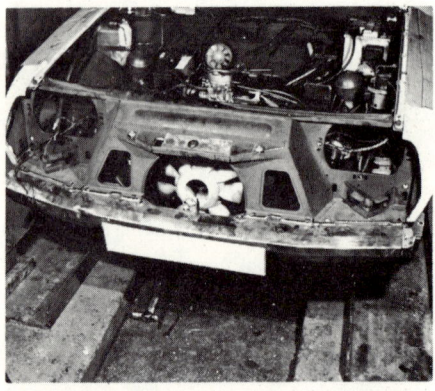

5.11b Fan panel and front bumper with end pieces removed

5.12a Removing the front bolts of the anti-roll bar bearing guard plate

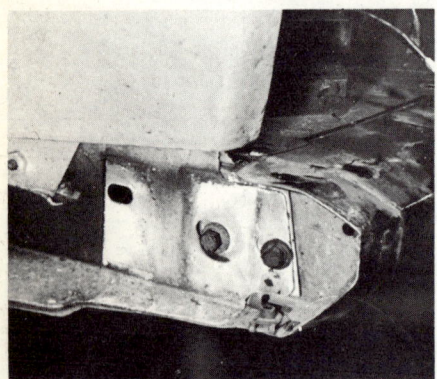

5.12b The end securing bolts of the lower finishing panel

5.12c Removing the lower finishing panel and front bumper

5.13a Uncoupling the driveshaft from the differential shaft

5.13b Removing the bolts securing the ball joints of the lower suspension arm

5.16a The heater distribution box

5.16b Heater box control cable attachment

5.18 Handbrake cable to brake unit connection

5.19 Releasing the clutch cable from the operating fork

5.20 Disconnecting the gearlever

5.24 Disconnecting the hydraulic pipes

5.26a The exhaust pipe support bolted to the gearbox housing

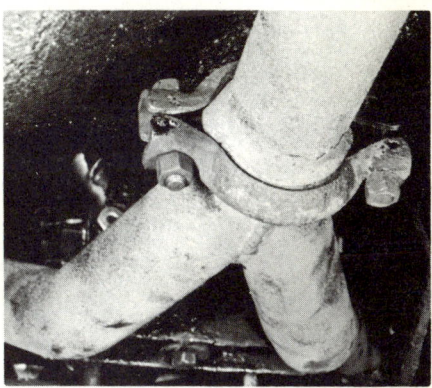

5.26b Exhaust clamps of 'Y' shaped connecting pipe

5.26c Gearbox rear flexible mounting

5.27 Pulling the engine/gearbox assembly forward

5.31 Removing the right-hand exhaust connecting pipe

6 Engine (only) - removal procedure

1 Carry out the operations described in Section 5, paragraphs 1 to 12, inclusive.
2 Disconnect the leads from the:

Distributor
Oil pressure warning lamp
Coil to the distributor (HT lead)
Starter motor
Oil thermal switch.

Release the electrical harness and lay it on the left-hand extension arm. Remove the distributor cap and rotor to prevent possible damage to these components when removing the engine.
3 Carry out the operations described in Section 5, paragraphs 15, 16, 21 and 22.
4 Disconnect the hydraulic circuits:

    a) *Disconnect the pump inlet flexible pipe from the hydraulic reservoir. Release it from the clip on the wheel arch and remove the rubber collar.*
    b) *Disconnect the pipe from the pressure regulator, remove the nuts securing the clips holding the pipe, free the clips and remove the pipe from the pressure regulator. Blank-off the ends of the pipes.*

5 On cars fitted with a torque converter remove the following:

    a) *Disconnect the pipe from the pressure regulator to the two-way union. Remove the bolt holding the pipe clip to the crossmember.*
    b) *Disconnect the leads from the electro-valve.*
    c) *Remove the bolts securing the pressure regulator and place the regulator on the right-hand extension.*
    d) *Remove the starter motor.*
    e) *Disconnect the flexible hose which supplies air to the converter oil cooler.*
    f) *Remove the three bolts, accessible through the starter motor aperture in the casing, holding the torque converter driveplate. Mark the relative position of the converter to the driveplate, so that it can be refitted in the same location.*

Note: To hold the torque converter in position while the engine is being removed it is necessary to fit a retaining bracket on the pressure regulator mounting. The Citroen bracket (Part No. 3186-T) is illustrated, but a suitable bracket can be made from sheet metal.
Caution: The electro-valve must **never** be disconnected from the control distributor of the converter.
6 Disconnect the exhaust pipes, by removing the plates from the lower heater ducts, the front connection collars and slackening the bolt of the central exhaust pipe support on the gearbox.
7 Fit a sling around the engine, positioned so that it will not damage any accessories, and using a hoist take the weight of the engine.
8 Remove the bolts from the flexible mounting at the rear of the crankcase and raise the engine and gearbox assembly until the clutch housing comes into contact with the upper crossmember of the suspension frame. Support the gearbox from underneath, taking care not to damage the clutch cable.
9 Make a final check to ensure that everything is disconnected and that cables and pipes are tucked to one side where they will not get caught up as the engine is removed.
10 Remove the four nuts securing the gearbox to the engine and carefully pull the engine forward, ensuring that the distributor does not foul the wheel arch and avoiding putting any strain on the gearbox input shaft.
11 Drain the engine oil and place the engine on a bench or wooden platform.

7 Engine and gearbox assembly - separating

1 Remove the four nuts securing the gearbox to the engine.
2 Withdraw the gearbox from the engine taking care not to strain the gearbox input shaft.
3 If a torque-converter is fitted, refer to Section 6, paragraph 5, for method of disconnecting the convertor-drive plate.
4 When removing the gearbox from the engine support the torque-converter so that it is retained with the gearbox.

Fig. 1.13. Hydraulic pipe connections

1 Pipe from pressure regulator   3 Clip securing nut
2 Pressure regulator securing bolt   4 Collar

Fig. 1.14. Hydraulic pipe connections

1 Pressure regulator securing bolts   3 Clip retaining bolt
2 Electro-valve leads   4 Supply pipe to two-way union

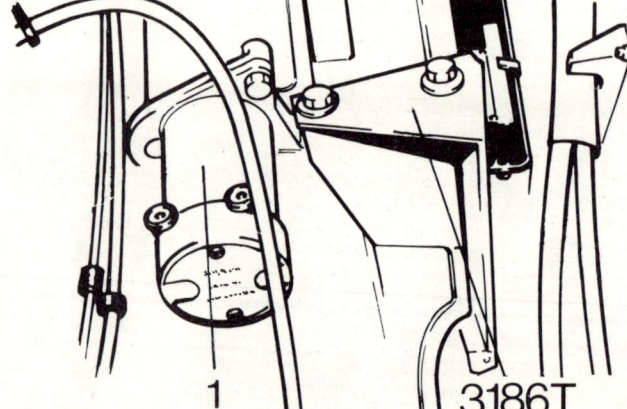

Fig. 1.15. Torque converter retaining bracket

1 Electro-valve

8 Engine - dismantling (general)

1   When the engine is removed from the car it, and particularly its accessories, are more vulnerable to damage. If possible mount the engine on a stand, or failing this, make sure it is supported in such a manner that it will not topple over whilst undoing tight nuts and bolts.

2   Cleanliness is important when dismantling the engine to prevent exposed parts from contamination. Before starting the dismantling operations clean the outside of the engine with paraffin, or a good grease solvent if it is particularly dirty. Carry out this cleaning away from the area in which the dismantling is to take place.

3   If a stand is not available carry out the work on a bench or wooden platform. Avoid working with the engine directly on a concrete floor, as grit presents a real source of trouble. .

4   As parts are removed clean them in a paraffin bath. However, do not immerse parts with internal oilways in paraffin as it is difficult to remove, usually requiring a high pressure hose. Clean oilways with nylon pipe cleaners.

5   It is advisable to have suitable containers to hold small items by their groups as this will help when reassembling the engine and also prevents possible losses.

6   Always obtain complete sets of gaskets when the engine is being dismantled. It is always a good policy to fit new gaskets in view of the relatively small cost involved. Retain the old gaskets when dismantling the engine with a view to using them as a pattern to make a replacement if a new one is not available.

7   When possible replace nuts, bolts and washers in their location as this helps to protect the threads and will also be helpful when the engine is being reassembled as it establishes their location.

8   Retain unserviceable items until the replacement parts are obtained so that the replacement parts can be checked against the old part to ensure that the correct item has been supplied.

9 Engine ancillaries - removal

Although the items listed may be removed separately with the engine installed (as described in the relevant Chapters) it is more appropriate to take them off after the engine has been removed from the car when extensive dismantling is being carried out.

Fuel system
Carburettor
Fuel pump

Ignition
Distributor
Spark plugs

Electrical components
Starter motor
Alternator.

10 Engine - dismantling procedure

1   Remove the clutch assembly, referring to Chapter 4. Remove the six flywheel retaining bolts and remove the flywheel.

2   Remove the upper duct covers.

3   Remove the hand starter dog, the fan and the alternator drivebelt. Remove the nuts securing the fan cowl to the three mounting studs and remove the cowl washers and spacers.

4   Remove the under cylinder ducts (G10 engines) by releasing the spring clip to free them from the oil return tubes of the cylinder heads.

5   Undo the union screws on the right and left-hand cylinder heads and on the carburettor heater box and remove the cylinder head lubricating pipe.

6   Remove the oil cooler and seals, the oil temperature thermal switch and the oil pressure switch.

7   Remove the inlet pipes, exhaust manifold pipes and the heating ducts.

8   Remove the nut and bolts securing the carburettor heater box and remove the box. Collect the O-ring between the heater box and the engine casing (early engines) or the pipe-intake manifold and carburettor assembly (later engines).

9   Remove the oil filter. As the oil filter is unscrewed oil will run over the top of the engine, have a cloth ready to mop up the oil.

10   Loosen the nuts holding the left-hand tension roller, compress the roller and remove the outer flange from the crankshaft outer drive pinion and the left-hand toothed belt. Slacken the nut holding the right-hand tension roller, compress the roller and remove the intermediate flange of the drive pinion and the right-hand toothed belt. Remove the inner drive pinion, protection plate and key from the crankshaft. Remove the tension rollers and thrust plates.

11   Restrain the camshaft wheels from turning, undo the securing nuts and remove the wheels.

12   Remove the cylinder head covers. Undo the eight cylinder head retaining nuts on each cylinder head and lift off the heads. Remove the oil return tubes, and the ducts beneath the cylinders (G103 engines).

13   Remove the four cylinders and mark them so that they will be refitted in the same positions. To avoid scoring of the pistons fit a piece of rubber tubing over the studs.

14   Remove the gudgeon pin retaining circlips situated towards the outside of the engine, ('a' and 'b' in Fig. 1.19) and push out the gudgeon pins using a suitable mandrel. Remove the pistons and place them and the gudgeon pins with their respective cylinders. Remove the piston rings. **Note**: It is important that the respective pistons and cylinders are kept together if they are to be refitted as they are a matched set.

15   Remove the five bolts securing the oil pump drive gear and remove the gear by levering it on two diametrically opposed points, taking care to avoid damaging the pump bearing. Collect the O-ring and remove the high pressure pump connecting rod, the oil pump cover plate and the oil pump pinions.

16   Place the crankcase with the left-hand half of the casing downwards and remove the assembly nuts. Separate the two halves of the casing, remove the front and rear crankshaft seals and lift out the crankshaft-connecting rod assembly. Remove the half bearings shells from each half of the casing. Remove the bolts securing the oil strainer. To assist the removal of the strainer, heat the casing around the strainer pipe at 'a' in Fig. 1.20. Remove the oil system relief valve by removing the retaining circlip and collecting the washer, spring washers, the piston, the spring, the sleeve and the spring cap. Remove the filter and oil cooler bypass valves.

11 Cylinder heads - dismantling

1   Loosen the locknuts and back-off the rocker adjusting screws under load. From each end of the rocker shafts remove the blanking bolts and copper seals, the spacers and the 'O' ring seals. Remove the rocker cover stud and with a 3 mm Allen key remove the grubscrew. Remove the rocker shafts, rocker arms and springs.

2   Remove the nuts securing the camshaft rear bearing, free the bearing by tapping lightly with a mallet on the end of the camshaft and remove the camshaft and bearing assembly. The camshaft and the rear bearing form an assembly which cannot be dismantled. Remove the front seal.

3   Position a 16 mm diameter rod, 'A' in Fig. 1.25, successively in place of each rocker arm shaft successively. And then a valve spring compression tool (Citroen tool Pt. No. 1652-T, is illustrated) compress the valve spring, using a block of wood under the valve head to prevent the valve opening. Remove the split cotters, cups, springs, thrust washers and seals. Remove the valve and the rod 'A'. Mark the valves so that if they are to be refitted they can be located in the same positions.

12 Cylinder heads - cleaning and renovation

1   After the cylinder heads have been dismantled they should be thoroughly cleaned to remove all carbon deposits in the combustion chambers. Avoid damaging the valve seats when removing the carbon. Examine the heads for cracks or other damage. If there are any visible cracks the head should be scrapped. Pay particular attention to the area around the valve seats and spark plug holes as these are where cracks are most likely to occur.

2   Slight pitting of the valves and valve seats can usually be rectified by lapping with carborundum paste. If the seats are badly pitted or burned they will require grinding. Valve seat angles and diameters are given in Fig. 1.27, but as this machinery requires special equipment you may decide to have it done by your local agent.

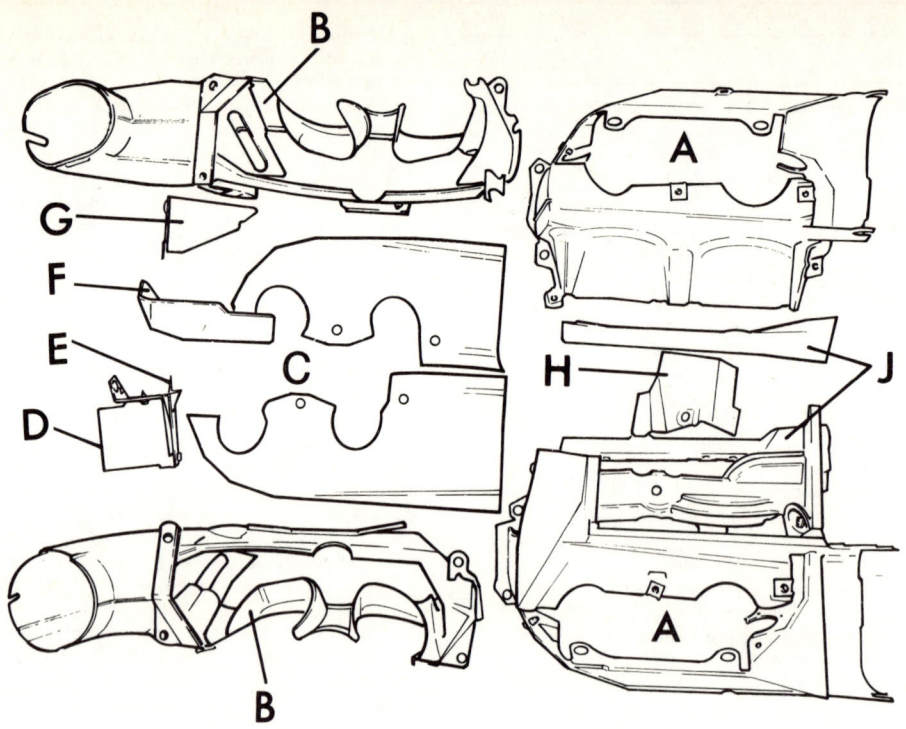

Fig. 1.16. Cooling and heating ducts - G10 engines

A *Cooling ducts*	*D* *Deflector*	*F* *LH mounting plate*	*H* *Deflector fitted towards*
B *Heating ducts*	*E* *RH mounting plate*	*G* *Screen*	*fan cowl*
C *Duct covers*			*J* *Ducts under cylinders*

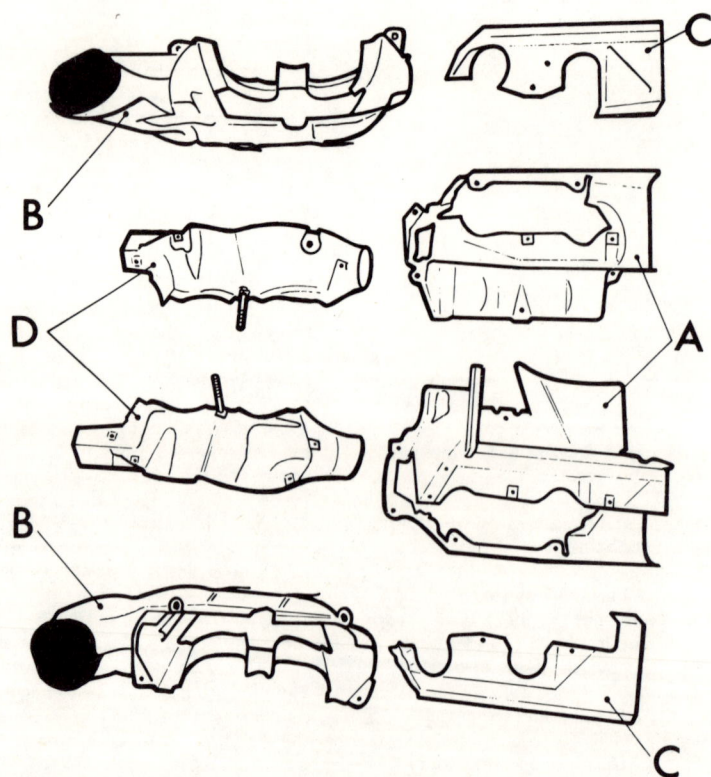

Fig. 1.17. Cooling and heating ducts - G103 engines

A *Cooling ducts*	*B* *Heating ducts*	*C* *Duct covers*	*D* *Ducts under cylinders*

Fig. 1.18. Removing the camshaft drivebelts

1 LH camshaft wheel   4 RH camshaft wheel
2 Crankshaft outer flange 5 LH tension roller
3 RH tension roller   6 Cylinder head lubrication pipe

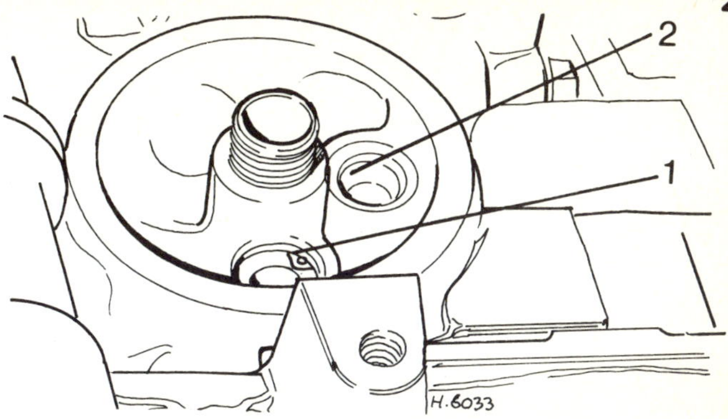

Fig. 1.19. Removing the gudgeon pin circlips

A Rubber tubing

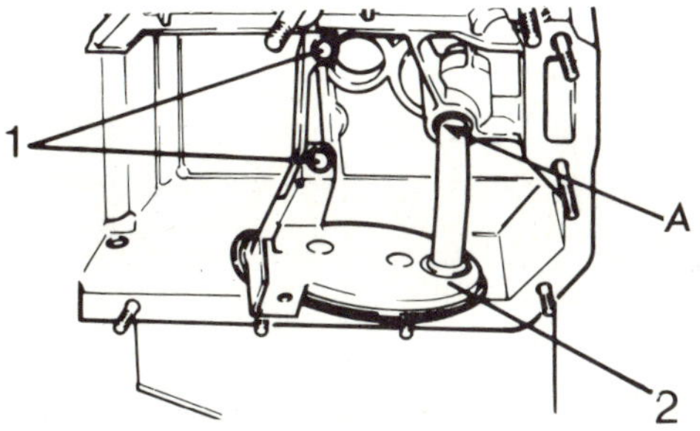

Fig. 1.20. Removing the oil strainer

1 Bolts   2 Strainer

Fig. 1.21. Removing the oil pressure relief valve

1 Filter bypass valve   2 Circlip

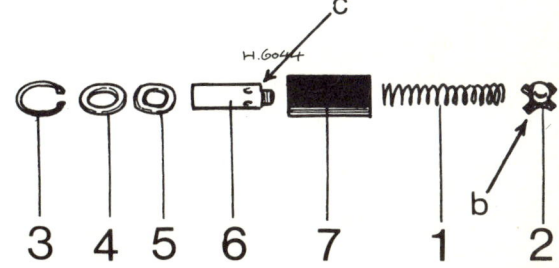

Fig. 1.22. Oil pressure relief valve

1 Spring   5 Spring washer
2 Spring cap   6 Piston
3 Circlip   7 Sleeve
4 Washer

Fig. 1.23. Dismantling a cylinder head

1 Adjusting screw   5 Grubscrew
2 Spacer   6 Stud
3 Blanking bolt   7 Rear bearing
4 Cup (early engines)

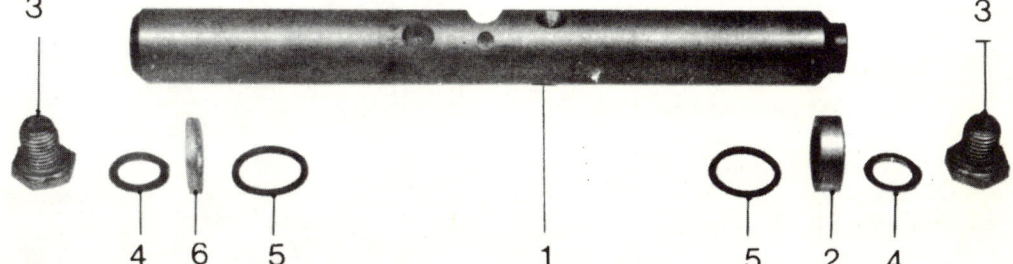

Fig. 1.24. Rocker arm shaft

1 Rocker shaft   2 Spacer   4 Copper seals   6 Spacer
                      3 Blanking bolts 5 'O' ring seals

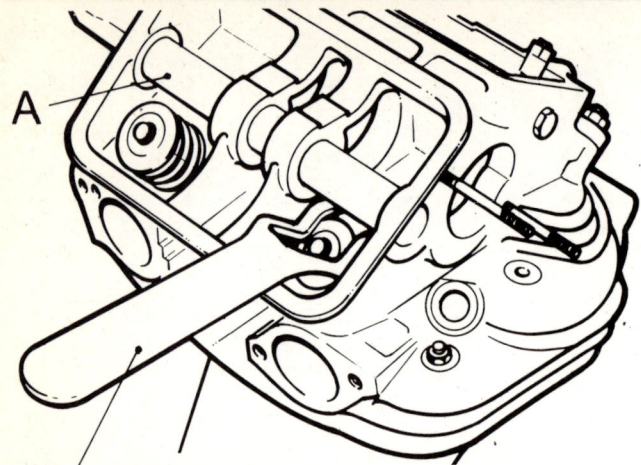

1652-T   Fig. 1.25. Removing the valves

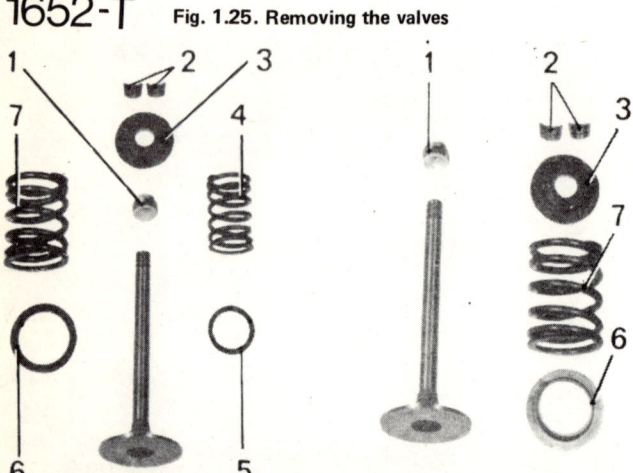

Fig. 1.26. Valve assemblies

1	Seal	5	Thrust washer
2	Split cotters	6	Thrust washer
3	Cup	7	Spring
4	Spring		

3   If the valves require grinding on a valve grinding machine, the chamfer of the valve heads is:

a) Intake valves = 120°
b) Exhaust valves = 90°

Make a slight chamfer at 'a' (Fig. 1.27) on the valve head to smooth the edge.

4   When lapping-in slightly pitted valves and valve seats with carborundum paste proceed as follows: Apply a little coarse grinding paste to the valve seat and using a suction valve grinding tool, lap the valve into its seat with a semi-rotary movement, lifting the valve from time-to-time. A light spring under the valve head will assist in this operation. When a dull matt even surface finish appears on both the valve and the valve seat, clean off the coarse paste and repeat the operation with a fine grinding paste until a continuous ring of light grey matt finish appears on both valve and valve seat. Carefully clean off all traces of grinding paste. Blow through the gas passages with compressed air.

5   Check the valve springs against the following load/dimensions.

Specifications:
G10 engine (early models)

2 Springs		Loaded length mm (in)	Load kg (lb)
Outer		32 (1.260)	23,5 ± 2 (51.7 ± 2)
		24,5 (0.965)	50 ± 3 (110 ± 6.6)
Inner		26,8 (1.055)	9,9 ± 0,9 (21.8 ± 2)
		19,3 (0.760)	21,1 ± 1,0 (46.5 ± 2.2)

G10 and G103 engines

1 Spring	Loaded length mm (in)	Load kg (lb)
	32 (1.260)	25,4 ± 2,5 (55.9 ± 5.5)
	24 (0.945)	59,6 ± 2 (131 ± 4.4)

6   Examine the rocker shafts, rockers and camshafts for wear or damage. If the camshaft rear bearing is defective the complete camshaft and bearing assembly must be renewed. Fit a new rear bearing seal. If necessary, replace the pin '1' (Fig. 1.28) and fit it positioned with the slot 'a' towards the outside of the camshaft. The fixing stud for the camshaft wheel must be fitted with Locktite and tightened to 2,5 to 3 kg f m (18 to 22 lb f ft).

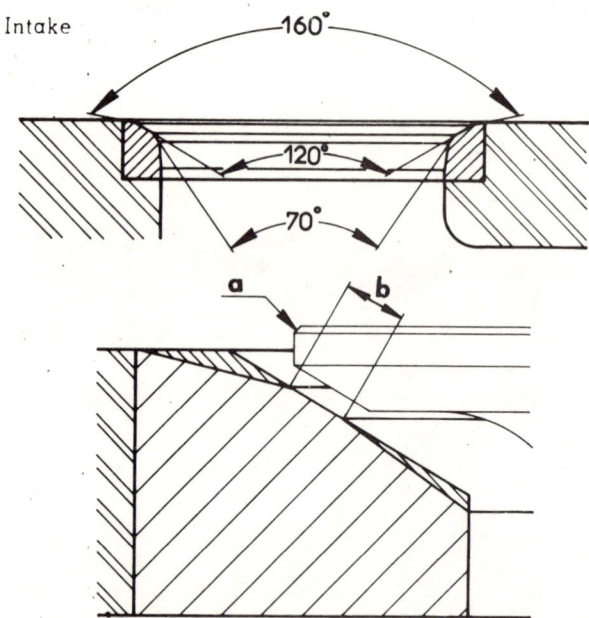

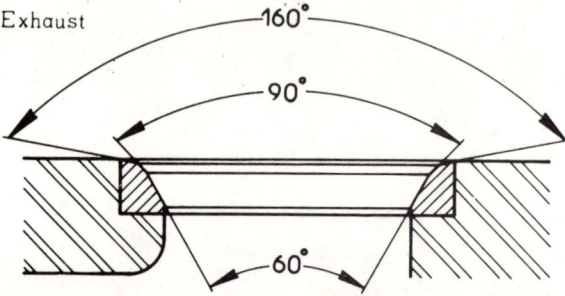

Fig. 1.27. Valve seat angles

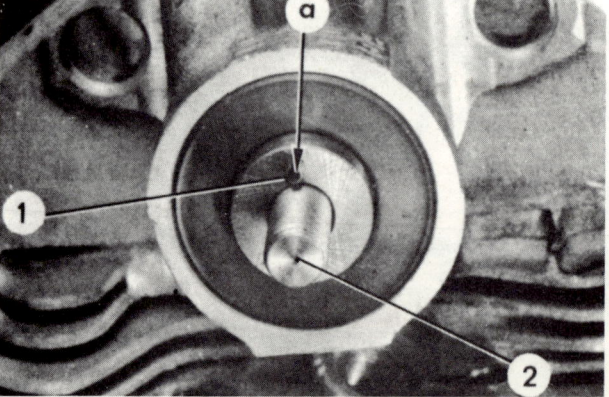

Fig. 1.28. Fitting a camshaft wheel stud

1 Pin   2 Stud

13 Cylinder heads - reassembly

Note: It is not possible to fit the single valve spring on cylinder heads equipped for two springs for valve.

1 Fitting of the valves is the reverse of the removal sequence. Always fit new valve seals on assembly. Ensure that the split cotters are seated correctly.

2 When fitting the joint between the rear bearing housing of the camshaft and the cylinder head, line-up the notch in the joint with the groove in the casing for the oil return of the cylinder head. Fit the joint dry. Oil the camshaft front seal bearing surface and fit the camshaft in the cylinder head. Fit the front seal. The seal must be fitted when the camshaft is in place, otherwise it will be damaged when fitting the camshaft. Tighten the camshaft securing nuts to 1,5 to 1,8 kg f m (11 to 13 lb f ft).

3 Fitting of the rocker shafts and arms is the reverse of the removal sequence. Note the markings on the rocker shafts for identification. The left-hand intake and right-hand exhaust shafts are identical and have no markings. The right-hand intake and the left-hand exhaust shafts are identical and are marked with an indentation 'd' (Fig. 1.29). This marking is very important for the correct fitting of the shafts in relation to the lubrication holes.

4 Oil the shafts and fit them in the cylinder heads with the shouldered ends 'c' towards the front of the camshaft. Temporarily fit a blanking screw on the end of the shaft, to allow the positioning of the shaft so that the grubscrew hole lines-up with the blend hold. Fit the grubscrew with the threads smeared with Locktite. Remove the blanking screw. When fitting the rocker cover fixing stud, fit the shortest thread in the cylinder head.

14 Crankshaft and connecting rods - general

1 The crankshaft and connecting rod assembly is a factory built unit and cannot be dismantled by the owner. A big-end bearing failure and damaged or worn main bearing journals necessitate the renewal of the complete assembly. Small-end bushes can be replaced but this requires special equipment and should be left to your Citroen agent.

2 The pilot bearing and oil seal in the rear of the crankshaft can be replaced as follows: Remove and discard the seal and bearing bush. Soak the new bush, for one hour, in clean engine oil before fitting it. Press the bush into the crankshaft to the dimensions shown in Fig. 1.30 and fit a new seal with the face bearing the manufacturers mark facing outwards.

15 Cylinders and pistons - cleaning and reassembly

1 It is not possible to renew cylinders and pistons separately as replacements are only sold in sets of four cylinder/piston assemblies. All four of which must be fitted to the same engine, as the difference in weight between two pistons must not exceed a few grams.

2 If the cylinder bores are worn this will result in excessive oil consumption and loss of power. A preliminary check for wear can be made by feeling the inside walls of the cylinder about ½ inch (12.7 mm) down from the top edge. If a ridge can be felt at any point, then the bores should be measured with an internal micrometer to ascertain

actual amount of wear. Take measurements at different positions in the bore to get a complete picture of wear and ovality.

3 If the same pistons are being refitted with only the rings being renewed, carefully clean the piston ring grooves with the aid of a broken piece of used ring. If there is excessive vertical clearance of the rings in the piston ring grooves the pistons require renewal.

4 Before fitting the new rings to the pistons check the ring gap by placing each ring in the cylinder in which it will be fitted, and using a piston, make sure they rest square in the bore near the bottom of the cylinder. Measure the gap between the ring ends with a feeler gauge: it should be between 0,30 to 0,45 mm (0.012 - 0.018 in).

5 When fitting the rings, note that they have a marking, 'HAUT', 'H' or 'TOP' on one of the faces near the gap, this marking must be positioned facing the top of the piston. Fig. 1.31 shows the location of the rings on the piston. The U—FLEX rings in their free state have an inside diameter greater than that of the piston and it is necessary to use a piston ring clamp when fitting the pistons into the cylinders.

6 There are two classes of cylinder (having different heights) marked by touches of green or red paint. Both cylinders fitted to one side of the engine must be of the same colour. Before fitting the pistons in the cylinders insert the gudgeon pin circlip on the same side 'b' (Fig. 1.32) as the fins 'c'. Position the piston ring gap at 120° spacing and fit the piston ring clamp. Fit the piston part way into the lower end of the corresponding cylinder, as marked at dismantling. Position the pistons in such a way that after fitting the connecting rod the figure at 'a' (compression ratio 9) is legible as illustrated and the fins 'c' are positioned as shown. Oil the gudgeon pin and insert it in the piston boss so as to leave a gap to enable the connecting rod small end to be fitted.

16 Flywheel starter ring gear - removal and replacement

1 Remove the flywheel starter ring by driving it off with a hammer.

2 Clean the contact areas of the replacement ring and the flywheel and ensure the surface is smooth and even.

3 Heat the ring with a blow torch, moving it round the ring all the time to ensure even expansion. Heat the ring to between 200 to 250° C (straw yellow colour) and fit the ring to the flywheel with the teeth lead-in (chamfer) towards the gearbox.

4 Check that the run-out on the starter ring does not exceed 0.3 mm (0.012 in).

17 Engine - reassembly (general)

1 To ensure maximum life with minimum trouble from a rebuilt engine, not only must everything be correctly assembled, but also must be spotlessly clean. All oilways must be clear, locking washers and spring washers must be fitted where indicated. Oil all bearings and other working surfaces thoroughly with engine oil during assembly.

2 Before assembly, renew any bolts, studs or screws with damaged threads and use of new spring washers is advisable.

3 Apart from having a supply of normal tools, a supply of clean rags and an oil can should be available.

4 Before starting work, clear the work area of any unwanted parts and arrange all the components nearby, prepared for reassembly.

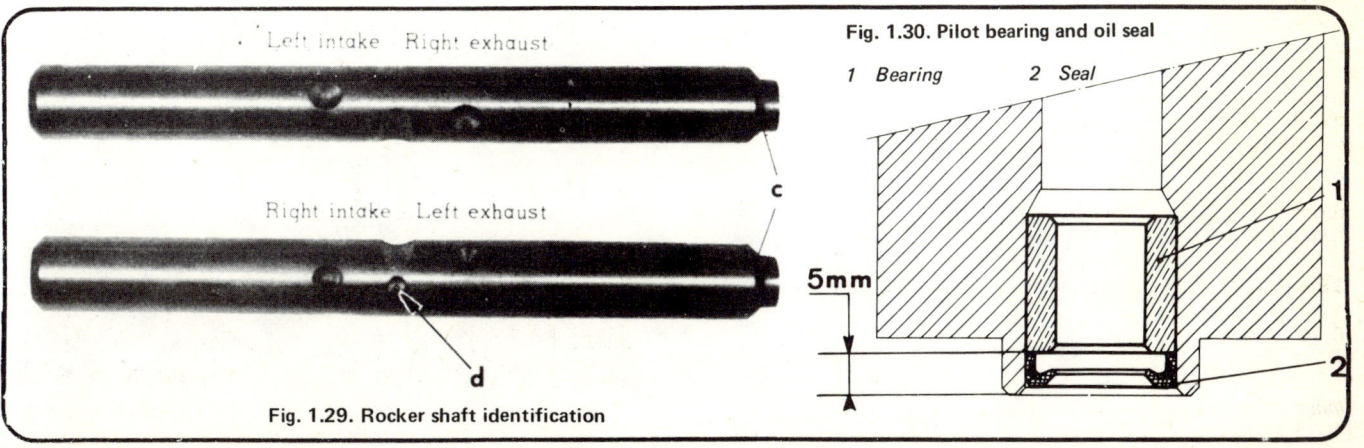

Fig. 1.29. Rocker shaft identification

Fig. 1.30. Pilot bearing and oil seal

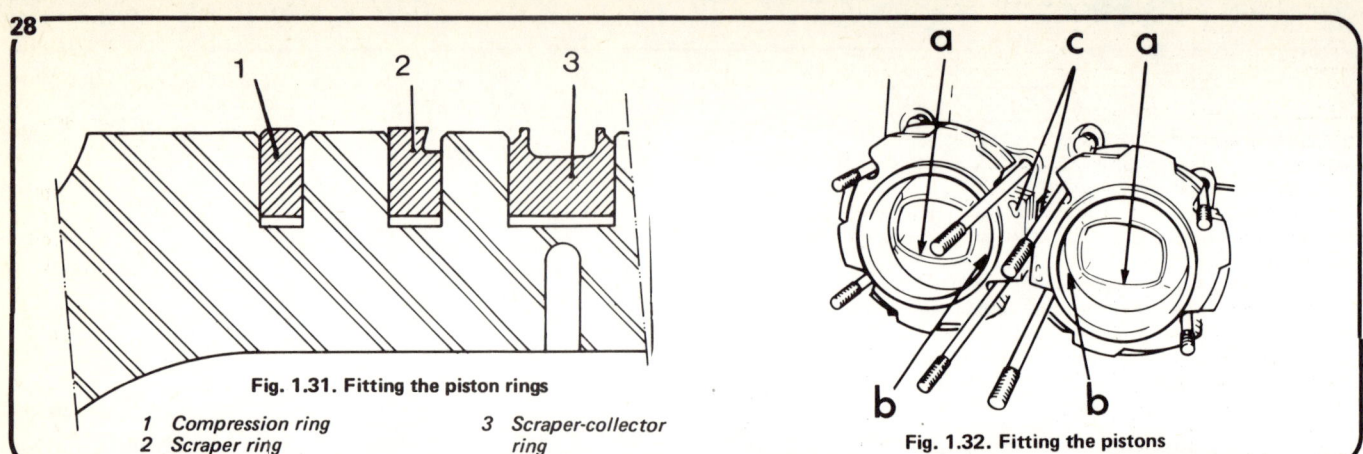

Fig. 1.31. Fitting the piston rings

1 Compression ring   3 Scraper-collector
2 Scraper ring   ring

Fig. 1.32. Fitting the pistons

13.1a Fitting a valve in the cylinder head

13.1b Fitting the valve seal

13.1c Valve spring and cup in position on the valve ready for fitting of the split cotters

13.1d Compressing the valve spring and fitting the split cotters

13.2a Fitting the left-hand camshaft

13.2b Fitting the right-hand camshaft

15.5 Fitting the piston in the cylinder using a piston ring clamp

15.6a Piston with gudgeon pin partly fitted in bore

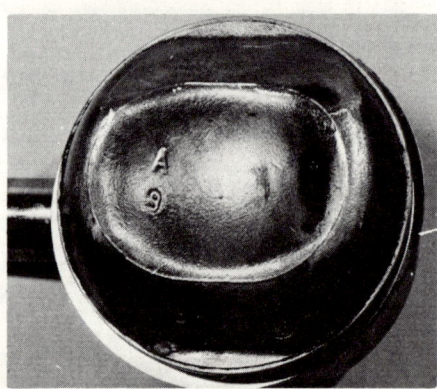

15.6b Fit the piston in the cylinder with the figure '9' the right way up

18 Engine - reassembly procedure

1   Fit the seal on the intake pipe of the oil strainer, smear the end of the pipe with Locktite and insert it in its housing on the engine casing. Insert the anti-emulsion shield between the engine casing and the strainer. Tighten the securing bolts to 1,4 kg f m (10 lb f ft).

2   Fit the oil filter bypass valve (white mark) as follows: Fit the valve, the washer and then the cup, secure the cup in the housing by tapping it in lightly. Fit the oil cooler bypass valve (green mark) in the same way. Smear the threads of the retaining plug with Locktite, fit with a copper washer and tighten to 4,5 to 5 kg f m (32 to 36 lb f ft).

3   Fit the lubrication system plugs with a copper washer, smear the threads with Locktite and tighten to 3,5 to 4 kg f m (25 to 29 lb f ft).

4   Make sure that the main bearing bores of the engine casings are clean and fit the bearing shells into the right and left-hand casings. Check that the bearing shells are properly engaged in the locating dowels and oil the bearing shells and journals of the crankshaft. Fit the crankshaft and connecting rod assembly in the left-hand casing and with a set of feeler gauges check that the endfloat of the crankshaft, measured at the centre bearing, is between 0,09 and 0,20 mm (0.0035 and 0.0078 in).

5   Smear the contacting face of the right-hand half engine casing with masti-joint HD 37 and place it on the left-hand half-casing. Fit the plain washers and nuts. Tighten the nuts '2' (Fig. 1.33), to 3,4 to 4,5 kg f m (24 to 32 lb f ft) and the nuts '1' to 1,2 to 1,5 kg f m (9 to 11 lb f ft). Check that the crankshaft rotates freely.

6   Oil the lip of the front and rear crankshaft seals and fit both seals carefully over each end of the crankshaft. Always fit new seals after each engine dismantling. Never fit the seals before assembling the half engine casings as this would crush the seals and cause oil leakage.

7   Refer to Fig. 1.22 and fit the oil pressure relief valve. Fit the cap with the lugs 'b' towards the bottom of the housing, the sleeve and the spring. Oil the piston and fit it, with the guide 'c' on the spring side, the spring washer, plain washer and circlip.

8   Oil and fit the oil pump pinions. Fit the cover plate so that the cavities 'b' (Fig. 1.35) are placed towards the inside of the engine casing and the small hole 'c' opposite cavity 'a' (Fig. 1.34). Place the hydraulic high pressure pump connecting rod in position. Temporarily fit a guide stud to assist assembly.

9   Fit the 'O'-ring seal, oil the shaft and eccentric. Place a shim between the wheel and the bearings at 'g' (Fig. 1.36) to prevent damaging the seal. Offer up the pump drive gear, to the guide stud with the groove 'd' of the connecting rod passage, positioned towards the high pressure pump, and engage the shaft in the central pinion. Turn the shaft in order to engage the flat-part 'e' into the oil pump pinion. Guide the high pressure pump connecting rod to engage it on the eccentric 'f' of the drive gear. Remove the guide stud and fit the five washers and retaining bolts, tighten to 1,5 to 1,8 kg f m (11 to 13 lb f ft). Remove the shim from between the wheel and the bearing. Check that the pump turns freely.

10   Oil the small-ends of the connecting rods, offer up the cylinder piston assemblies to the connecting rods, as shown in Fig. 1.32 and complete the fitting of the gudgeon pins in the pistons. Fit the gudgeon pin circlips, ensure that they are fully engaged in their grooves. Oil the pistons and inside of the cylinders and completely engage the cylinder. On G103 engines fit the under cylinder cooling ducts.

11   Fit and lubricate the 'O' rings on the oil return tubes and engage the longest ends into their engine casing housings. Turn the crankshaft to bring the pistons to their mid-stroke position and fit the cylinder heads while guiding the oil return tubes into position. Fit the washers and nuts, screw them up finger tight then torque tighten them initially, in the sequence shown in Fig. 1.37 to 0,8 to 1 kg f m (5.8 to 7.2 lb f ft). Before tightening the right-hand cylinder head, position the cylinders to allow for the fitting of the brake unit (early G10 engines). Finally tighten the cylinder head nuts, in the same sequence to 1,6 to 1,8 kg f m (12 to 13 lb f ft) for the 12 mm nuts and 2 to 2,5 kg f m (15 to 17 lb f ft) for the 13 mm nuts.

12   The two camshaft wheels are identical. Fit a wheel on the end of each camshaft and engage it on the locating pin. Fit the washer and securing nut, restrain the wheel from turning and tighten the nut to 8,2 kg f m (59 lb f ft).

13   The two tensioner rollers are identical. Fit the rollers, engaged with the locating pins, on the roller shafts, fit the support plates, washers and nuts. Do not tighten the nuts at this stage.

14   Fit the protective plate, (Fig. 1.38) the key on the crankshaft and the inner drive pinion, the intermediate flange and the outer drive pinion. Position the pinions so that groove 'a' is outwards on the outer pinion and towards the crankcase on the inner pinion.

15   When fitting the timing belts make sure that there is no trace of oil or grease on the belts, pinions or rollers. On a given engine always fit belts from the same manufacturers.

Turn the engine to bring the mark 'a' (Fig. 1.39), located on the intermediate flange, towards the top of the centre-line of the engine. Position the marks 'b', 'c' and 'd' on the camshaft wheels and the oil pump as shown in Fig. 1.39. Compress the tensioner roller in the direction of the arrows and tighten the securing nuts.

16   Fit the right-hand belt (the shorter of the two) so that the white marks on the belt coincide with the marks 'a' and 'd' in such a way that:

a - d = 42 teeth, tensioner side (G10 engines)
a - d = 43 teeth, tensioner side (G103 engines)

Fit the left-hand belt so that:

The white marks coincide with marks 'a' and 'b'
The yellow mark coincides with the mark 'e'

In this position:

a - b = 32 teeth (G10 engines)
a - b = 33 teeth (G103 engines)
a - c = 25 teeth (both engine types)

Fit the outer flange on the crankshaft. Slacken the roller securing nuts to release the rollers and then retighten the nuts.

17   The valve clearances are adjusted with the engine cold. Successively adjust each of the rocker arms as follows:

a)   Turn the engine until the heel of the rocker to be adjusted is on the back of the corresponding cam (valve completelty closed).
b)   Loosen the adjusting screw locknut and, using a feeler gauge and a cranked screwdriver, adjust the clearance between the heel of the rocker and the back of the cam to 0,2 mm (0.008 in). The clearance for both inlet and exhaust valves is the same.
c)   Tighten the locknut while holding the adjusting screw from turning. Re-check that the valve clearance is still correct.

18   Tension the timing belts: With the crankshaft marking and camshaft wheels positioned as shown in Fig. 1.39, turn the crankshaft through 90° in its normal direction of rotation. Loosen the left-hand tensioner roller securing nut and retighten it to 1,8 kg f m (13 lb f ft). Turn the crankshaft in its normal direction of rotation through one complete turn and carry out the same operation on the right-hand tensioner roller.

19   Ensure that there is no roughness on the joint faces of the rocker cover and cylinder head and that they are clean and dry. Stick the gasket on the rocker covers with Bostik 1400. Carefully oil the rocker arms, shafts and cams. The lower and upper cylinder head rocker covers are different, take care when fitting them. The rocker cover with the oil filler orifice is fitted on the left-hand side. Take care to centre the covers correctly as poor centring or insufficient tightening of the fixing nut could lead to a total loss of the engine oil. Tighten the nut to 0,8 to 1,0 kg f m (6 to 7 lb f ft).

20   Fit the cooling ducts 'a' (Figs. 1.16 and 1.17).

a)   Left-hand side, fit the duct on the engine casing.
b)   Right-hand side:
Fit the brake unit (G10 engines only).
Fit the duct on the right-hand cylinder head.
Fit the bolt '3' in Fig. 1.40 with the rear support plate of the air filter under the duct plate.
Fit the bolt '4' with the front support plate of the air filter under the duct plate (G10 engines only).

21   Fit the cylinder head lubrication pipes, tighten the union screws to 1,8 to 2 kg f m (13 to 14.5 lb f ft) and check that there is a minimum clearance of 5 mm (0.2 in) between the pipes and the camshaft wheels. Fit the oil pressure switch with a new seal and tighten it to 2,2 kg f m (16 lb f ft).

22 Oil the seal of the oil filter cartridge. Fit the seal and screw the cartridge as tight as possible by hand, then tighten it a further ½ to ¾ of a turn with a strap wrench.

23 When refitting the flywheel always fit new securing bolts. Make sure you fit the correct bolts, they are identified by a circle marked on the centre of the head. Ensure that both contact faces of the flywheel and crankshaft are clean and the dowel properly located. Oil the bolt threads, fit the bolts and restrain the flywheel from turning while tightening the bolts to 6,4 to 6,9 kg f m (46 to 50 lb f ft). On cars with automatic transmission a driveplate is fitted in place of the flywheel and the fixing bolts must be treated with Locktite.

24 Fit the exhaust pipes and tighten the nuts to 1,5 kg f m (11 lb f ft).

25 Fit a new seal on the oil temperature thermal switch and tighten it to 2,5 kg f m (18 lb f ft).

26 Fit the clutch assembly, referring to Chapter 4.

27 Fit new oil seals on each tube of the oil cooler. Fit the cooler and tighten the bolts to 1,8 kg f m (13 lb f ft).

28 Fit the starter motor, as described in Chapter 11.

29 Fit the breather tube ensuring that it does not touch the cooling duct. Fit the dipstick guide.

30 Fit the heating ducts (Figs. 1.16 and 1.17).

Fit the front right-hand deflector 'H'
Fit the rear left-hand screen 'G'.
Fit the assembly of rear right-hand mounting plate 'E' and deflector 'D'.
Couple up the heating ducts, fit washers under the heads of all screws.

31 Fit the carburettor heater box or inlet pipe manifold and carburettor assembly. Tighten the bolts to 1,8 kg f m (13 lb f ft). Connect the pipe from the exhaust to the heater box.

32 Fit the hydraulic pump: During handling of the pump, hold the pump piston to prevent it coming out of its cylinder. Check that the contact faces of the pump and the engine casing are clean. Fit a new 'O' ring seal between the pump and the casing. Offer up the pump to the connecting drive rod and fit the pin. If necessary, turn the engine to bring the connecting rod to its tdc (top-dead-centre) position. Check that the piston is correctly located in the pump cylinder and that the 'O' ring is in place on the engine casing. Fit the pump over the mounting studs and bring the baseplate up to the engine casing without forcing it. Fit and tighten the securing nuts to 1,3 to 1,4 kg f m (9.5 to 10 lb f ft). Fit the cover on the pump body, connect the delivery pipe. Fit the bracket fixing the pipe onto the cylinder head.

33 Fit the alternator tensioner and the alternator, do not tighten the alternator bolts at this stage. Fit the cylinder head lubrication pipe supports.

34 On G10 engines, engage the ducts 'J' (Fig. 1.16) on the oil return tubes of the cylinder heads. The upper part of the duct must be engaged between the third and fourth cooling fin of the cylinder.

35 On the fan cowl mounting studs fit a flat washer on each side of the spacer, fit the fan cowl and tighten the nuts.

36 Fit the fanbelt on the alternator pulley and engage it on the fan pulley. Fit the fan on the end of the crankshaft, the starter dog and locknut. Position the starter dog so that it is horizontal when the engine is at ignition point. Adjust by loosening the locknut and turning the threaded sleeve as necessary. Tighten the locknut to 18 kg f m (130 lb f ft). The starter dog should have 4 to 5 mm of thread visible after tightening the nut.

37 Fit the upper duct covers with the spark plug lead support fixed on the the centred bolt.

38 Fit the carburettor, fuel pump, distributor, spark plugs and pressure regulator, referring if necessary to the appropriate Chapters.

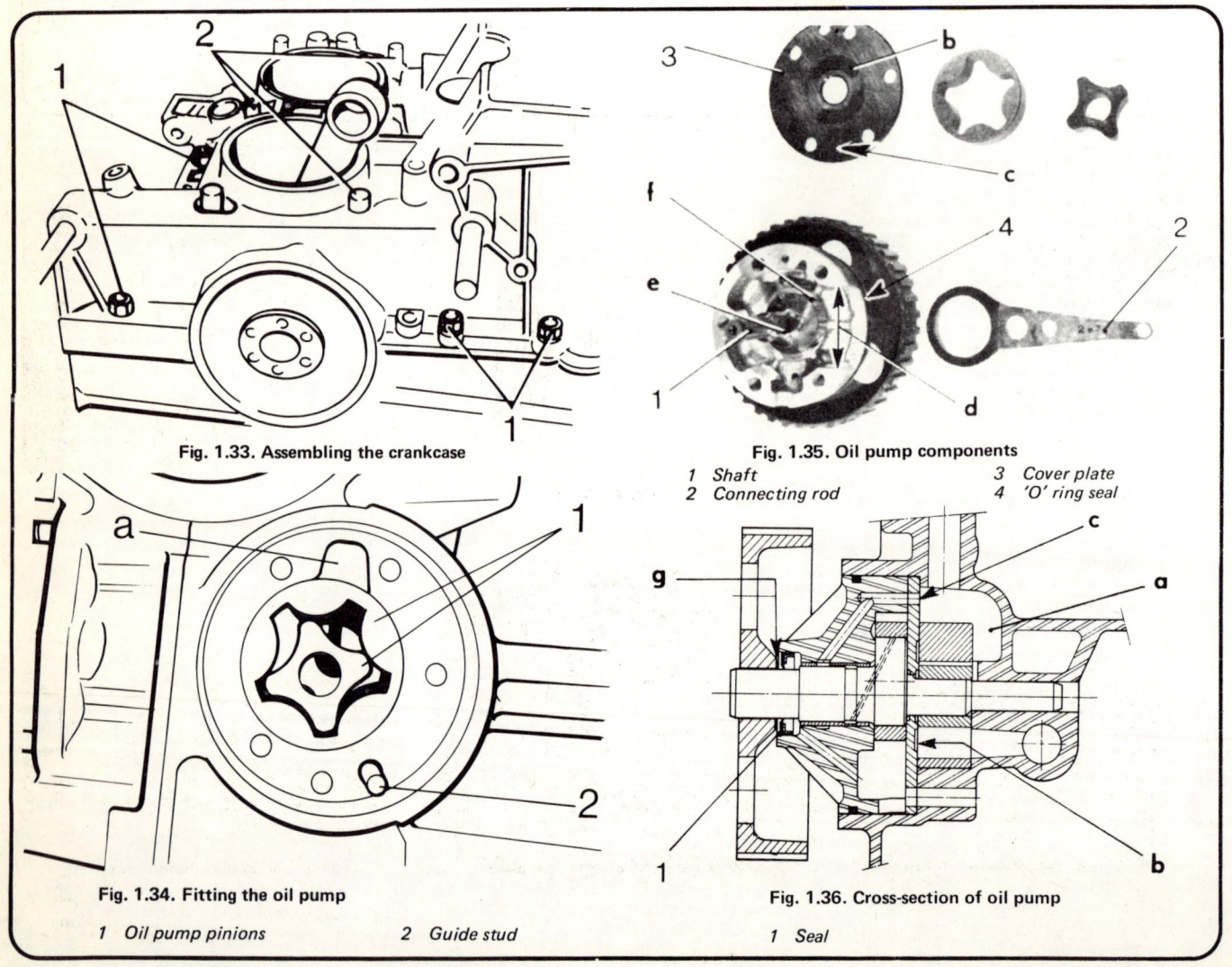

Fig. 1.33. Assembling the crankcase

Fig. 1.35. Oil pump components

1   Shaft   3   Cover plate
2   Connecting rod   4   'O' ring seal

Fig. 1.34. Fitting the oil pump

1   Oil pump pinions   2   Guide stud

Fig. 1.36. Cross-section of oil pump

1   Seal

Fig. 1.37. Tightening sequence of cylinder head nuts

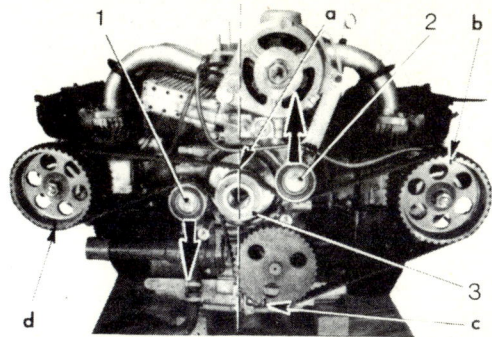

Fig. 1.39. Fitting the timing belts

1 Tension roller nut   3 Outer flange
2 Tension roller nut

Fig. 1.38. Crankshaft timing gears

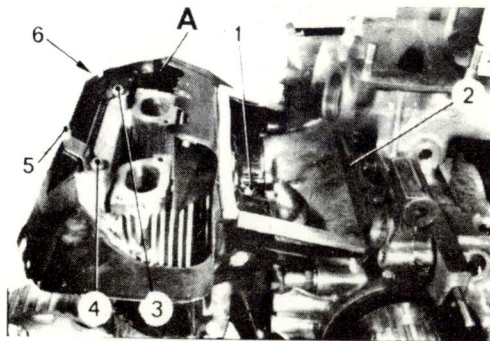

Fig. 1.40. Fitting the cooling duct

1 Nut   4 Protective plate
2 Outer pinion   5 Inner pinion
3 Intermediate flange   6 Tension roller

1 Brake unit (G10 engines only)   4 Bolt
2 Seal   5 Front support plate
3 Bolt   6 Rear support plate

18.1 Fitting the oil strainer and anti-emulsion shield

18.2a The oil cooler bypass valve

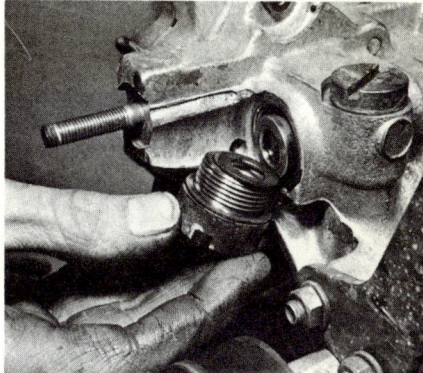

18.2b Fitting the oil cooler bypass valve and retaining plug

18.4a The left-hand half-casing

18.4b Fitting the main bearing shells

18.4c Fitting the crankshaft and connecting rod assembly in the left-hand half-casing

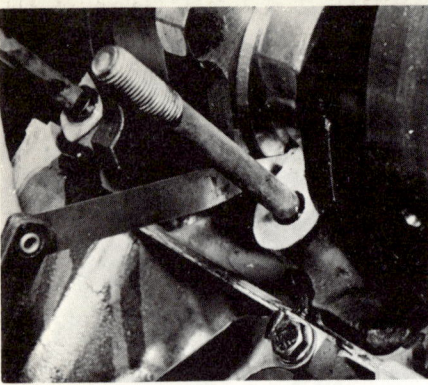

18.4d Measuring the crankshaft endfloat with a feeler gauge

18.6 Fitting the crankshaft rear seal

18.8a Fitting the oil pump pinions

18.8b Fitting the cover plate

18.8c Placing the hydraulic pump connecting rod in position

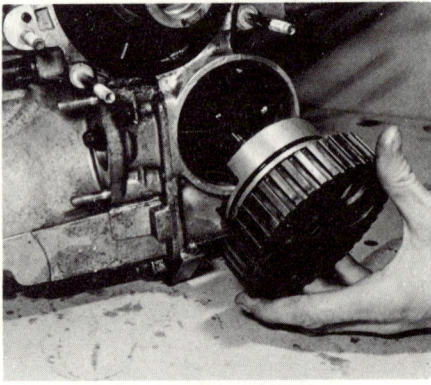

18.9 Fitting the oil pump drive gear

18.10a Fitting the piston and cylinder assembly

18.10b Gudgeon pin fitted in position

18.11a Fitting the oil return tubes

18.11b Piston at mid-stroke position

18.11c Replacing the right-hand cylinder head

18.12 Fitting the drive wheel on the right-hand camshaft

18.13a A timing belt tensioner roller

18.13b Fitting the right-hand tensioner roller, support plate, washer and nut

18.14a Fitting the inner protective flange plate and key on the crankshaft

18.14b Replacing the inner belt drive pinion, the intermediate flange and the outer drive pinion

18.16a Right-hand drivebelt fitted

18.16b Left-hand drivebelt fitted

18.16c Lining-up the marks on the belts and flanges

18.17 Adjusting the rocker arm clearance

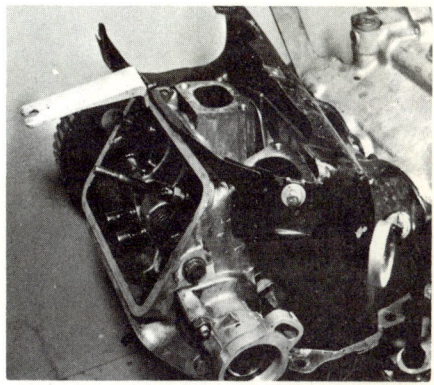

18.20a Replacing the left-hand cooling duct

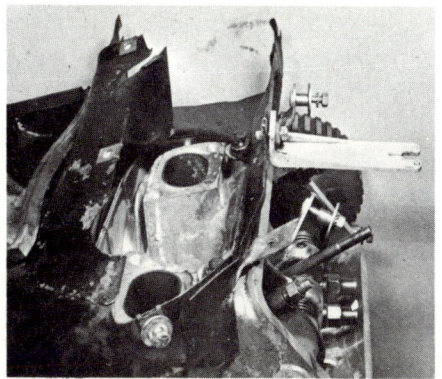

18.20b Replacing the right-hand cooling duct

18.21 Connecting the lubricating pipe to the right-hand cylinder head

18.22 Replacing the oil filter cartridge

18.23a Flywheel bolt identification marking

18.23b Flywheel bolted in position

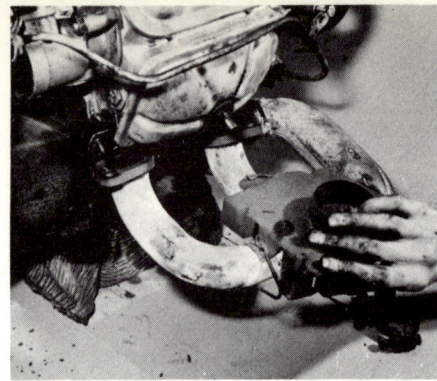

18.24 Fitting the right-hand exhaust manifold pipes

18.27a Fitting new seals on the oil cooler tubes

18.27b Replacing the oil cooler

18.28 Replacing the starter motor

18.29a The crankcase breather

18.29b Crankcase breather fitted in position

18.29c Fitting the dipstick guide

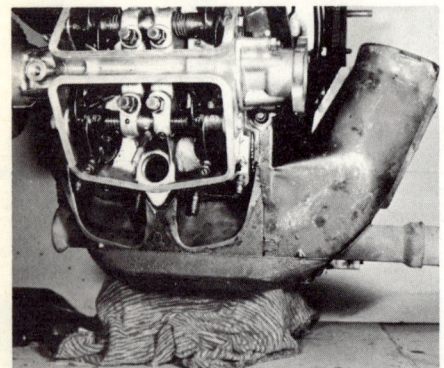

18.30 Assembling the left-hand heating duct

18.31a Replacing the carburettor and intake manifold pipes assembly

18.31b Connecting the pipe from the exhaust to the intake manifold

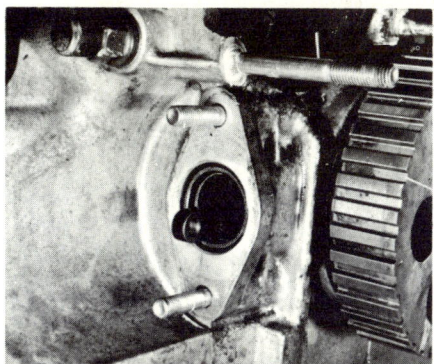

18.32a Hydraulic pump connecting rod and mounting flange

18.32b Fitting the hydraulic pump

18.33 Replacing the alternator

18.34 Engaging the under cylinder cooling duct on the oil return tubes (G10 engines only)

18.36 Fitting the fan and the starter dog nut

19.2 Don't forget to put oil in the engine before starting-up

19 Engine - replacement in car

1   Replacement of the engine is a reversal of the removal operations. Do not forget to fit the driveshafts and connect up the exhaust pipe.
2   Carry out the following checks before starting the engine:

    a) *Fuel pipes to pump and carburettor connections tightened.*
    b) *Sump drain plug tightened and oil in the engine.*
    c) *Gearbox oil level correct and plugs tightened.*
    d) *Ignition wiring and spark plug leads connected.*
    e) *Oil pressure and temperature sender units connected.*
    f) *Choke and throttle cable connected.*
    g) *Starter motor and alternator leads connected.*
    h) *Hydraulic oil reservoir filled.*
    j) *Hydraulic pipe connections made and tightened.*
    k) *Fully charged battery fitted and leads connected.*

20 Engine - initial start-up after assembly

1   Carry out a visual examination of the engine compartment, for rags or tools which may have been overlooked, before starting the engine.
2   Prime the high pressure pump by freeing the pump suction pipe from the reservoir and filling the pump with LHM fluid through the pipe. Slacken the pressure regulator bleed screw.
3   Set the choke and start the engine. Quickly replace the suction pipe in the reservoir and tighten the pressure regulator bleed screw.
4   Run the engine at a fast idle, and check for oil leaks and leaks from the hydraulic system.
5   Select the high suspension position and top-up the hydraulic reservoir, as described in Chapter 6.
6   When the engine running temperature has been reached, adjust the idling speed, as described in Chapter 2, and road-test the car.
7   After 600 miles (1000 km) running, change the engine oil, and retighten the cylinder head bolts to the correct torque loading with the engine cold. Check the valve clearances.

21 Fault diagnosis - engine overleaf

21 Fault diagnosis - engine

Symptom	Reason/s	Remedy
Engine will not turn over when starter-switch is operated	Flat battery Bad battery connections Bad connections at starter motor and/or solenoid switch	Check that battery is fully charged and that all connections are clean and tight.
	Starter motor jammed	Engage a gear and rock the car back and forward. If ineffective remove the starter.
	Defective solenoid	Remove the starter and check the solenoid.
	Starter motor defective	Remove and overhaul the starter.
Engine turns over but fails to start	No spark at plug	Check ignition system in accordance with procedures given in Chapter 3.
	No fuel reaching the engine	Check fuel system in accordance with procedures given in Chapter 2.
	Too much fuel reaching the engine (flooding)	Check the fuel system as above.
Engine starts but runs unevenly and misfires	Ignition and/or fuel system faults	Check the ignition and fuel systems as though the engine had failed to start.
	Incorrect valve clearances	Check and reset clearances.
	Burnt out valves	Remove engine and overhaul as necessary.
	Worn piston rings and cylinders	Remove engine and overhaul as necessary.
Lack of power	Ignition and/or fuel system faults	Check the ignition and fuel systems for correct timing and carburettor settings.
	Incorrect valve clearances	Check and reset clearances.
	Burnt out valves	Remove engine and overhaul as necessary.
	Worn piston rings and/or cylinders	Remove engine and overhaul as necessary.
Excessive oil consumption	Oil leaks from pipe unions and gaskets of lubrication system	Identify source of leak and rectify as appropriate.
	Oil leaks from crankshaft oil seals	Remove engine and replace seals.
	Worn valve guides and/or defective valve stem seals	Remove engine and rectify as appropriate.
	Worn piston rings and cylinders (indicated by excessive blue smoke from exhaust)	Remove engine and overhaul as necessary.
Excessive mechanical noise from engine	Wrong valve clearances	Adjust valve clearance.
	Worn crankshaft bearings	Remove engine and overhaul as necessary.
Unusual vibrations	Misfiring on one or more cylinders	Check ignition system.
	Loose mounting bolts	Check tightness of bolts and condition of flexible mountings.

Note: When investigating starting and uneven running faults do not be tempted into snap diagnosis. Start from the beginning and follow it through. It will take less time in the long run. Poor performance from an engine in terms of power and economy is not normally diagnosed quickly. In any event the ignition and fuel system must be checked first before assuming any further investigation needs to be made.

Chapter 2 Carburettors; fuel and exhaust systems

Contents

Specifications

Fuel pump
Type ... ... Guiot or AC Delco mechanical
Delivery pressure ... ... 250 m b (3.5 psi)

Fuel filter
To February 1972 ... ... In fuel tank
From February 1972 ... ... Guiot G20 (disposable)

Air Cleaner ... ... Dry element, cleanable

Fuel tank capacity ... ... 43 litres (9.75 Imp. gallons)

Carburettor - Solex 28 CIC series CIT 118

	1st choke	2nd choke
Venturi bore	21	21
Main jet	110	90
Emulsion tube	1 P 1	2 U 1
Slow running jet	50	—
Accelerator pump injector	35	—
Float	Double polyamide	

Carburettor - Solex 28 CIC series CIT 133

	1st choke	2nd choke
Venturi bore	19	19
Main jet	100	70
Emulsion tube	1 P 1	2 P 2
Slow running jet	50	—
Accelerator pump injector	45	—
Bypass jet	—	40
Econostat jet	—	140
Float	Double polyamide	

Carburettor - Solex 28 CIC^2 series CIT 137

	1st choke	2nd choke
Venturi bore	19	19
Main jet	100	75
Emulsion tube	1 P 2	2 P 3
Idling jet	45	—
Constant richness idling jet	35	—
Accelerator pump injector	50	—
Bypass jet	—	50
Econostat jet	—	160
Float	Double plastic	

Carburettor - Solex 28 CIC[3] series CIT 131

	1st choke	2nd choke
Venturi bore	19	19
Main jet	100	80
Air correction jet	1 P 3	2 P 4
Idling jet	50	—
Constant richness idling jet	30	—
Accelerator pump injector	50	—
Econostat jet	—	130
Bypass jet	—	40
Float	Double plastic	

Carburettor - Weber 30 DGS (W50.00)

	1st choke	2nd choke
Venturi bore	20	20
Main jet	100	100
Air correction jet	AD 1	AD 2
Emulsion tube	F 20	F 20
Slow-running jet	45	45
Accelerator pump injector	50	—
Sprayers (mixture jets)	4, 5	4, 5
Float	Brass-weight 11 g	

Carburettor - Weber DGS 1 (W51.00)

	1st choke	2nd choke
Venturi bore	20	20
Main jet	100	107
Air correction jet	AD 2	AD 2
Emulsion tube	F 20	F 20
Idling jet	45	45
Accelerator pump injector	50	—
Sprayers (mixture jets)	4, 5	4, 5
Float	Brass-weight 11 g	

1 General description

1 The fuel system comprises a fuel tank at the rear of the car, a mechanical fuel pump mounted at the rear of the right-hand cylinders and a Solex or Weber carburettor. Early models have a filter in the tank suction pipe, on later models an in-line filter is fitted between the tank and the pump. A dry type element is fitted in the air cleaner/silencer. Those models fitted with anti-pollution type carburettors have an air valve assembly which thermostatically controls the temperature of the intake air.

2 The fuel pump draws petrol from the fuel tank and delivers it to the carburettor. The level of the petrol in the carburettor is controlled by a float operated needle valve. Petrol flows past the needle until the float rises sufficiently to close the valve. The pump will then freewheel under slight back pressure until the petrol level drops in the float chamber. The needle valve will then open and petrol will continue to flow until the level rises again.

3 The petrol/air charge is drawn into the cylinders on the induction stroke via the heater box which is heated from the oil system on early models and by exhaust gases on the later models.

2 Air cleaner assembly - removal and replacement

1 Disconnect the breather pipe and the hot air pipe. Release the clip securing the elbow duct to the carburettor and remove the bracket retaining nuts. Remove the cleaner assembly.

2 Unclip the cover and withdraw the element. Clean the dust from the element and examine it for defects. Clean the interior of the casing and casing cover. Examine the ducts and flexible pipes for damage.

3 Fitment of a new or cleaned element and replacement of the cleaner assembly is the reversal of the removal sequence.

3 Preheating of the air intake system - general

1 Warm air enters the control valve body from the heating duct and ambient air enters through the elbow at the side of the valve body. The temperature of the air entering the air cleaner casing is controlled by a flap valve which regulates the amount of warm air and air at ambient temperature. The flap valve is actuated by a thermostat, refer to Fig. 2.1 and the warm air enters the control valve body at 'a' and air at ambient temperature enters at 'b'.

2 During the warm up of the engine it is possible to check the movement of the flap valve by observing the mark which is on the end of the flap valve spindle. The operation of the flap valve may also be checked by inserting a thin rod into the ambient air intake and checking the flap movement.

3 Remove the control valve assembly and check the thermostat as follows:

   a) That at ambient temperature below 36° C (97° F) the flap valve, Fig. 2.1, closes the duct 'b'.
   b) Immerse the thermostat element in cold water and slowly heat the water to progressively raise the temperature. Check that when the temperature reaches $39 \pm 3°C$ ($102 \pm 5°F$) the flap valve progressively closes the warm air duct (preheated air) and stays in that position.
   c) Let the water cool and check that when the temperature falls below $39 \pm 3°C$ ($102 \pm 5°F$) the flap valve closes the ambient air intake duct.

4 A defective control valve is not repairable by an owner and must be renewed.

2.2 Removing the air cleaner element

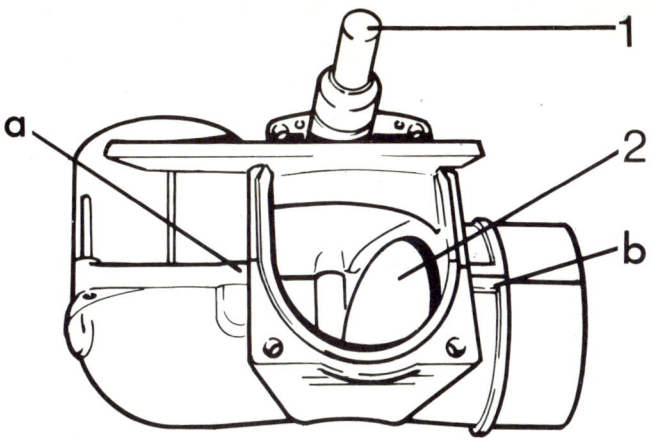

Fig. 2.1. Air control valve assembly

1   Thermostat   (a) Warm air duct
2   Flap valve   (b) Ambient air duct

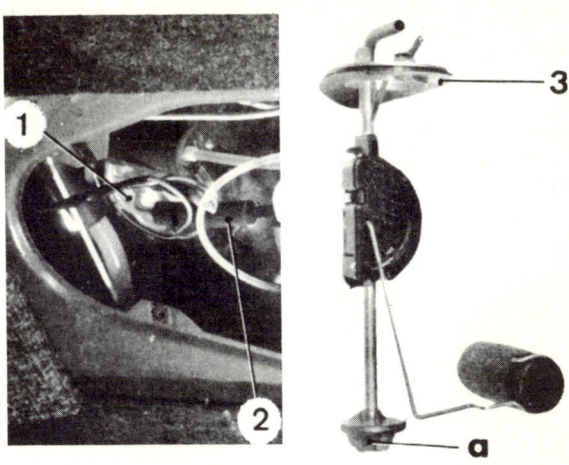

Fig. 2.2. Suction pipe and sender assembly

1   Locking ring   3   Gasket
2   Flexible fuel pipe   (a) Filter

4 Fuel filter - general

1   On models to February 1972 a cleanable fuel filter was fitted in the fuel tank, later models have a disposable unit fitted in the fuel line between the tank and the fuel pump. It is mounted in front of the rear axle, underneath the car on the right-hand side.

2   To remove, clean and replace the fuel tank filter proceed as follows:

a) Disconnect the earth lead from the battery.
b) Remove the cover plate from inside the boot.
c) Disconnect the two transmitter leads and uncouple the flexible suction pipe from the sender.
d) Remove the transmitter locking ring from the tank, by rotating it 60° in an anti-clockwise direction, and then carefully withdraw the suction pipe and sender assembly.
e) Clean the filter element in petrol and blow out with compressed air.
f) First insert the float into the tank and then the suction pipe.
g) Correctly locate the gasket, fit the locking ring and turn it 60° clockwise to lock.
h) Connect the transmitter leads, couple up the flexible suction pipe to the sender and fit the cover plate.
j) Connect the earth lead to the battery, switch on the ignition and check the operation of the fuel gauge sender.

3   The in-line filter fitted to models from February 1972 cannot be cleaned and must be renewed every 1200 miles (20,000 km). When fitting a replacement filter ensure that it is installed correctly with the arrow on the unit, indicating the petrol flow, pointing in the right direction.

4.3 The in-line fuel filter

5 Fuel pump - general

1   The mechanical diaphragm type pump is mounted on the rear bearing housing of the right-hand camshaft and is operated by an eccentric cam ring at the end of the camshaft. An insulation spacer is fitted between the pump flange and the camshaft bearing housing to reduce heat transfer from the engine to the pump. No instructions are given for the repair of a defective pump by the owner. Test procedures are described: if the pump is found to be defective it should be renewed.

6 Fuel pump - removal and replacement

1   Disconnect the inlet pipe from the fuel tank and the delivery pipe to the carburettor. Remove the two securing nuts and washers and lift off the pump. Replacement is a straightforward reversal of the removal sequence.

6.1 Fuel pump inlet and delivery pipe connections

7 Fuel pump - testing

1   Illustrated in Fig. 2.3 is the Citroen test set 4005-T used for fuel pump pressure testing. If the owner wants to make up a kit he will require a pressure gauge, a two way union with a shut-off cock and flexible piping.
2   Disconnect the fuel feed to the carburettor and fit the test set between the pump and carburettor. Carry out the following checks:

   a) *Unscrew the knurled knob approximately one and a half turns and start the engine.*
   b) *Screw the knob in completely and check that the stabilized pressure does not exceed 0.25 kg/sq. cm (3.5 psi).*
   c) *Stop the engine and check that the pressure does not drop abruptly.*
   d) *Slacken the knurled knob, start the engine and allow it to run for a few seconds. Stop the engine and check that the pressure does not drop abruptly.*

Remove the test set and reconnect the fuel feed to the carburettor.
3   Remove the fuel pump, as described in Section 6, and check the travel of the pump pushrod as follows:

   a) *Using a depth gauge, Fig. 2.4, measure the distance between the upper face of the spacer and the actuating eccentric of the camshaft, first at the high and then at the low position. Turn the engine with the starting handle or the starter ring to facilitate this operation. The distance should be between 21.5 and 22 mm (0.846 and 0.866 in) for the high position of the eccentric and 26.5 to 27 mm (1.043 to 1.063 in) for the low position of the eccentric.*
   b) *Measure the distance 'm' (Fig. 2.5), between the spring cap and the end of the pump spindle, this must not be less than 4 mm (0.16 in).*

Replace the pump as described in Section 6.

8 Carburettors - general description

1   Two makes of carburettor are fitted, Solex and Weber. Both are of a downdraught twin choke type with manually operated choke control. Both types are conventional in operation and have a primary and main jet system and a mechanically operated acceleration pump. Both makes of carburettor incorporate exhaust emission control, anti-pollution features except the Solex CIT 118 and 133 series.

9 Carburettor - removal and replacement (Solex and Weber)

1   The removal and replacement procedure is the same for both Solex and Weber carburettors.
2   Remove the air cleaner assembly, as described in Section 2.
3   Disconnect the choke and throttle cables from the carburettor.
4   Disconnect the flexible fuel feed pipe from the carburettor and blank the end with a 7 mm diameter bolt.
5   Remove the four securing nuts and lift off the carburettor and the insulation spacer.
6   Replacement of the carburettor is the reverse of the removal sequence. Clean off the old jointing compound from the carburettor mounting flange, the spacer and the heater box. Smear both faces of the spacer with LOWAC sealing compound and fit it on the heater box with the hole positioned on the right-hand side.

10 Carburettors (Solex) - general

1   The modification standard of Solex carburettors is recognised by a series of CIT numbers which are marked on the carburettors. Identification of the jets and their location is shown in Fig. 2.13.
2   The position of the stop screws '2' and '4', shown in Fig. 2.6, for the butterflies of the primary and secondary chokes is obtained by using a micro-measuring device and these screws must not be altered under any circumstances.

Only the idling air screw may be adjusted to obtain the correct idling speed.
3   If the engine is running badly check the condition of the following before carrying out any adjustments to the carburettor:

   Air cleaner
   Valve clearance
   Ignition system
   Spark plugs
   Strobe timing of the distributor
   Throttle and choke linkage

Adjustments should be carried out with the engine at normal running temperature, engine oil temperature 70 to 80ºC (158 to 176ºF).
4   If the car is not fitted with a tachometer, a workshop tachometer will have to be fitted for setting the idling speed, 900 to 950 rpm for models with manual transmission and 850 to 900 rpm for models with semi-automatic transmissions.

11 Idling - adjustment (Solex series CIT 118 and 133 carburettors)

1   Ensure that the throttle butterflies, for the primary and secondary chokes, close properly.
2   Slacken the pressure regulator bleed screw.
3   Preset screw '3' (Fig. 2.6) by screwing it in fully without forcing and then unscrew it six full turns. Preset screw '1' by screwing in fully and then unscrewing four complete turns.
4   Adjust the air screw '1' to bring the idling speed to that specified in Section 10.
5   Find the peak idling speed by slowly adjusting the volume control screw '3' in or out, as necessary, then screw it in so as to cause the idling speed to fall by between 10 and 20 rpm.
6   If the final speed obtained is different from that specified in Section 10, reset it, and repeat the operations as paragraph 5 above.

12 Choke control - adjustment (Solex series CIT 118 and 133 carburettors)

1   Refer to Fig. 2.7. With the choke lever in position indicated and peg 'a' in firm contact with lever '3', a 0.5 mm diameter rod must pass snugly, but freely, between the edge of the secondary throttle butterfly and the body of the carburettor. If necessary, adjust screw '2' to obtain this setting.

13 Idling - adjustment (Solex series CIT 137 and 131 carburettors)

1   Refer to Fig. 2.8. Do not alter the butterfly stop screws '2' and '4' of the primary and secondary chokes.
2   Connect up an exhaust gas analyser.
3   Slacken the hydraulic pressure regulator bleed screw.
4   With the engine running at normal temperature, adjust screw '1' to obtain an idling speed of 900 to 950rpm.
5   Using screw '3' adjust the mixture to obtain a CO reading of 2 to 3.5 percent and a CO_2 reading of 10 to 13 percent.
6   Operations 4 and 5 are to be carried out simultaneously until the specified idling speed is obtained with the CO and CO_2 readings within the specified limits.

14 Throttle closing damper - adjustment (Solex series CIT 137 carburettors)

1   The throttle closing damper is fitted to delay the rate of closure of the throttle when the accelerator pedal is released suddenly.
2   To check the closing delay run the engine at 2500rpm, release the accelerator pedal suddenly and check that the rpm falls to 1000 within 2 to 5 seconds.
3   Adjust the throttle closing damper, if necessary, as follows:

   a) *Slacken the nut '1', Fig. 2.9.*
   b) *Screw in the throttle closing damper to reduce the closing delay or screw it out to increase the closing delay.*

c) Tighten the nut '1' and recheck the timing of the closing delay.

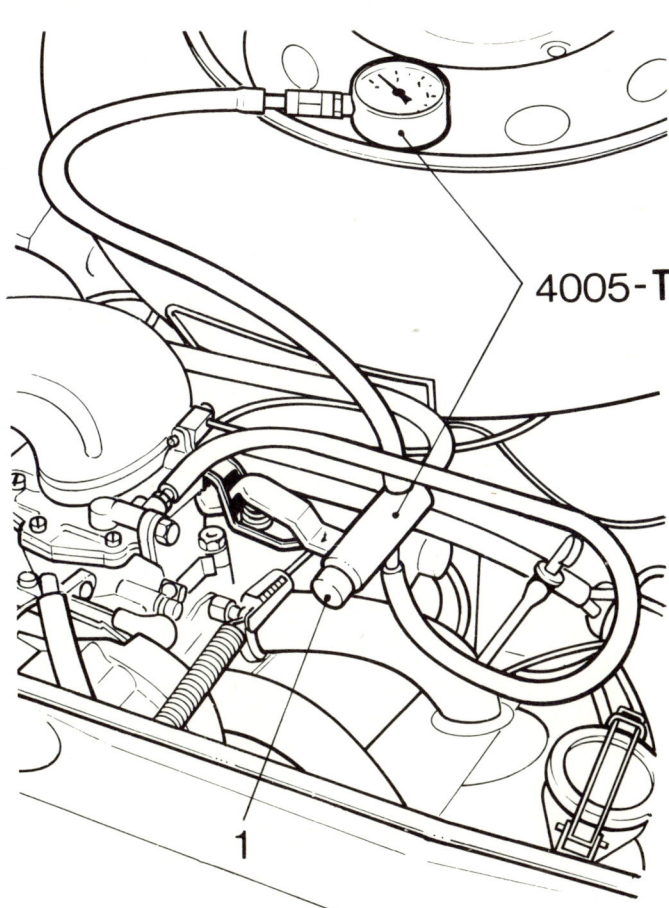

Fig. 2.3. Checking the fuel pressure

1   Knurled knob

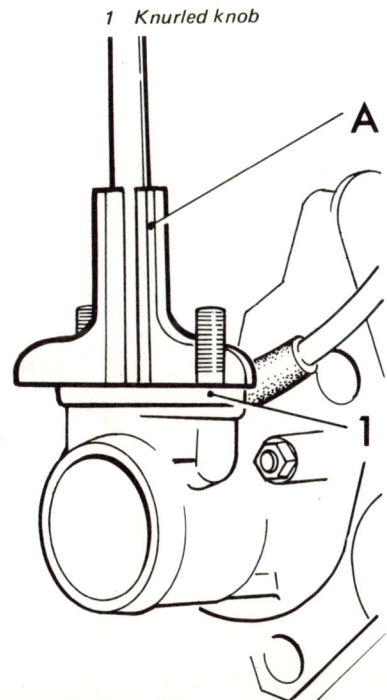

Fig. 2.4. Checking the pump pushrod travel

1   Insulation spacer   A   Depth gauge

Fig. 2.5. Measuring the fuel pump spindle

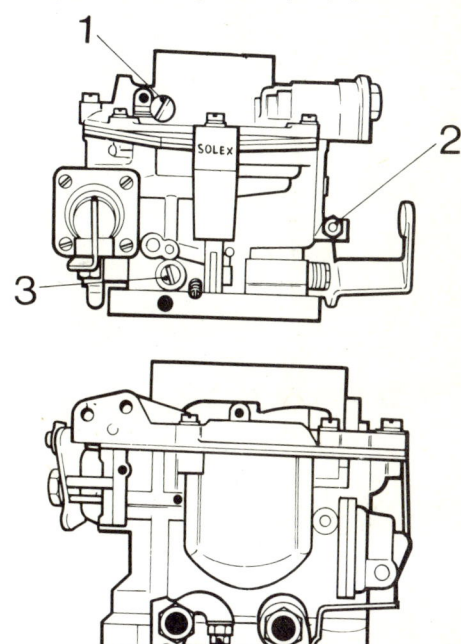

Fig. 2.6. Carburettor adjusting screws

1   Idling air screw   3   Volume control screw
2   Primary butterfly stop screw 4   Secondary butterfly stop
                                       screw

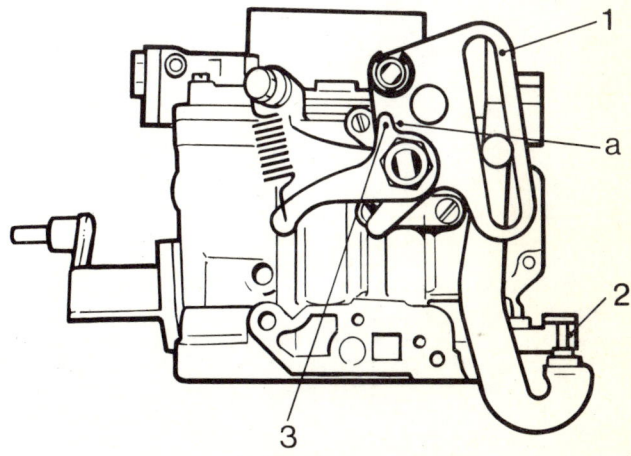

Fig. 2.7. Choke adjustment

1   Choke lever   3   Lever
2   Adjusting screw

Fig. 2.8. Idling adjustment

1 *Adjusting screw*	4 *Secondary butterfly stop screw*
2 *Primary butterfly stop screw*	5 *Choke control*
3 *Mixture screw*	6 *Choke adjusting screw*

Fig. 2.9. Throttle closing damper - adjustment

1 *Locking nut*	2 *Throttle closing damper*

15 Choke control - adjustment (Solex series CIT 137 carburettors)

1   With the choke control '5' (Fig. 2.8) at the first notch (starting from the no-choke position) check that a 0.35mm (0.014in) diameter rod goes through easily, but snugly, between the secondary throttle butterfly and the body of the carburettor. Adjust as necessary with screw '6' to obtain the correct setting.

16 Choke control - adjustment (Solex series CIT 131 carburettors)

1   On carburettors for cars produced up to June 1973 and fitted with the choke lever 'A' (Fig. 2.10), adjust as follows: With the choke lever

positioned as shown in Fig. 2.11, peg 'C' in firm contact with lever '3', a 0.35 - 0.40mm (0.013 - 0.015in) diameter rod must pass freely, but snugly, between the edge of the secondary throttle butterfly and the body of the carburettor. If necessary, adjust screw '2' to obtain this setting.
2   On carburettors for cars produced since June 1973 and fitted with choke lever 'B', adjust as for those fitted with lever 'A' except that a rod of 0.25 - 0.35mm (0.010 - 0.013in) is used.
3   It is important that before any adjustment of the choke control, the difference in profile of the slots in the choke levers should be noted: 'a' for lever 'A' and 'b' for lever 'B'. **Note:** It is recommended that the choke control assembly 'A' be replaced by the assembly 'B'.

17 Float level - adjustment (Solex carburettors)

1   Remove the air cleaner, as described in Section 2. Disconnect the fuel feed pipe and remove the cover retaining screws. Lift off the cover and float assembly.
2   With the cover and float assembly positioned as shown in Fig. 2.12, the dimension measured between the float centre-line and the joint face of the cover (gasket fitted) must be:

> a) *Carburettors CIT 118 series - 'h' = 20 ± 1mm (0.79 ± 0.04in)*
> b) *Carburettors all other series - 'h' = 18 ± 1mm (0.71 ± 0.04in)*

If necessary, alter the position of the float by moving lug 'a' to obtain dimension 'h' for the type of carburettor being adjusted.
3   Fit the carburettor cover and ensure that the float does not touch the walls of the float chamber. Connect the fuel feed pipe. Fit the air cleaner assembly, refer to Section 2.

18 Cleaning - general (Solex carburettors)

Use only petrol and compressed air to clean jets and air bleeds. Do not clean them with probes as this may alter the calibration.
Remove the top cover as described in Section 17.
The position of the jets and air bleeds of a Solex 28 CIC 3 carburettor is illustrated in Fig. 2.13 and earlier series carburettors will not have all the jets as shown.

19 Carburettors (Weber) - general

The Weber 30DGS (W50.00) fitted to G10 engines and the Weber 30DGS1 (W51.00) fitted to G103 engines are very similar and the idling speed and the float adjustment is the same for both carburettors. The position of the jets and air bleeds of a 30DGS (W50.00) carburettor are illustrated in Fig. 2.14. Both carburettors have exhaust emission control anti-pollution systems and exhaust gas analyser equipment is required when adjusting the idling speed.

20 Idling speed - adjustment (Weber carburettors)

1   Before adjusting the idling speed, refer to Section 10 and carry out the checks listed in paragraph 3.
2   Do not alter the setting of the secondary butterfly stop screw as this is set, using a micro-measuring device, by the manufacturer.
3   Ensure that the throttle butterflies in the primary and secondary chokes close fully.
4   Run the engine to obtain a normal operating temperature of 70° to $80^{\circ}C$ (158° to $176^{\circ}F$) and slacken the pressure regulator bleed screw.
5   Adjust screw '1' to obtain the correct idling speed:

> a) *850 to 900rpm - for cars with semi-automatic transmission*
> b) *900 to 950rpm - for cars with manual transmission.*

6   Using screw '5' adjust the mixture to obtain a CO reading 2 to 3.5 percent and a CO_2 reading of 10 to 13 percent. Obtain these readings with the engine idling speed as specified in paragraph 5 above. Both operations must be carried out simultaneously. The specified CO and CO_2 readings are for an ambient air temperature of between 15° and $30^{\circ}C$ (61° and $86^{\circ}F$).

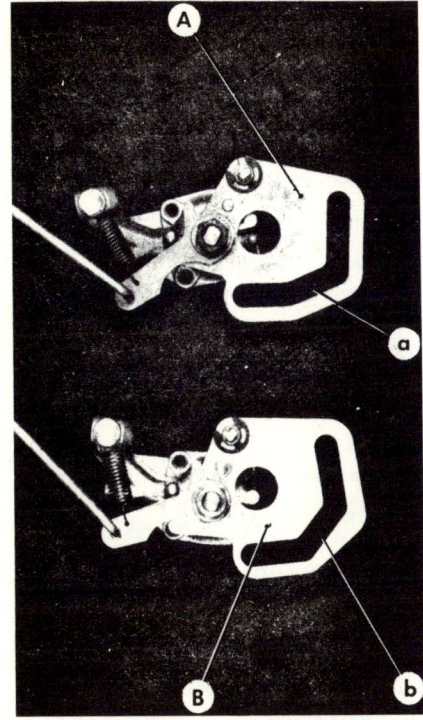

Fig. 2.10. Choke lever assemblies

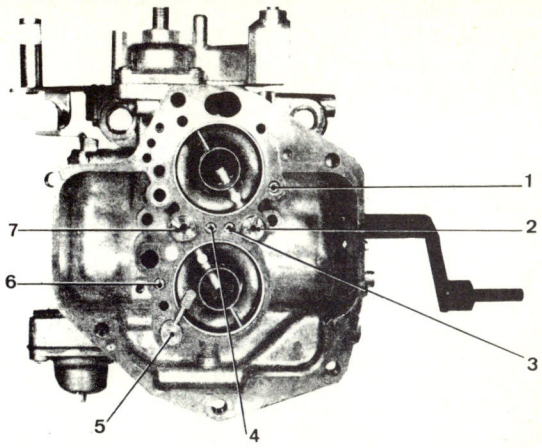

Fig. 2.13. Solex carburettor - cover removed

1 Bypass jet for primary choke
2 Air jet for secondary choke
3 Econostat for secondary choke
4 Constant richness idling jet
5 Accelerator pump injector
6 Idling jet
7 Air jet for primary choke
Main jet for primary choke at bottom of well for jet 7.
Main jet for secondary choke at bottom of well for jet 2.

Fig. 2.14. Weber carburettor - cover removed

1 Air correction jet for primary choke
2 Idling jet for primary choke
3 Mixture jet for primary choke
4 Accelerator pump injector
5 Mixture jet for secondary choke
6 Idling jet for secondary choke
7 Air correction jet for secondary choke
8 Main jet for secondary choke
9 Main jet for primary choke

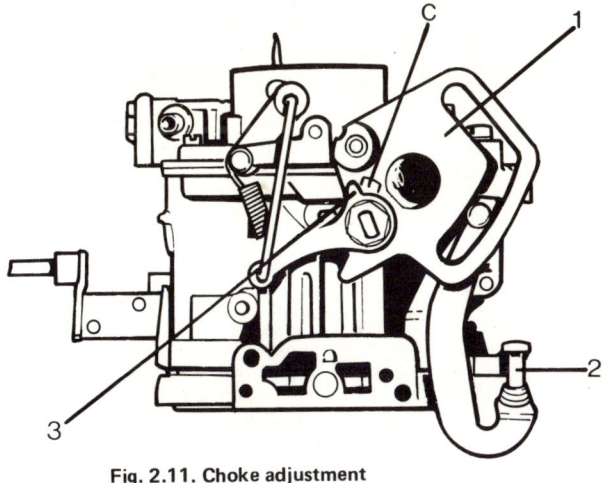

Fig. 2.11. Choke adjustment

1 Choke lever
2 Adjusting screw
3 Lever

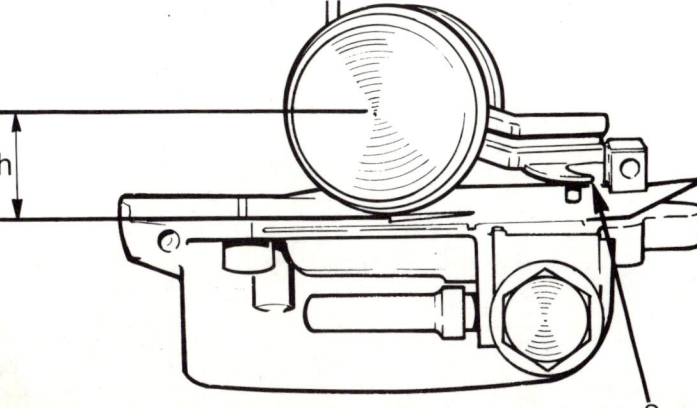

Fig. 2.12. Float level adjustment

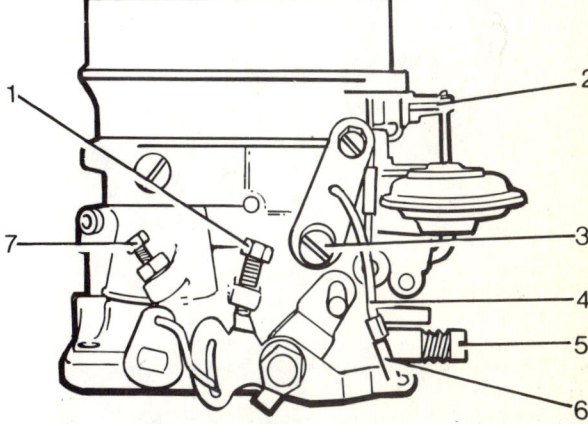

Fig. 2.15. Weber carburettor adjustment

1 Primary butterfly stop screw
2 Circlip
3 Choke lever clamp screw
4 Connecting rod
5 Mixture screw
6 Clip
7 Secondary butterfly stop screw

21 Primary butterfly - adjustment (Weber carburettors)

1   When the choke is operated, the linkage opens the primary
butterfly by a preset amount. To adjust the setting it is necessary
to remove the carburettor, as described in Section 9.
2   With the primary butterfly fully closed measure the gap between
the edge of the butterfly and the body of the carburettor. For 30DGS
(50.00) carburettors the gap should be 1.25 to 1.35mm (0.049 to
0.053in) and for 30DGS1 (51.00) 1.0 to 1.1mm (0.039 to 0.043in).
3   Adjust, if necessary, by bending the connecting rod, refer to Fig.
2.15 to obtain the correct setting.

22 Float level - adjustment (Weber carburettors)

1   Remove the air cleaner assembly, as described in Section 2. Disconnect the fuel feed pipe.
2   Remove the carburettor cover. Refer to Fig. 2.15 and remove
the clip and its rubber washer and disconnect the connecting rod from
the throttle butterfly control lever. Disconnect the choke lever from
the carburettor body by removing the choke lever clamp screw and its
spring. Disconnect the control lever from the capsule by removing the
circlip. Remove the five cover securing screws and lift off the cover and
float assembly.
3   Hold the cover and float assembly vertically as shown in Fig. 2.16,
with the needle valve ball not depressed. Measure the distance 'a'
between the joint face of the cover (gasket in position) and the float.
This measurement must be 6.5 ± 0.25mm (0.255 ± 0.010in), if necessary, adjust lug 'b' to bring this dimension within the limits specified.
4   Ensure the gasket is in good condition, or renew it, and refit the
cover and float assembly in the reverse sequence of the removal
operations. Connect the fuel feed pipe and refit the air cleaner assembly.

23 Cleaning - general (Weber carburettors)

1   When cleaning the carburettor use only petrol and compressed air.
Never use a probe in the jets or air bleeds as this may well affect the
calibration.
2   Removal of the cover and float assembly, as described in Section 22,
gives access to the jets and air bleeds, the positions of which are shown
in Fig. 2.14.

24 Carburettor - dismantling (Solex and Weber)

1   Other than removing the carburettor cover and float assembly, as
described in Sections 17 and 22, it is unlikely that the owner will need
to further dismantle the carburettor, bearing in mind that the secondary
butterfly stop screws are set by the manufacturers and must not be
altered. If the butterfly spindles, which run directly in the body of the
carburettor, become worn a complete replacement carburettor will be
required.

25 Exhaust system - general

1   The exhaust system consists of separate pipes from each cylinder
head, joined in a 'V' section to the single pipe leading to the silencer.
2   The front piping as fitted to models using exhaust gases to heat the
inlet casing (early models use engine oil) is illustrated in Fig. 2.17..
3   When fitting the exhaust piping ensure that it is routed correctly
and that the clamps and securing bolts are tightened evenly. Components subject to stress and strains are liable to fracture.
4   When any one part of the system requires renewal, consideration
should be given to renewing the complete system as, apart from accidental damage, when one part fails the rest of the system is not likely
to last long.

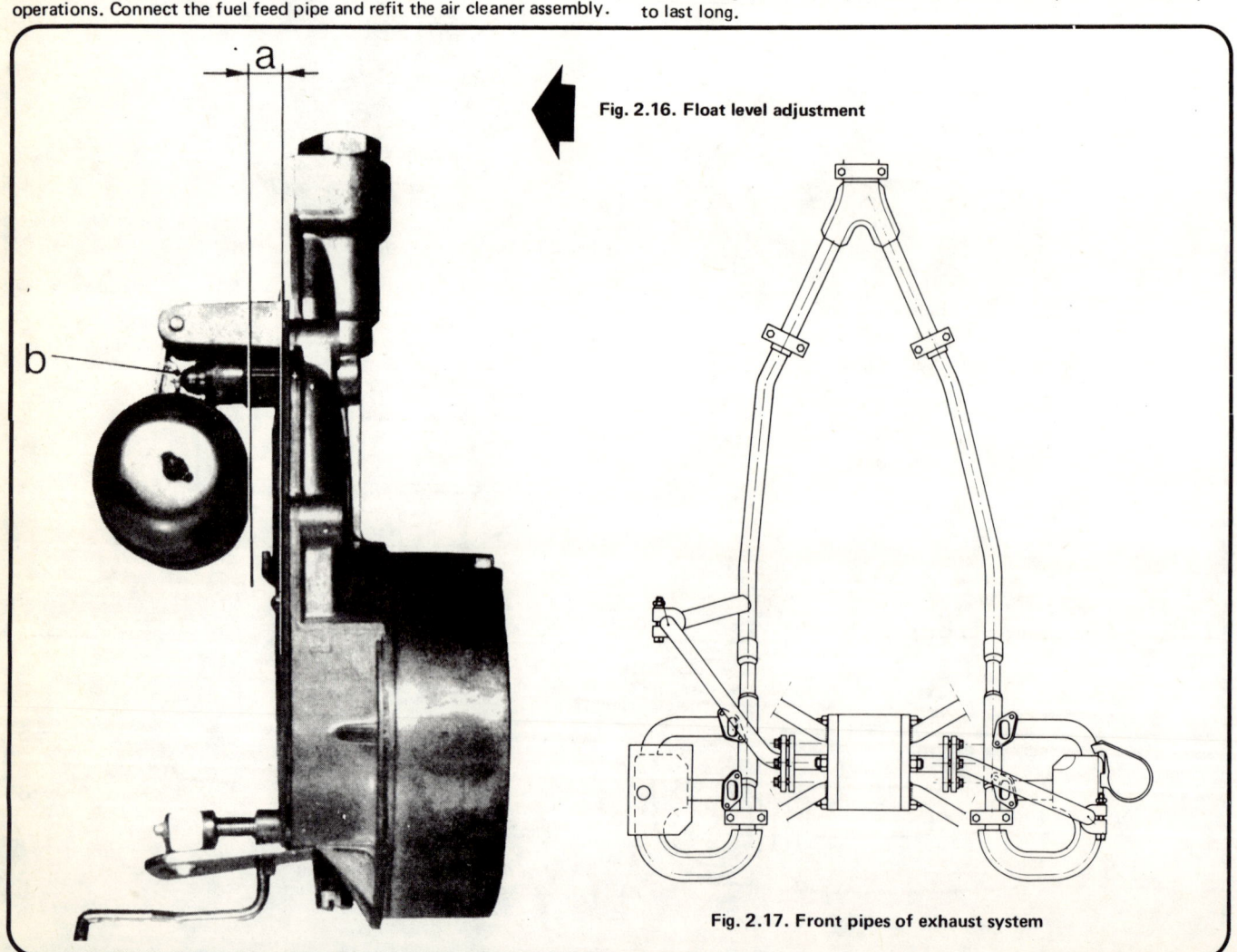

Fig. 2.16. Float level adjustment

Fig. 2.17. Front pipes of exhaust system

26 Fault diagnosis - carburettors and fuel system

Unsatisfactory engine performance and excessive fuel consumption are not necessarily the fault of the fuel system or carburettor. In fact they more commonly occur as a result of ignition faults. Before working on the fuel system it is necessary to check the ignition system. Even though a fault may lie in the fuel system it will be difficult to trace unless the ignition is correct. The table below, therefore, assumes that the ignition system is in order.

Symptom	Reason/s	Remedy
Smell of petrol when engine is stopped	Leaking fuel lines or unions	Repair or renew as necessary.
	Leaking fuel tank	Fill tank to capacity and examine seams and joints. Repair as necessary.
Smell of petrol when engine is idling	Leaking fuel line between pump and carburettor	Check pipe and unions and tighten or repair.
	Overflow of fuel from float chamber due to wrong level setting or ineffective needle valve or punctured float	Check fuel level setting and condition of float and needle valve. Renew if necessary.
Excessive fuel consumption for reasons not covered by leaks or float chamber faults	Worn needle valve	Renew needle valve.
	Sticking needle valve	Check correct movement of needle valve.
Difficult starting, uneven running, lack of power, cutting out	One or more jets blocked or restricted	Dismantle and clean out float chamber and jets.
	Float chamber fuel level too low or needle valve sticking	Dismantle and check fuel level and needle valve.
	Fuel pump not delivering sufficient fuel	Check pump delivery and replace if necessary.

Chapter 3 Ignition system

Contents

Specifications

Spark plugs
To June 1972:
SEV - Marchal	34 S
Eyquem	755 S
Gap	0.6 to 0.7 mm (0.024 to 0.028 in)

From June 1972:
SEV-Marchal	34 HS
AC	40.8 x LS
Eyquem	800 LS
Champion	N 6 Y
Beru	230/14/3A
Bosch	W 280 T 30
Gap	0.65 to 0.8 mm (0.026 to 0.032 in)

Coil (alternatives)
Ducellier	2777 C
SEV-Marchal	E 44910312
Marelli	BZR 206 A

Distributor
	SEV-Marchal (cassette type)	Ducellier
January 71 to December 71	41301002	4310 A
December 71 to September 72	41301202	4431 A
From September 72	41301302	4451 A

Rotation (seen from drive end)	Clockwise
Firing order	1 - 4 - 3 - 2
Contact breaker gap	0.35 to 0.45 mm (0.014 to 0.018 in)
Cam dwell angle	55 to 59°

Ignition timing
Static setting	10° BTDC
Mark on flywheel:	
Cars to October 71	Rod hole corresponding to 10° initial advance before TDC
Cars from October 71	A chisel mark on flywheel and a sector graduated in crankshaft degrees fixed to the crankcase.
Condenser	0.25 - 0.30 UF

1 General description

In order that the engine can run it is necessary for an electrical spark to ignite the fuel/air mixture in the combustion chamber at exactly the right moment in relation to the engine speed and load.

The ignition system is based on feeding low tension voltage from the battery to the ignition coil where it is converted to high tension voltage. The high tension voltage is powerful enough to jump the spark plug gap in the cylinders many times a second under high compression pressures, providing that the system is in good condition and that all adjustments are correct.

The ignition system is divided into two parts, the low tension and the high tension circuits. The low tension (or primary) circuit consists of the battery, lead to the control box, lead to the ignition switch, lead from the ignition switch to the low tension or primary coil windings terminal and the lead from the low tension coil windings to the contact breaker points and condenser on the distributor. The high tension circuit consists of the high tension or secondary coil windings, the heavy duty ignition lead from the centre of the coil to the centre of the distributor cap, the rotor arm, the spark plug leads and spark plugs. The system functions in the following manner: High tension voltage is generated in the coil by the interruption of the low tension circuit. The interruption is effected by the opening of the contact breaker points in the low tension circuit.

High tension voltage is fed via the carbon brush, in the centre of the distributor cap, to the rotor arm of the distributor.

The rotor arm revolves at half engine speed inside the distributor cap and each time it comes in line with one of the four metal segments in the cap, which are in turn connected to the spark plug leads, the opening and closing of the contact breaker points causes the high tension voltage to build up, jump the gap from the rotor arm to the appropriate metal segment. From the sequence the electrical charge travels via the spark plug lead to the spark plug, where it finally jumps the spark plug gap before going to earth.

The ignition is advanced and retarded automatically, both mechanically and by a vacuum device, to ensure that the spark occurs at the right instant for the particular load at the prevailing engine speed. As engine speed increases centrifugal action of rotating weights pivoting against the tension of small springs advances the contact breaker cam in relation to the distributor shaft and so advances the timing. The vacuum control is connected via a small bore pipe to the carburettor and according to the varying intake depression it advances or retards the ignition timing.

Distributors of SEV-Marchal make have cassette type contact breaker sets which are discarded and replaced by a new cassette. Ducellier distributors have conventional type points. The distributor is fitted at the rear of the left-hand cylinder head and is secured on two studs which engage in elongated holes. To adjust the contact breaker points the distributor must first be removed from the engine as the points are not accessible when the engine is fitted in the car.

Fig. 3.1 diagrammatically illustrates the ignition circuit and the layout and numbering of the cylinders. The firing order, 1 - 4 - 3 - 2, is the same for both engines.

2 Distributor - removal and replacement

1   Mark the flanges of the distributor and its mounting so that the distributor can be refitted in its original position.
2   Remove the distributor cap and take note of the position of the rotor arm.
3   Remove the retaining nuts and withdraw the distributor.
Note: Do not turn the crankshaft when the distributor is removed. If the crankshaft is moved whilst the distributor is removed, the ignition timing will have to be reset.
4   No overhaul procedures are described for either make of distributor. Testing of the centrifugal and vacuum advance device requires special testing equipment and this should be entrusted to a service station which you know is equipped to test distributors.
5   To replace the distributor set the rotor arm to the same position it was at when the distributor was removed. Refit the distributor and the two retaining nuts, turn the distributor to line up the marks which were made on the flanges and tighten the retaining nuts.
6   If a new distributor is being fitted the ignition will have to be retimed, as described in Section 8.

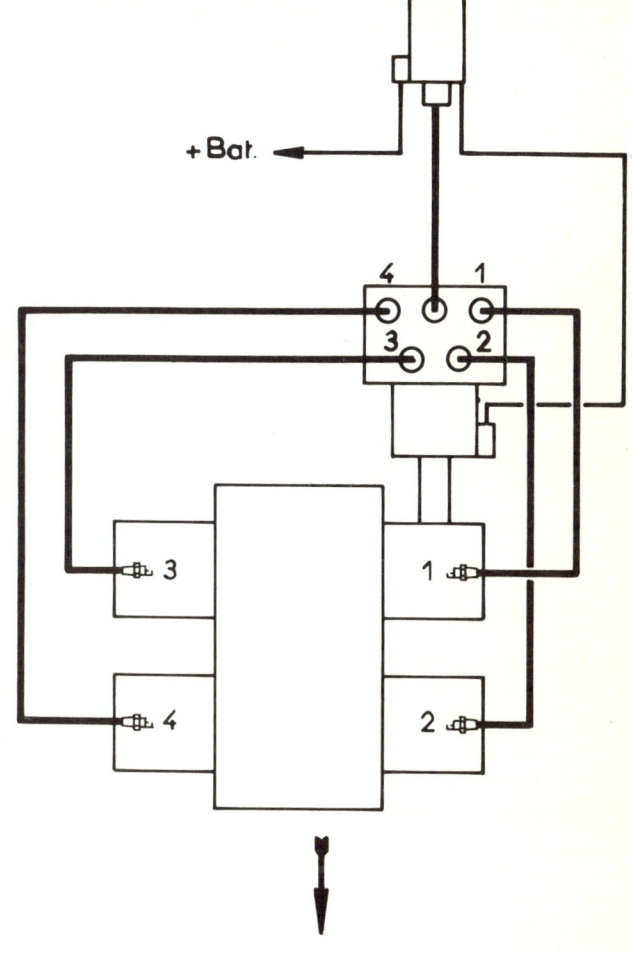

FRONT OF VEHICLE

Fig. 3.1. Ignition and cylinder layout diagram

3 Contact breaker points - adjustment

1   Remove the distributor as described in Section 2. Remove the rotor and the seal.
2   Turn the distributor shaft until one cam lobe lifts the contact heel to its highest point. Slacken the points locking screw and adjust the points gap to 0.35 to 0.045 mm (0.014 to 0.018 in) by moving the adjustable contact with a small screwdriver inserted through the adjacent slot.
3   Tighten the locking screw and re-check the gap.
4   Replace the distributor as described in Section 2.

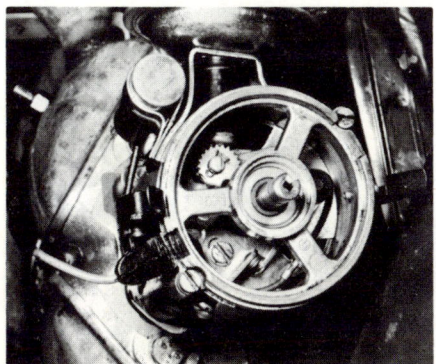

2.2 Distributor with cap, rotor and seal removed

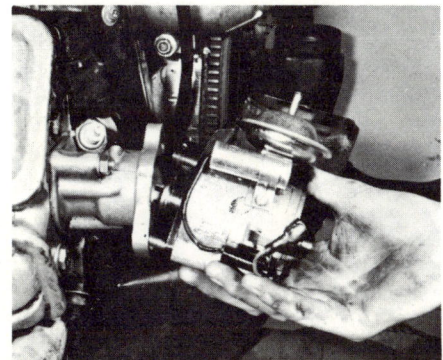

2.3 Removing the distributor

2.5 Distributor fitted in position on the engine

3.2 Measuring the points gap with a feeler gauge

4 Contact breaker points - removal and replacement

1   Remove the distributor as described in Section 2. Remove the rotor and the seal.

2   SEV-Marchal distributors have a disposable, cassette type set of points. Remove the casette and fit a replacement cassette.

3   Ducellier distributors have a conventional set of points. Remove the two screws securing the top bearing housing and remove the housing. Remove the retaining clip and locking screw and lift out the contact points.

4   Check the condition of the points, if they are rough and pitted it will be necessary to replace them.

5   Fit the contact points and adjust the gap as described in Section 3. Refit the distributor, as described in Section 2.

5 Spark plugs and HT leads - general

1   The correct functioning of the spark plugs is vital for the correct running and efficient operation of the engine. The spark plugs fitted as standard are as listed in the Specifications at the beginning of this Chapter.

2   At intervals of 6,000 miles (10,000 Km) the plugs should be removed, examined and cleaned. If worn excessively they must be renewed. The condition of the spark plug can give some indication of the overall condition of the engine.

3   If the insulator nose of the spark plug is clean and white, with no deposits, it is an indication that the mixture is too weak, or that too hot a plug is fitted. (A hot plug transfers heat away from the electrode slowly - a cold plug transfers it away quickly).

4   If the tip and insulator nose is covered with sooty black deposits, then this is indicative that the mixture is too rich. Should the plug be black and oily, then it is likely that the engine cylinders and piston rings are worn, as well as the mixture being rich.

5   A properly tuned engine, under normal running conditions, will have a light deposit of a greyish brown colour on the electrodes.

6   If there are traces of long brown tapering stains on the outside of the white portion of the spark plug, then the plug will have to be renewed, as this shows that there is a faulty joint between the plug body and the insulator, and that pressure is being allowed to leak past.

7   If possible clean the spark plug in a sand blasting machine as this will remove carbon deposits more thoroughly than cleaning by hand. The machine will also test the condition of the spark plugs under pressure conditions. Any plug that fails to spark at the recommended pressure should be discarded.

8   The spark plug gap is of considerable importance as its efficiency will be seriously affected if the gap is too large or too small. Set the spark plug gap to 0.65 to 0.75 mm (0.026 to 0.030 in).

9   Set the gap by measuring it with a feeler gauge, and then bend open, or close, the outer electrode until the correct gap is obtained. Never

bend the centre electrode as this will probably crack the insulation and cause plug failure.

10   To help get the spark plug thread correctly seated in the cylinder head when replacing the plugs, push a rubber tube over the insulator and screw the plug in as far as possible with the tube. Finish tightening the plug to 2 - 2.5 kg f m (14 - 18 lb f ft) with a torque wrench.

11   No routine maintenance is required for the plug leads other than being kept clean by wiping them regularly and checking for deterioration of the insulation and loose connections.

6 Coil and condenser - general

The coil is mounted on the left-hand wheel arch and the condenser is secured to the distributor by a clip. Checking the coil and condenser is dealt with in Section 9.

7 Ignition timing - general

1   There should be little need to retime the ignition except after engine overhaul or if the distributor has been renewed. When setting the timing it is essential that the contact breaker points are in good condition and that the gap is correctly set, as described in Section 3.

2   Two methods of determining the static timing point are used, on early G10 engines, a 5 mm diameter rod is inserted in a hole in the crankcase to lock the flywheel and on all later G10 engines and G103 engines a graduated timing scale is attached to the crankcase and the flywheel is marked.

8 Ignition timing - adjustment

1   On G10 engines fitted with a distributor reference GA 2 - GD 1, proceed as follows:

a) *Set No. 1 cylinder to TDC at the end of compression stroke (remove the rocker cover from the left-hand cylinder head and check that both valves are closed) and insert a 5 mm diameter rod through the hole in the left-hand side of the crankcase to engage with the hole in the flywheel. This determines the static timing position, 10° before TDC.*

b) *Turn the distributor shaft until the rotor arm is pointing to the position of No. 1 segment of the distributor cap, refer to Fig. 3.1, and fit the distributor on its mounting studs. Fit the retaining nuts finger-tight.*

c) *Connect a 12 volt timing lamp, 'A' in Fig. 3.2, between the earth and the terminal 'a' of the condenser on the distributor.*

d) *Switch on the ignition and slowly turn the distributor body in the direction of the arrow shown in Fig. 3.4. Stop turning the distributor the moment the lamp lights up, indicating that the points are just opening. Tighten the retaining nuts and switch off the ignition. Disconnect the timing lamp and fit the distributor cover.*

2   For G10 and G103 engines fitted with distributors with reference numbers: GA2 - GD1, GA4 - GD1, GA5 - GD2 and GA3 - GD4 proceed as follows:

a) *Set No. 1 cylinder to the end of the compression stroke (both valves closed), then turn the engine so that the mark, 'b' in Fig. 3.5 on the flywheel is aligned with th the 10° graduation on the timing scale. Use of a mirror will help in aligning the mark accurately.*

b) *Turn the distributor shaft until the rotor arm is pointing to the position of No. 1 segment of the distributor cap and fit the distributor with the retaining nuts finger-tight.*

c) *Connect a timing lamp between the terminal 'RUP' of the ignition coil and earth.*

d) *Switch on the ignition and slowly turn the distributor body in the direction of the arrow in Fig. 3.4. Stop p turning the distributor the moment the lamp lights up, indicating that the points are just opening.*

e) *Tighten the retaining nuts and switch of the ignition. Disconnect the timing lamp and fit the distributor cap.*

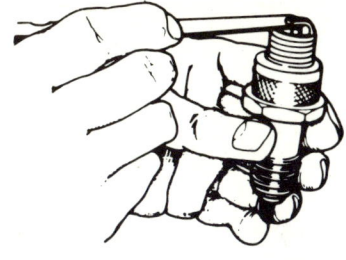
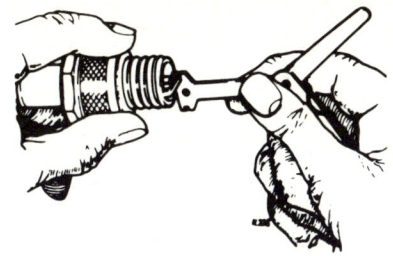

Checking plug gap with feeler gauges

Altering the plug gap. Note use of correct tool

Fig. 3.2a. Spark plug maintenance

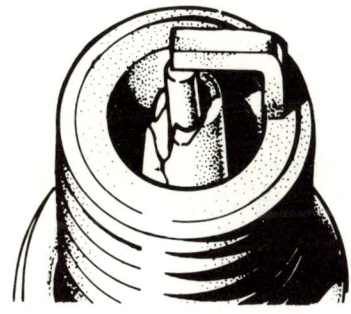

White deposits and damaged procelain insulation indicating overheating

Broken porcelain insulation due to bent central electrode

Electrodes burnt away due to wrong heat valve or chronic pre-ignition (pinking)

Excessive black deposits caused by over-rich mixture or wrong heat valve

Mild white deposits and electrode burnt indicating too weak a fuel mixture

Plug in sound condition with light greyish brown deposits

Fig. 3.2b. Spark plug electrode condition

Fig. 3.3. Timing the ignition

8.2 Setting the timing marks

Fig. 3.4. Setting the static ignition timing

1   Distributor retaining bolts

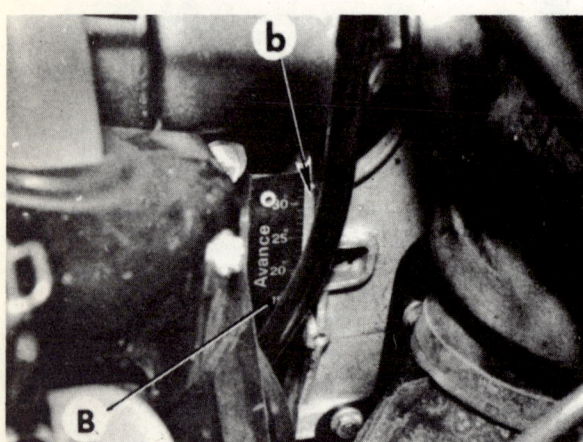

Fig. 3.5. Checking the timing

9   Fault diagnosis - ignition system

There are two main symptoms indicating ignition faults. Either the
engine will not start or is difficult to start and misfires. If it is a
regular misfire the fault is most likely to be in the secondary or high
tension circuit. If the misfiring is intermittent, the fault could be in
either the high or low tension circuits. If the engine stops suddenly, or
will not start at all, it is likely that the fault is in the low tension
circuit. Loss of power and overheating, apart from faulty carburation
settings is normally due to faults in the distributor or incorrect
ignition timing.

Engine fails to start

1   If the engine fails to start and the car was running normally when it
was last used, first check that there is petrol in the fuel tank. If the
engine turns over normally on the starter motor and the battery is
evidently well charged, then the fault may be in either the high or low
tension circuits. First check the HT circuit. **Note:** If the battery is known
to be fully charged, the ignition warning light comes on and the starter
motor fails to turn the engine, check the tightness of the leads on the
battery terminals and also the secureness of the earth lead to its
connection on the body. It is quite common for the leads to have
worked loose, even if they look and feel secure. If one of the battery
terminal posts get very hot when trying to operate the starter motor,
this is a sure indication of a faulty connection to that terminal.
2   One of the commonest reasons for bad starting is wet or damp
spark plug leads and distributor. If condensation is visible internally,
dry the cap with a cloth and also wipe over the leads.
3   If the engine still fails to start, check that current is reaching the
plugs. Disconnect each plug in turn at the spark plug end, and hold the
end of the lead about 3/16th inch (5 mm) away from the cylinder head
(not the rocker cover); turn the engine over on the starter. Sparking
between the end of the cable and the cylinder head should be fairly
strong with a regular blue spark. Hold the lead with rubber or plastic
gloves to avoid electric shocks. If current is reaching the spark plugs,
remove them, clean and reset the gap. The engine should now start.
4   If there is no spark at the plug leads take off the HT lead from the
centre of the distributor cap and hold it to the cylinder head as before.
Spin the engine on the starter. A rapid succession of blue sparks between
the end of the lead and the cylinder head indicates that the coil is in
order and that the distributor cap is cracked, the rotor arm faulty, or
the carbon brush in the top of the distributor cap is not making good
contact with the spring on the rotor arm. Possibly the contact breaker
points are burnt, pitted or dirty, if so clean or renew them as described
in Section 4.
5   If there are no sparks from the end of the lead from the coil, check
the connection at the coil end of the lead and if it is in order check
out the low tension circuit.

6 Switch on the ignition and turn the crankshaft so that the contact breaker points are open, then using a 12V bulb and two lengths of wire, or a zero-to-20 range voltmeter if available, test between the low tension wire to the coil and earth. No reading indicates a break in the supply from the ignition switch. Check the connections at the switch to see if any are loose and if so, refit them. A reading shows a faulty coil or condenser, or broken lead between the coil and the distributor.
7 Take the condenser wire off the points and with the points open, test between the moving point and earth. If there is now a reading then the condenser is faulty and will have to be renewed.
8 With no reading from the moving point to earth, take a reading between earth and the negative terminal of the coil. A reading here shows a broken wire, which will have to be renewed, between the coil and the distributor. No reading indicates that the coil is defective and must be replaced. Remember to fit the condenser wire to the points assembly. For these tests it is sufficient to separate the points with a piece of dry paper while testing with the points open.

Engine misfires
1 If the engine misfires regularly run it at a fast idling speed. Remove and replace each spark plug lead from its spark plug in turn. If the plug is firing properly this will accentuate the uneven running but will make no difference if the plug is defective. Remove the insulator from the lead to the faulty plug and hold the end about 3/16th inch (5 mm) away from the cylinder head (not the rocker cover) with the engine running. If the spark is strong and regular the fault must lie in the spark plug.
2 The plug may be loose, the insulation may be cracked, or the electrodes may have burnt away giving too wide a gap. Either renew the plug, or clean it, reset the gap and then test it.
3 If there is no spark at the end of the plug lead, or if it is weak and intermittent, check the ignition lead from the distributor to the plug. If the insulation is cracked or perished, renew the lead. Check the connection at the distributor cap.
4 If there is still no spark, examine the distributor cap carefully for tracking. This can be recognised by a very thin black line running between two or more segments, or between a segment and some other part of the distributor. These lines are paths which now conduct current across the cap, thus letting it run to earth; if this is the case it means the distributor cap will have to be renewed.
5 Apart from the ignition timing being incorrect, other causes of misfiring have already been dealt with in the previous sub-Section.
6 If the ignition timing is too far retarded, the engine will tend to overheat and there will be a noticeable drop in power. If this happens and the ignition timing is correct, then the carburettor should be checked as it is likely that this is where the fault lies.

Chapter 4 Clutch and manual gearbox

Contents

Specifications

Clutch

Type	Single dry disc, diaphragm spring
Disc (G10 engine)	6 springs of all the same colour
Disc (G103 engine)	2 grey, 2 blue, 2 white springs
Lining	Ferodo A755
Lining thickness - new	7.7 mm (0.30 in)

Gearbox

Number of gears	4 forward, 1 reverse
Ratios:	
1st	3.82 : 1
2nd	2.38 : 1
3rd	1.52 : 1
4th	1.12 : 1
Reverse	4.18 : 1
Speedometer drive	2.17 : 1

Differential unit

Location	Integral with gearbox
Ratio:	
G10 Engine	4.375 : 1
G103 Engine	4.125 : 1

Gearbox and differential tolerances

Endfloat of 1st/2nd synchro-hub (max)	0.05 mm (0.002 in)
Endfloat of 3rd/4th synchro-hub (max)	0.05 mm (0.002 in)
Clearance of half-washers between 2nd and 3rd gearwheels (max) ...	0.05 mm (0.002 in)
Crownwheel and pinion backlash (max)	0.13 to 0.27 mm (0.005 to 0.011 in)
Total preload on differential bearings	0.05 mm (0.002 in)

Oil grade ... ... EP 80

Oil capacity ... ... 1.4 litre approx. (2.5 Imp. pints)

1 General description

1   Two types of transmissions are available on GS models, a manual
transmission with a four speed gearbox, and a semi-automatic transmission. The drive, transmitted to the front wheels through the
differential gearing in the gearbox and the drive shaft is very similar
on both types. The semi-automatic transmission is described in Chapter
5.
2   The clutch is a cable operated single dry plate diaphragm type. When
the clutch pedal is depressed the clutch springs are compressed which
releases the pressure plate pressure thereby freeing the driven plate
(disc), which is splined to the gearbox primary shaft through the
control shaft. When the clutch driven plate is freed there is no drive
from the engine to the gearbox, and when engaged, drive is transmitted
from the engine to the gearbox. Fig. 4.1 shows a cross-section
through the clutch.
3   The four forward speed gears are in constant mesh through synchro
units. Reverse gear is engaged through a separate layshaft and idler gear,
and is meshed with a gear which is integral with the 1st and 2nd synchro-
unit. Gear selection is obtained by the gear lever operating the selector
forks, which select gears on the primary shaft which then mesh with
the appropriate gear on the pinion shaft.
4   Various gear ratios have been used. The speedometer drive is taken
from the gearbox. The power flow through the gearbox is shown in
Fig. 4.4.

2 Clutch - maintenance

Routine maintenance is confined to checking the clutch pedal free-
movement. If all the adjustment is nearly taken up, this is an indication
that the Ferodo lining on the disc is almost at the limit of permissible
wear.

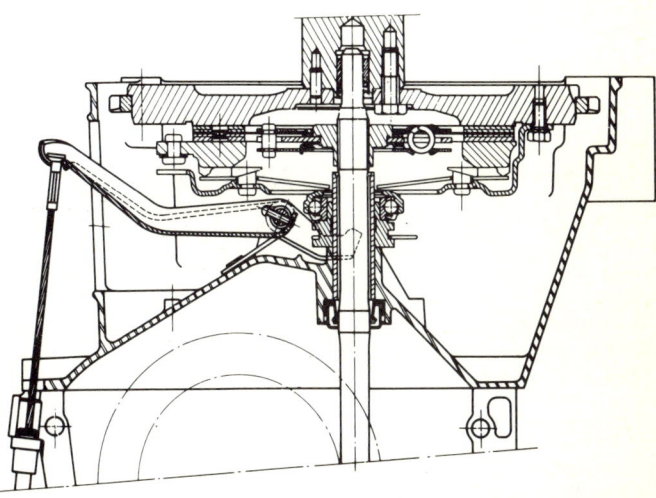

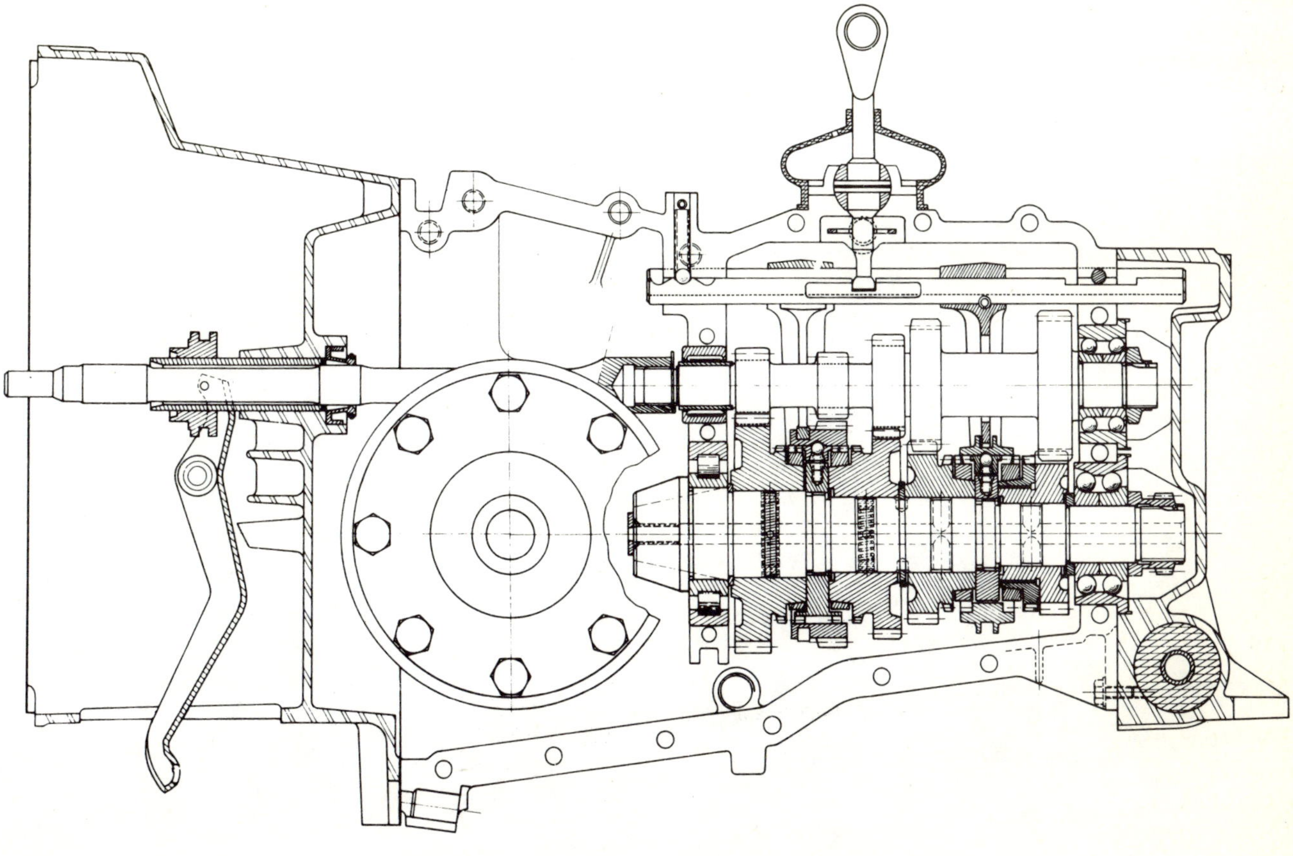

Fig. 4.1. Cross-section through the clutch

Fig. 4.2. Longitudinal section - manual gearbox

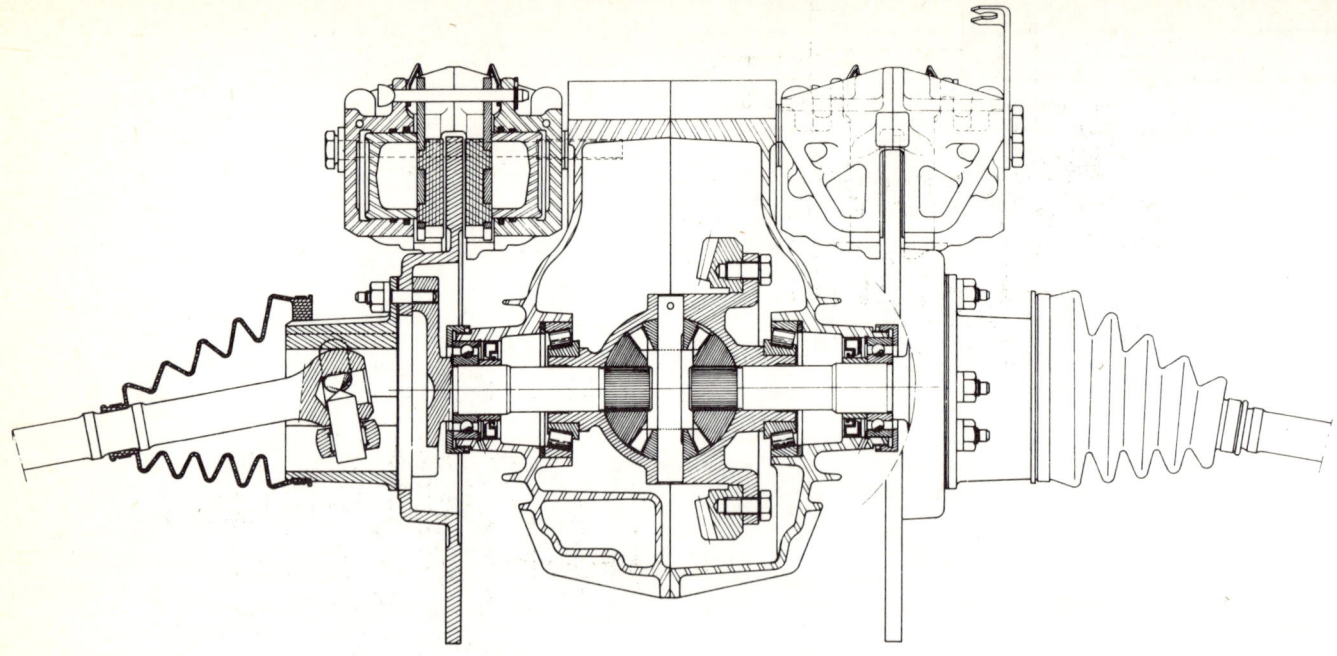

Fig. 4.3. Transverse section - manual gearbox

3 Clutch cable - removal and replacement

1   Open the bonnet. Remove the spare wheel, slacken off the locknut and cable adjusting nut. Get an assistant to depress the clutch pedal while you chock the clutch release fork, release the pedal and remove the cable end from the release fork. Disconnect the other end from the pedal linkage on the bulkhead and remove the cable from its support on the gearbox casing.
2   Replacement is the reverse of the removal sequence. Adjust the release bearing clearance as described in Section 4.

4 Clutch - adjustment

1   Remove the spare wheel.
2   Refer to Fig. 4.5 and slacken the locknut. Turn the adjusting nut to obtain a clearance of 3.2 to 4.8 mm (0.125 to 0.190 in) between the fixed tube and the adjusting nut. This setting will give the clutch pedal 15 to 20 mm (0.6 to 0.8 in) free movement.
3   Tighten the locknut and replace the spare wheel.

5 Clutch - removal

1   Removal of the clutch necessitates the removal of the engine as described in Chapter 1, Section 6. Before removing the clutch cover

bolts, mark the position of the cover in relation to the flywheel, so that it can be put back in the same position.
2   Restrain the flywheel from turning and slacken the cover assembly retaining bolts a little at a time, working in a progressively diagonal sequence so that the diaphragm spring pressure is released evenly to prevent any distortion.
3   When all the spring pressure on the bolts has been released, remove the bolts, washers, clutch cover assembly and clutch disc.

6 Clutch - inspection and renovation

1   Examine the Ferodo lining of the clutch disc for wear and contamination by oil. If the linings are dark in colour this indicates oil contamination caused by oil leaking past the crankshaft rear seal, or the gearbox seal. Check that there are no loose or broken damper springs or rivets on the disc and that the splines of the hub are in good condition.
2   Examine the friction faces of the flywheel and clutch pressure plate for scoring, caused by the heads of the rivets on the clutch driven plate, as a result of excessive wear of the linings. If there is deep scoring of the flywheel it will have to be machined, (this is specialist work), or renewed. Heavy scoring of the pressure plate or broken pressure spring necessitate the replacement of the clutch cover assembly.
3   Whenever the engine is removed for any reason, always examine the clutch operating mechanism and replace any worn parts as described in Section 12.

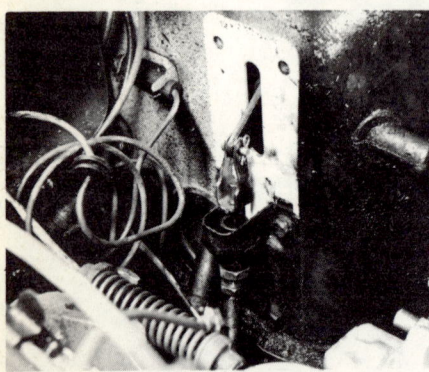

3.1a Disconnecting the clutch cable from the pedal linkage on the bulkhead

3.1b Clutch cable support on the gearbox housing

5.3 Removing the clutch cover assembly and clutch disc

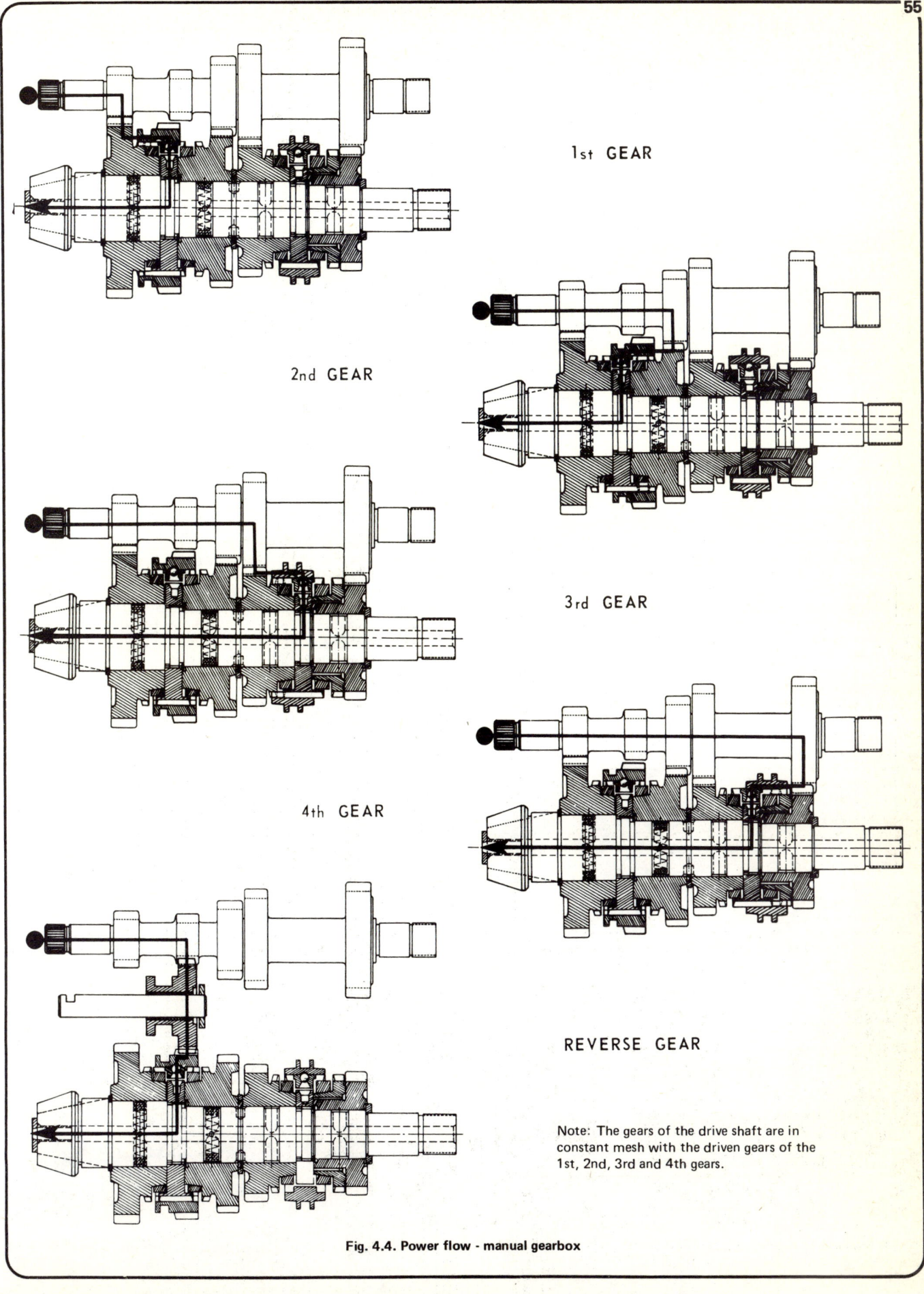

1st GEAR

2nd GEAR

3rd GEAR

4th GEAR

REVERSE GEAR

Note: The gears of the drive shaft are in
constant mesh with the driven gears of the
1st, 2nd, 3rd and 4th gears.

Fig. 4.4. Power flow - manual gearbox

Fig. 4.5. Clutch adjustment

1 Adjusting nut	3 Fixed tube
2 Locknut	

7 Clutch - replacement

1 If the original clutch cover assembly is being refitted, line-up the marks made at removal, position the driven plate and fit the cover assembly to the flywheel. Fit the washers and retaining bolts, screw them in evenly just enough to grip the driven plate but not enough to prevent it being moved.

2 Before tightening the retaining bolts it is necessary to line-up the centre of the driven plate with the centring bush of the crankshaft. This is easily done if you have an old control shaft or a mandrel with the same spigot and spline diameter as the control shaft. It can also be lined up by eye, but this is not so reliable. If the driven plate is not centred correctly, it will be impossible to fit the engine to the gearbox and the central shaft may get damaged while attempting to do so.

3 With the driven plate correctly positioned, proceed to tighten the retaining bolts in a progressive and even manner at a torque of 1.8 kg f m (13 lb f ft). Remove the centralising tool.

4 Replace the engine in the car as described in Chapter 1.

7.3 Clutch cover assembly bolted in position on the flywheel

8 Gearbox - removal and replacement

The gearbox cannot be removed as a separate unit. It is removed with the engine, as an engine and gearbox assembly, as described in Chapter 1, Section 5. Separation of the gearbox from the engine is described in Chapter 1, Section 7.

9 Gearbox - dismantling (general)

Before dismantling the gearbox decide if it is worthwhile from a cost point of view. If it is in a generally poor condition then the cost of parts could be more than an exchange unit. Another point to consider is that special equipment is required to adjust the crownwheel and pinion.

10 Gearbox - dismantling procedure (stage 1)

1 Drain off the oil and position the gearbox on the bench with the left-hand half-casing lowermost. Remove the brake calipers, as described in Chapter 8, Section 4.

2 On each side loosen the differential output shaft ring nuts with a chain or strap wrench. Unscrew the ring nuts fully and withdraw the shafts and bearings (if necessary, tap lightly with a mallet).

3 Remove the spring clip and the clutch thrust bearing. Remove the fork shaft retaining screw and withdraw the shaft by passing it through one of the vents of the clutch housing. Collect the spring, the anti-rattle bushes and the fork.

4 Remove the rear cover and the clutch housing. Refer to Fig. 4.7, and blank off the orifice (a) with a finger, remove the split pin and collect the blanking disc from the orifice.

5 Remove the nuts and bolts securing the half-casings together and lift off the right-hand casing, taking care to collect the lockball, the ball and socket guide and the guide thrust spring.

6 Remove the plate which holds the return spring, the ball and socket, the plunger, the spring and the lockball.

7 Remove the shaft and fork of the 3rd and 4th gear and the lockball. Remove the control shaft and primary shaft assembly. Remove the bevel pinion assembly.

8 Remove the differential assembly. Remove the roller bearing outer races from the half-casings and mark them so as to identify them with their corresponding bearings. To avoid having to reset the backlash on reassembly, identify and mark the position of the adjusting shims.

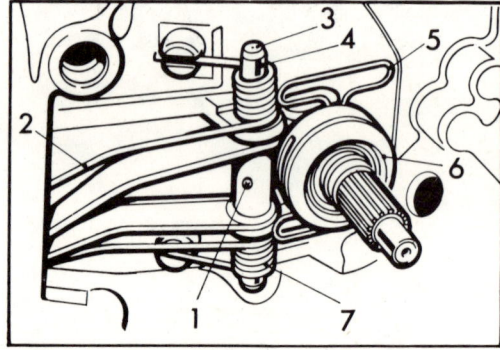

Fig. 4.6. Clutch release mechanism

1 Screw	5 Spring clip
2 Fork	6 Thrust bearing
3 Bush	7 Spring
4 Shaft	

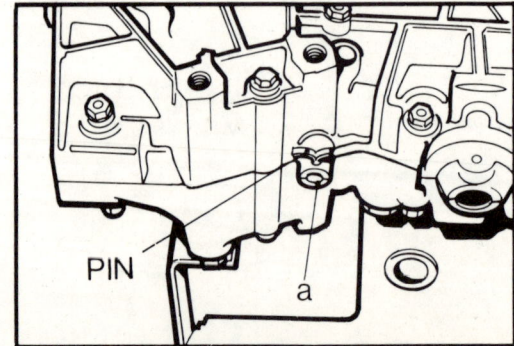

Fig. 4.7. Removing blanking disc

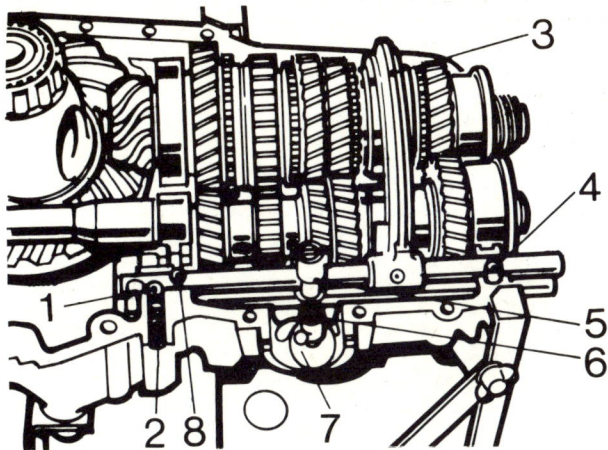

Fig. 4.8. Dismantling the gearbox

1 Lockball	5 Plate
2 Spring	6 Ball and socket guide
3 Selector fork	7 Ball and socket
4 Plunger	8 Lockball

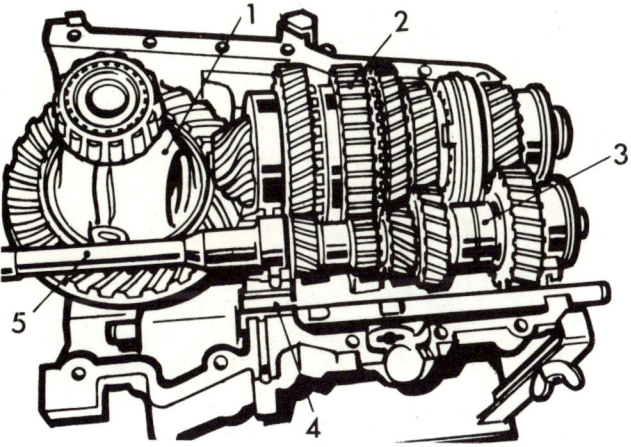

Fig. 4.9. Dismantling the gearbox

1 Differential unit	4 Lockball
2 Bevel pinion shaft assembly	5 Control shaft
3 Primary shaft	

11 Gearbox - dismantling procedure (stage 2)

1 Strip down the left-hand half-casing:

   a) Remove the cylindrical pin, which is free in its housing, the reverse idler gear shaft and the gear.

   b) Remove the reverse gear lever by unscrewing the lever spindle from the underside of the half-casing and remove the lever.

   c) Remove the reversing light switch (if fitted), or the blanking plug.

   d) Place a finger over the orifice (a) in Fig. 4.10, free the reverse gear control shaft towards the rear and collect the lockball and its spring from the housing.

   e) Remove the circlip (if fitted) retaining the differential output shaft seal and drive out the seal with a suitable tube.

2 Strip down the right-hand half-casing:

   a) Place a finger on the lockball orifice and free the 1st and 2nd gear shaft and fork assembly towards the rear and collect the lockball and its spring. Remove the stop pin by positioning the shaft/fork assembly against the rear bearing to avoid any damage as the pin is removed using a 5 mm pin punch.

   b) Remove the differential output shaft seal, refer to paragraph 1 (e) above.

3 Strip down the control shaft/primary shaft assembly:

   a) Remove the circlip and separate the control shaft from the primary shaft.

   b) Remove the needle bearing, the retaining nut, which is locked by peening, and the bearing.

4 Strip down the bevel pinion shaft assembly:
Note: The bearing surfaces of the bevel pinion shaft have been subjected to a special surface treatment and it is essential that precautions are taken to prevent any scratches or other damage that could risk causing seizure of the operating parts.

   a) Remove the speedometer drive/nut, which is locked by peening, the bearing and the pinion shaft, adjusting shim, the idling pinion of the 4th gear and the synchro-ring. Identify the adjusting shim to avoid having to adjust the position of the pinion shaft in the casing unless the pinion shaft or casing is being replaced.

   b) To avoid damage to the bearing surface of the shaft wrap a piece of 0.10 mm (0.004 in) thick foil, 'A' in Fig. 4.13,, round the shaft. Hold it against the circlip, separate the ends of the circlip with pliers and slip the foil under the circlip. Remove the circlip over the foil.

   c) Remove the 3rd and 4th gear synchro-hub, the 3rd gear synchro-ring and idling pinion. The 3rd and 4th gear synchro-rings are identical but must be kept as a matched set with the corresponding pinions if they are not being renewed.

   d) Release the washer and remove the two half-washers. Remove the 2nd gear pinion, the needle cage, (or the dowels and spring), and the 2nd gear synchro-ring.

   e) Using a piece of foil as before, remove the circlip, as described in (b) above. Remove the 1st and 2nd gear synchro-hub, the 1st gear synchro-ring, the 1st gear idling pinion and the dowels and their springs.

   f) If it is necessary to remove the front bearing inner race, a press and piece of tube of 50 mm diameter is required. Remove the circlip, the thrust washer and the bearing. Press off the inner race.

5 To dismantle the differential assembly remove the locking pin and drive out the differential gear shaft. Remove the differential gears and the planet gears. Remove the crownwheel retaining bolts. If the bearings are to be replaced, remove them using a three claw extractor with a suitable centre pad.

6 Strip down the differential output shafts:
   There are two types of output shaft, the earlier type 'A' in Fig. 4.17 and the later type, 'B'.

   a) Grease the visible thread (b) and then remove the nut from 'type A' shaft.

   b) Using a universal type extractor, having a central screw fitted with a ball to avoid damaging the end (a) of the shafts, remove the bearing.

7 Release the speedometer socket from the rear cover and uncouple the speedometer drive gear. Remove the seals.
8 From the clutch housing remove the control shaft seal by levering it out with a screwdriver.

12 Gearbox components - preparation for reassembly (general)

1 Clean all the parts thoroughly and examine them for defects. Check the gears for chipping and cracks. If the bevel pinion shaft requires renewal, this will also mean a new crownwheel, and in that case you may think it more economical to exchange the gearbox. It is important that no grinding or any type of re-work be carried out on the specially treated surfaces of the pinion shaft. Oil all parts before fitting with EP 80 oil.

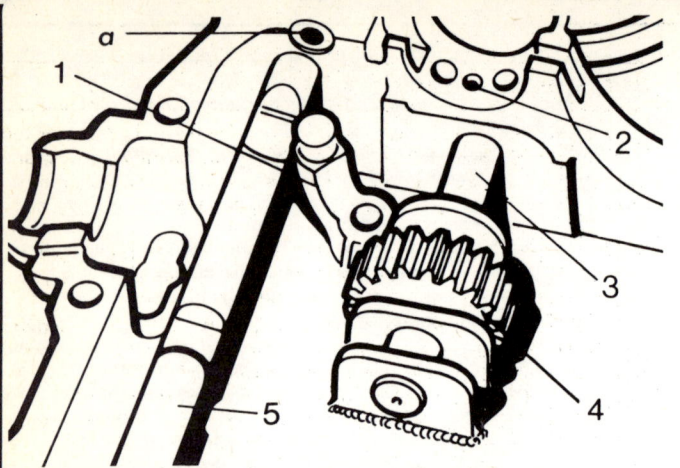

Fig. 4.10. Removing the reverse idler gear

1	Lever	4	Idler gear
2	Pin	5	Reverse gear selector
3	Shaft		shaft

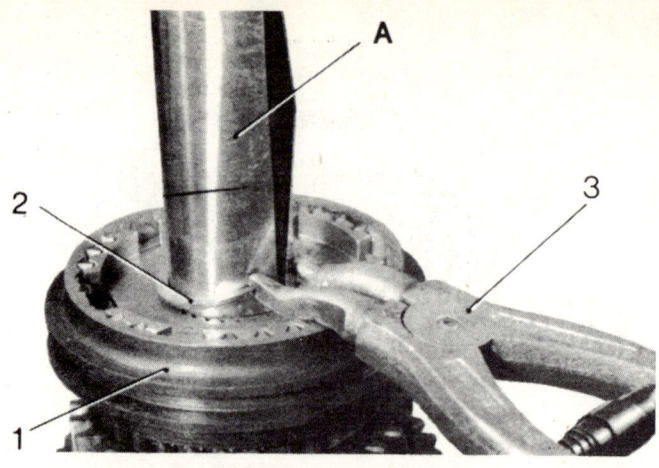

Fig. 4.13. Removing the circlip

A	Foil	2	Circlip
1	3rd & 4th synchro unit	3	Pliers

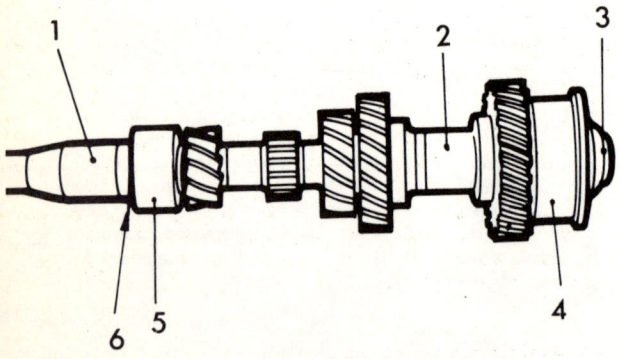

Fig. 4.11. Control shaft and primary shaft assembly

1	Control shaft	4	Bearing
2	Primary shaft	5	Needle bearing
3	Nut	6	Circlip

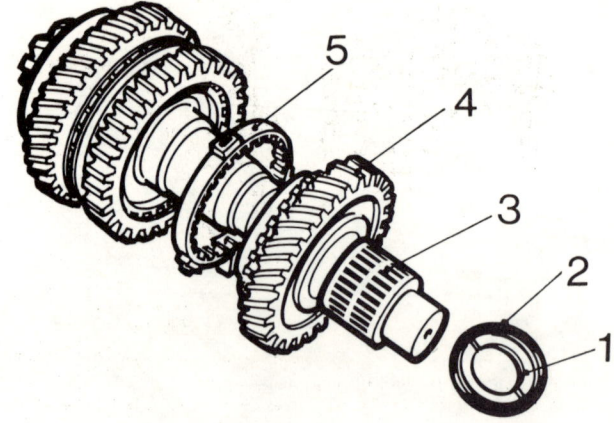

Fig. 4.14. Bevel pinion shaft assembly - dismantling

1	Half-washers	4	2nd gear pinion
2	Washer	5	2nd gear synchro-ring
3	Needle cage		

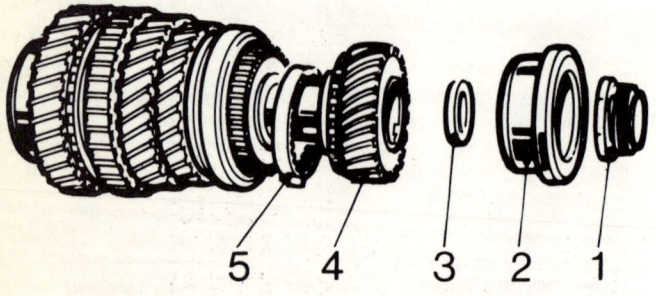

Fig. 4.12. Bevel pinion shaft assembly - dismantling

1	Speedometer drive/nut	4	4th gear pinion
2	Bearing	5	4th gear synchro ring
3	Shim		

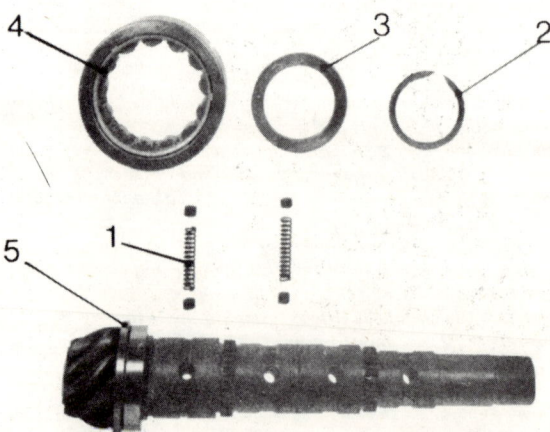

Fig. 4.15. Pinion shaft bearing removal

1	Dowels and spring (if fitted)	4	Bearing
2	Circlip	5	Inner race
3	Thrust washer		

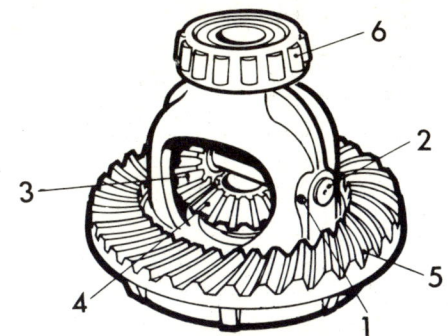

Fig. 4.16. The differential unit

1 Pin
2 Shaft
3 Differential gear
4 Planet gear
5 Crownwheel
6 Bearing

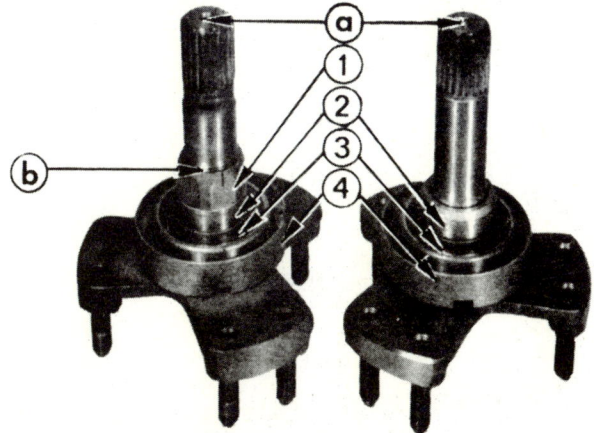

Fig. 4.17. The output shaft

1 Nut
2 Bush
3 Bearing
4 Ring nut

13 Differential shafts - preparation for reassembly

1 Fit the ring nut in position and press on the bearing using a piece of tube with an inside diameter of 26 mm.
2 Fit the bush against which the seal bears, ensure that the bush does not have any scratches or damage.
3 On the earlier type shafts fit the nut and tighten it to 14 to 16 kg f m (100 to 115 lb f ft).

14 Bevel pinion - preparation for reassembly

1 Press on the inner race with the aid of a 45 mm inside diameter tube. Fit the roller bearing with the smaller bore of the bearing on the gear side of the pinion shaft. Fit the thrust washer with the engraved face away from the bearing. Fit the circlip using the same precautions and method as at removal. Refer to Section 11.
2 Fit the retarding dowels and their springs (if fitted), the 1st gear pinion, the 1st gear synchro-ring and the synchro unit of the 1st gear with the selector fork groove towards the 1st gear pinion.
3 Adjust the axial clearance, 'J1' as in Fig. 4.18, of the synchro-hub of the 1st and 2nd gear by selecting a circlip of suitable thickness which will ensure that the clearance does not exceed 0.05 mm (0.002 in). A range of circlips, 1.30 to 1.58 mm thick, in steps of 0.04 mm are available. When fitting the circlip use the same precautions and method, as described at removal in Section 11.
4 Fit the 2nd gear synchro-ring, the retarding dowels and their springs and the 2nd gear pinion.
5 Adjust the clearance of the thrust bearings of the 2nd and 3rd gear wheels by selecting adjusting half-washers of suitable thickness. Half-washers are available in steps of 0.03 mm (0.0012 in). With the half-washers in place, the clearance at 'J2' as in Fig. 4.19, between the half-washers and the side of the groove must not exceed 0.05 mm. The two half-washers fitted must be of the same thickness. Fit the retaining washer.
6 Fit the 3rd gear pinion, the 3rd gear synchro-ring and its 3rd and 4th gear synchro-unit.
7 Adjust the end clearance of the synchro-hub of the 3rd and 4th gears using the same procedure as for the synchro-hub of the 1st and 2nd gears. See paragraph 3. This clearance, 'J3' as in Fig. 4.19, must not exceed 0.05 mm.
8 Fit the 4th gear synchro-ring and pinion, an adjusting shim of known thickness and the bearing, with the shoulder towards the rear of the bevel pinion shaft. Fit the speedometer drive/nut and tighten to 10 to 12 kg f m (72 to 86 lb f ft). Do not lock the nut, by peening, at this stage. **Note: To hold the bevel pinion shaft while tightening the nut clamp the 1st gear pinion, interlocked with the bevel pinion by the slider of the 1st and 2nd gears in a vice fitted with light-alloy vice grips**

15 Control shaft and primary shaft - reassembly

1 Fit the ball bearing with the shoulder pointed towards the rear and fit the retaining nut. Tighten the nut to 7 to 8.5 kg fm (50 to 62 lb f ft) and lock by peening.
2 Fit the needle bearing and couple up the control shaft to the primary shaft. Fit the retaining clips.

13.2 Differential shaft with ring nut, bearing and bush fitted

14.1a Fitting the roller bearing on the bevel pinion shaft

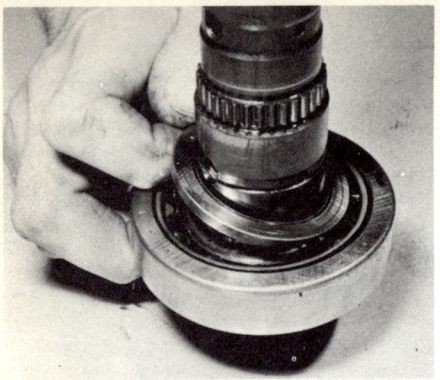
14.1b Fitting the thrust washer

14.1c Using a piece of foil to protect the specially treated surfaces of the shaft while fitting the circlip

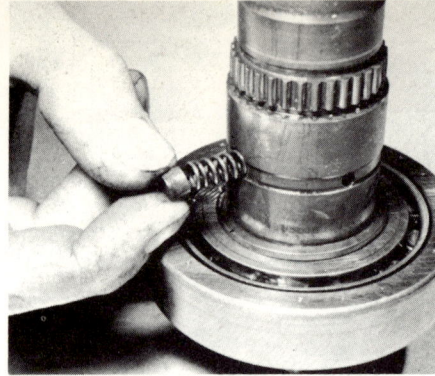
14.2a Replacing the retarding dowel and spring ...

14.2b ... the retarding dowels in position while fitting the 1st gear pinion

14.2c 1st gear synchro-ring and synchro-unit with selector fork groove towards 1st gear pinion

14.3 Fitting the circlip retaining the synchro-hub of 1st and 2nd gear

14.4a Locating the spring and dowels of the 2nd gear pinion

14.4b Fitting the 2nd gear pinion

14.5a The adjusting half-washers

14.5b The half-washers fitted in position and the retaining washer

14.6a Fitting the 3rd gear pinion and 3rd gear synchro-ring

14.6b The 3rd/4th gear synchro-unit

14.6c Fitting the 3rd/4th gear synchro-unit

14.7 The circlip retaining the 3rd/4th gear synchro-unit

14.8a Fitting the 4th gear synchro-ring and pinion

14.8b Fitting the adjusting shim

14.8c Fitting the pinion shaft rear end bearing

14.8d Fitting the speedometer drive/nut

14.8e Clamping the bevel pinion shaft in a vice with soft jaw grips and tightening the speedometer drive/nut

15.1a Fitting the primary shaft ball bearing

15.1b Fitting the bearing retaining nut

15.1c Retaining nut locked by peening

15.2a Fitting the needle bearing on the primary shaft

15.2b Coupling the control shaft to the primary shaft and secured with spring clip

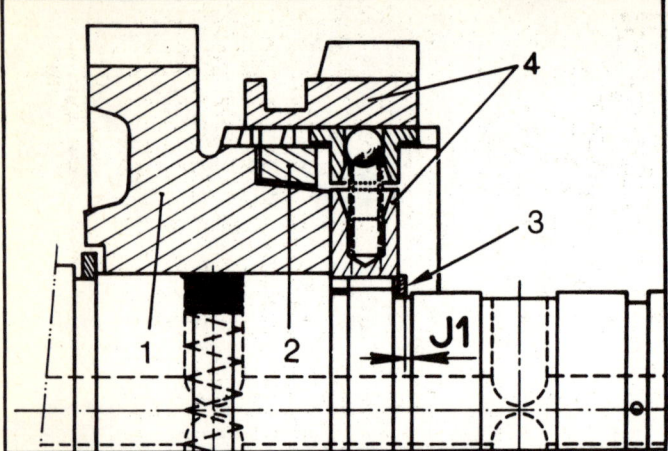

Fig. 4.18. Adjustment of 1st and 2nd gear synchro-unit axial clearance

1	1st gear pinion	3	Circlip
2	1st gear synchro hub	4	Synchro-unit

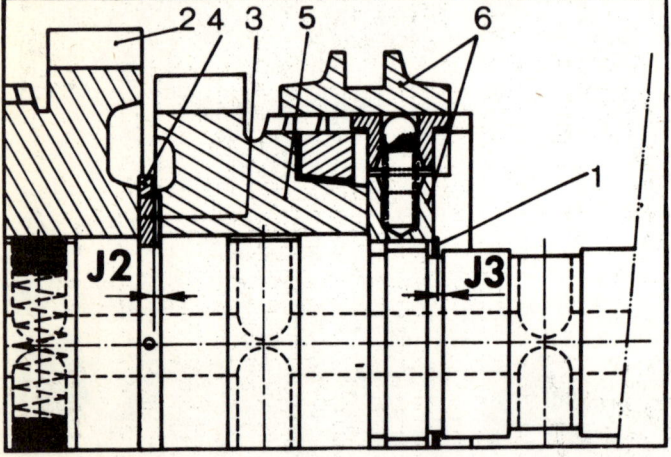

Fig. 4.19. Adjustment of 2nd and 3rd gear thrust bearings

1	Circlip	4	Washer
2	2nd gear pinion	5	3rd gear pinion
3	Half-washer	6	3rd & 4th gear synchro-unit

16 Clutch housing - preparation for reassembly

1   Fit a new control shaft seal in the clutch housing.
2   Fit the two bushes in the coils of the springs with the shoulders placed face-to-face. Lightly oil the spindle. Hold the fork and its spring in place, fit the spindle through one of the orifices in the housing and then in the spring of the fork and its bearings.
3   Position the spindle and tighten the retaining screw. Fit the two free ends of the spring to rest on the bosses of the housing.
4   Fit the thrust bearing and the spring clip locking the bearing to the fork.

17 Half-casings - preparation for reassembly

1   On each half-casing, grease the differential shaft bore and the edge of the seals. Fit the seals in the bore with the lip of the seal towards the inside of the half-casing. On gearboxes with a retaining circlip fitted fit the seal and then fit the circlip so that one end of the circlip is 10 mm (0.40 in) from the drain hole in the bearing housing.
2   In the right-hand half-casing, fit the selector fork shaft of the 1st and 3rd gears on the rear bearing with the notch towards the front. Fit the fork on the shaft and fit the locking pin. Position the fork and shaft assembly against the rear bearing when driving in the locking pin.
3   Fit the spring and lockball into the housing. Use a 5 mm diameter rod to compress the spring while fitting the shaft into the front bearing. All five lockballs and their springs are identical.

4   In the left-hand half-casing fit the spring and lockball of the reverse gear selector shaft in the housing. Use a round bar to compress the spring and fit the selector shaft. Fit the reverse gear lever and tighten the spindle to 2.7 to 3.3 kg f m (21 to 25 lb f ft).
5   Fit the reverse idler pinion shaft in the rear boss. Fit the reverse pinion, with the groove towards the differential, and the spacer. Engage the reverse gear lever in the groove and complete fitting the reverse pinion shaft. Fit the locking pin fully in its housing. This pin which locks the primary shaft needle bearing must protrude slightly beyond the face of the bearing housing.

18 Differential unit - reassembly

1   If the crownwheel, bearings or differential casing is being renewed, it will be necessary to determine the required thickness of the adjusting shims, as described in Section 21. Assembly should not take place until this has been done. If the above parts are not being renewed, proceed with the assembly.
2   Press the inner races on the casing and ensure that the roller bearings are identified and matched to their respective inner races. Fit the crownwheel, treat the threads of the retaining bolts with Loctite and tighten them to 4.8 to 5.5 kg f m (35 to 38 lb f ft).
3   Fit the two planet gears and hold them in place with the differential shafts. Fit the differential gears and shaft with the locking pin hole lined up correctly. Fit the locking pin.

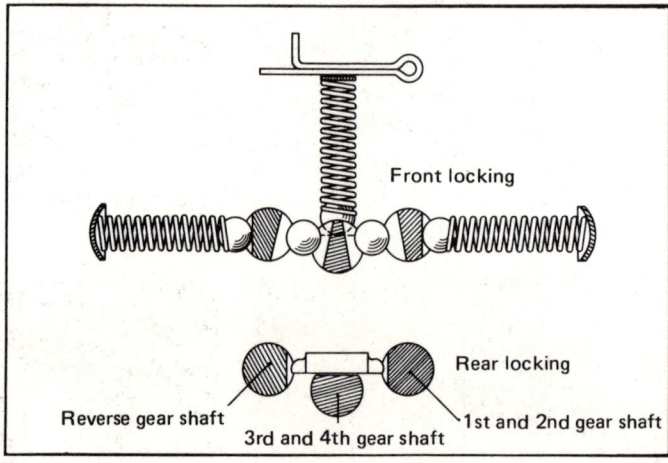

Fig. 4.20. Gear selector shaft lockballs and springs

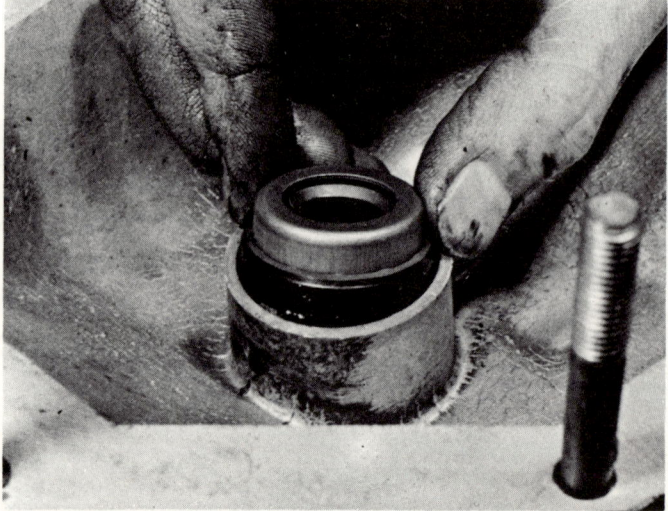

16.1 Fitting a new control shaft seal in the clutch housing

16.4 Clutch thrust bearing and retaining clip

17.1 Fitting the differential shaft seal in the half-casing bore

17.2 Fitting the 1st/3rd gear selector fork and shaft assembly

17.4a Fitting the reverse gear selector shaft detent spring in its housing

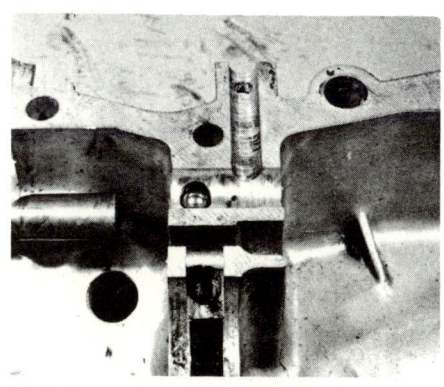
17.4b The lockball in its housing

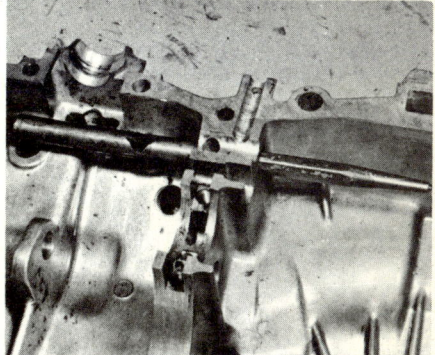
17.4c Holding down the spring and lockball with a pin punch while fitting the selector shaft

17.4d The reverse gear lever fitted in position

17.5a Reverse gear shaft and pinion in position

17.5b Fitting the reverse gear shaft locking pin

19 Bevel pinion/crownwheel - adjustment (general)

1   The bevel pinion shim along with the differential shims are used to adjust the differential crownwheel and the bevel pinion to achieve the correct engagement of the gearteeth and to preload the differential bearings. This adjustment is most important. Giving the teeth the correct engagement will ensure silence and long service from the crownwheel and pinion.

2   The bevel pinion and crownwheel are paired and marked with identical inscriptions engraved on face, 'F1', of the pinion shaft and the side, 'F3', of the crownwheel as in Fig. 4.21. On some pairings the mark of the pinion is on the face, 'F2'. Never separate a crownwheel and pinion pairing.

3   In addition to the pairing marks, two dimensions are engraved on the side, 'F3', of the crownwheel. The larger dimension represents the distance 'L1' from the intersection 'a' of the bevel gear centre line to the thrust face of the roller bearing on the bevel pinion shaft. The smaller dimension represents the distance 'L2' of the intersection 'a' of the bevel gear centre-line to the thrust face of the crownwheel on the casing. These dimensions are obtained by adjusting the position of the bevel pinion and of the crownwheel with shims whose thickness have to be determined. To do this a Citroen adjusting kit 3184-T (a dial gauge and a surface plate) will be required.

20 Bevel pinion - position adjustment

1   Fit the bevel pinion shaft assembly in the left-hand half-casing. Fit the rear cover and hold it in place with two bolts.

2   Fit the cap, 'A' of kit 3184-T, and hold in place with the screw 'a', screwed into the plastic cap on the end of the bevel pinion. Fit the

dial gauge on support 'B' and place the support on a surface plate. Zero the dial on the large needle of the gauge and note the position of the integrating needle, datum point.

3   Fit the support 'B' into the bore of the differential bearing, using handle 'C', pivot the support first in one direction and then in the other and stop at the exact point when the needle changes direction. Rotate the bevel pinion shaft and check any variation in the dial reading. If the variation exceeds 0.2 mm change the position of cap 'A'.

4   Pull rod 'd' to bring the needle to the datum point and then allow it to return slowly, counting the number of revolutions and fractions of a revolution made by the large needle until the stem again contacts the cap. This measurement is equivalent to dimension 'E' in Fig. 4.24. 'K1' + 'K2' is a gauge dimension of 78 mm and is marked on support 'B' at 'b' in Fig. 4.23.

5   If, for example, 'L1' in Fig. 4.21 is 82 mm and dimension 'E' is 4.44 mm, the position of the bevel pinion is 'K1' + 'K2' + 'E' or 78 + 4.44 - 82.44 mm. Therefore the pinion is too far from the differential centre line: 82.44 - 82 = 0.44 mm, and it is necessary to replace the existing adjusting shim with one that is 0.44 mm thicker. Shims are available in steps of 0.04 mm. If the distance read is smaller than the dimension on the bevel pinion then a thinner shim will be required.

6   Remove the adjusting equipment, the rear cover and the bevel pinion shaft assembly. Remove the nut from the pinion shaft and the bearing. Replace the existing shim with one of the correct thickness. Fit the bearing and the nut, tighten to 10 to 12 kg f m (72 to 80 lb f ft) and lock by peening into the groove on the shaft.

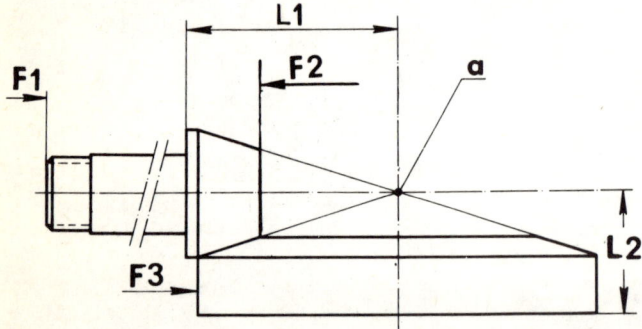

Fig. 4.21. Bevel wheel and crownwheel identification

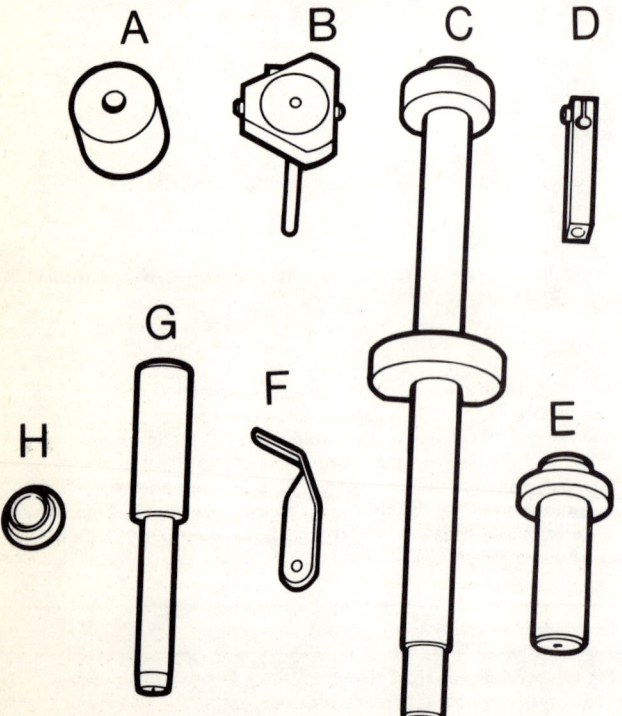

Fig. 4.22. Crownwheel and pinion adjusting kit - 3184T

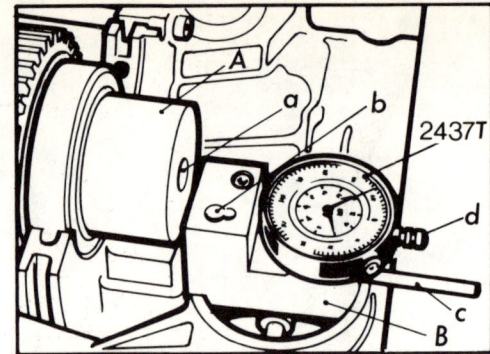

Fig. 4.23. Adjusting the bevel pinion shaft position

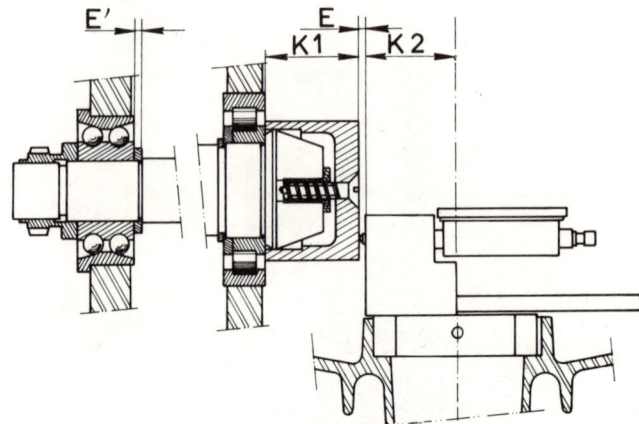

Fig. 4.24. Selecting bevel pinion shaft adjusting shim

20.6 Locking the speedometer drive/nut by peening

21 Crownwheel - position adjustment

1   Fit the outer races of the left- and right-hand differential bearings in their housings without the shims. Fit the differential roller bearings and fit the differential casing in the left-hand casing. Fit the mandrel 'C', in the pinion shaft position. Fit the right-hand half-casing and rear cover, as described in Section 16 (without sealing compound).

2   Fit the dial gauge on the straight edge 'D' and place it on a surface plate. Adjust the gauge position so that it will operate between 8 and 9 mm. Zero the dial opposite the large needle and note the position of the integrating needle (datum point). The dimension 'K1' + 'R', in Fig. 4.25, equals 35 mm. This dimension is engraved on the straight edge 'D'.

3   Fit the straight edge on the crownwheel bearing face of the differential casing, with the dial gauge probe trucking the end of the mandrel. Move the differential casing back and forward and stop at the exact moment at which the needle changes direction. Note the gauge reading. Pull back the probe of the dial gauge to the datum point then, release it slowly and count the number of revolutions or fractions of a revolution made by the large needle until the probe touches the mandrel. This measurement is dimension 'E' in Fig. 4.25. .

4   If, for example, the large needle rotates through 7.46 turns, then dimension 'E' is 7.46 mm. The bearing face of the wheel is 35 + 7.46 = 42.46 mm distance from the bevel pinion centre line. Therefore, if 'L2' in Fig. 4.21 is 40 mm, to obtain this dimension would require a shim of 42.46 - 40 = 2.46 mm. As the preloading of the bearings is evaluated at 0.025 mm per bearing the thickness of the shim which must be fitted between the left-hand half-casing and the outer race is 2.46 + 0.025 = 2.485 mm. Shims are available in steps of 0.05 mm, so the nearest thickness would be 2.50 mm.

5   Place the gearbox with right-hand half-casing lowermost and measure dimension 'E' as described for the left-hand half-casing. Assume this to be 2.45 mm, therefore the crownwheel bearing face is 35 + 2.45 = 37.45 mm from the bevel pinion centre line. The shim required would be 40 - 37.45 = 2.55 mm. Without taking into consideration the bearing pre-loading the total thickness of shims (left and right) would be 2.46 + 2.55 = 5.01 mm. With preloading of 0.05 mm for the two bearings the total thickness would be 5.06 mm. As the shim for the left-hand side is 2.50 mm, the right-hand shim would be 5.06 - 2.50 = 2.56 mm, so the nearest thickness would be 2.55 mm.

6   Assemble the differential, as described in Section 12, paragraph 9.

22 Gearbox - reassembly procedure

1   Fit the differential in the left-hand half-casing. Check that the reverse gear idler is in the neutral position and fit the bevel pinion shaft assembly. Fit the control/primary shaft assembly, turn the needle bearing so that the end of the locking pin of the reverse gear shaft enters the locking notch in the bearing.

2   At this stage, check the crownwheel to pinion backlash. If the crownwheel and pinion shaft adjustment has been carried out the backlash should be correct, however it is advisable to check it. Fit the right-hand half-casing and the rear cover. Tighten the rear cover bolts first and then the casing assembly bolts. Mount a dial gauge on the left-hand casing so that its probe rests on the side of a tooth of the crownwheel and measure the movement of the wheel while holding the bevel pinion. The backlash should be between 0.13 and 0.27 mm. Take three readings spaced at 120° intervals, the difference between any two

readings should not exceed 0.1 mm, otherwise the wheel is out of true, and must be replaced, or there is a foreign body between the crownwheel and the differential casing flange. Remove the dial gauge, the rear cover and the right-hand half-casing.

3   Oil the 3rd and 4th gear shaft and fork assembly, check that the 1st and 2nd gear and the 3rd and 4th gear synchro units are in neutral. Fit the 3rd and 4th gear fork and shaft and engage the fork with the groove in the synchro-unit. Fit the 3rd and 4th gear lockball and spring.

4   Fit the interlock plunger of the 1st and 2nd and reverse gear shafts. Fit the spring holder plate noting that the springs are of different thickness wire. The one with its thicker wire should be fitted towards the reverse gear idler. Grease the ball joint and fit it in the left-hand half-casing, with the groove towards the right-hand half casing.

5   On the right-hand half-casing, stick the lockball in its housing with grease. Stick the spring and guide of the ball joint in their housing with grease. Smear the joint faces of the two half-casings with Curtylon sealing compound. To prevent the sealing compound from entering the casing smear only the outer half width of the joint faces.

6   Check that the planet gears are correctly positioned and fit the right-hand half-casing, ensuring that the 1st and 2nd gear fork engages correctly, that the spring holder plate fits into its housing and that the guide fits in the ball joint groove. Fit the assembly bolts but do not tighten fully until after the rear cover has been fitted.

7   Fit a new seal and 'O' ring and replace the speedometer socket in the rear cover. Smear the joint face of the cover with Curtylon sealing compound and fit the rear cover. Tighten the cover retaining bolts to a torque of 2.5 to 3 kg f m (18 to 21 lb f ft) then slightly loosen the bolts holding the rear cover to the right-hand half-casing. Finally tighten the assembly bolts of the half-casings to 1.4 to 1.5 kg f m (10 to 11 lb f ft) in the sequence shown in Fig. 4.26. Tighten the bolts holding the rear cover to the right-hand half-casing to 2.5 to 3 kg f m (18 to 21 lb f ft).

8   Fit the lockball, spring and disc of the 3rd and 4th gear selector fork shaft. Compress the disc and spring with a 5 mm diameter rod and fit a new split pin.

9   Smear the outer half width of the clutch housing joint face with Curtylon sealing compound and fit the housing, taking care that the oil seal is not damaged by the splines of the control shaft. Tighten the retaining nuts to 1.3 to 1.5 kg f m (9.5 to 11 lb f ft).

10   Fit the differential output shafts, tap them lightly with a mallet to position the bearing. Tighten the ring nuts to 6 to 10 kg f m (43 to 72 lb f ft) and lock them by peening. Fit the brake calipers as described in Chapter 8, Section 5.

11   Fit the drain, level and filler plugs. Fit the reversing light switch or blanking plug. When fitting the switch, smear the threads with Mast-Joint HD 37 and tighten to 1.2 to 1.5 kg f m (9 to 10 lb f ft).

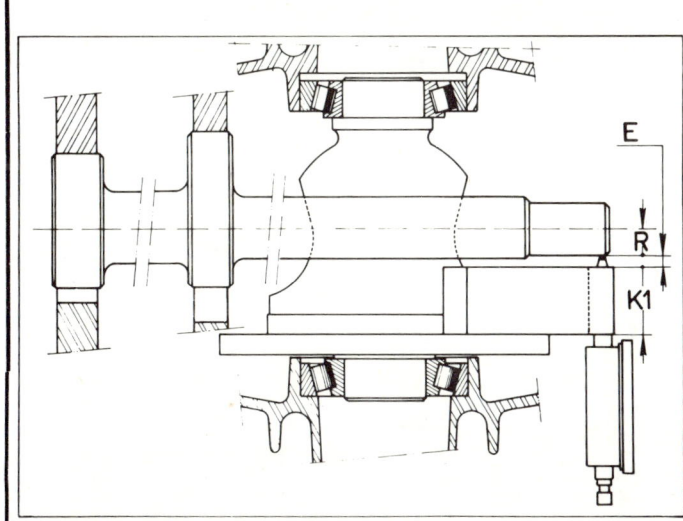

Fig. 4.25. Selecting differential bearing adjusting shims

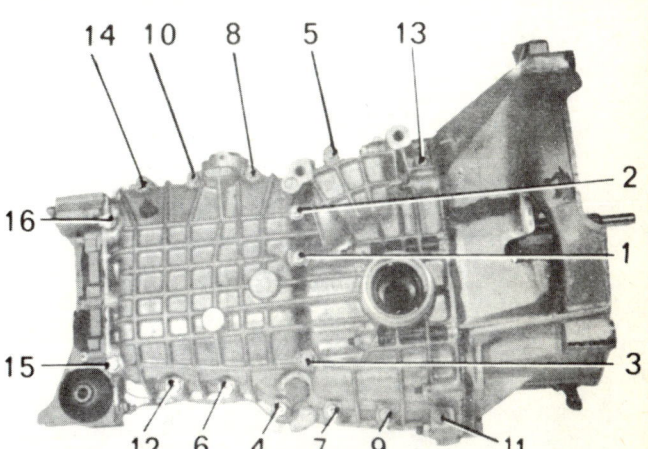

Fig. 4.26. Tightening sequence of assembly bolts

22.1a The differential unit in position in the left-hand half-casing

22.1b Placing the bevel pinion shaft assembly in the left-hand half-casing

22.1c The control and primary shaft assembly fitted in position

22.3 Placing the 3rd/4th gear selector fork and shaft assembly in position

22.4a Fitting the interlock plunger of the 1st/2nd and reverse gear selector shafts

22.4b Fitting the spring holder plate

22.4c Positioning the ball joint with the groove upwards

22.5 Ball joint guide fitted in right-hand half-casing

22.6 Fitting the right-hand half-casing to the left-hand half-casing

22.7a Fitting the rear cover

22.7b Assembly bolts with cap nuts

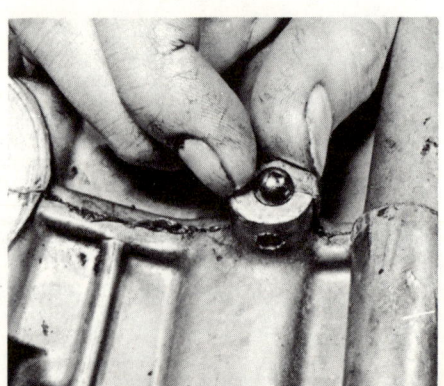

22.8a Fitting the lockball of the 3rd/4th gear selector fork shaft in its housing ...

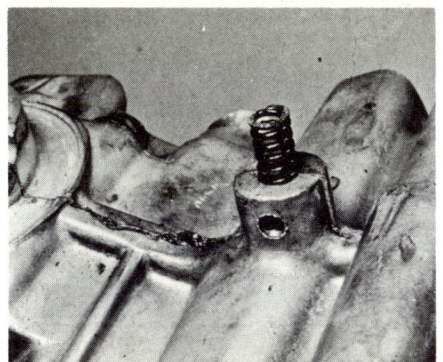

22.8b ... and then the spring ...

22.8c ... and the disc ...

22.8d ... retained by a split pin

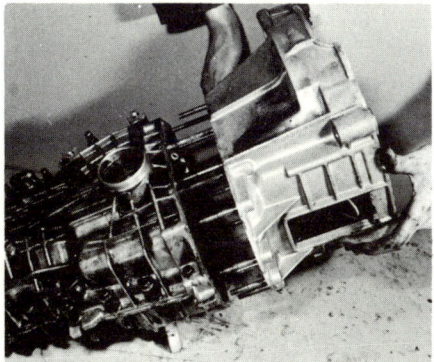

22.9 Fitting the clutch housing to the gearbox

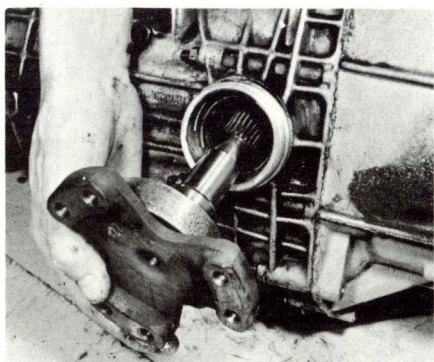

22.10a Fitting a differential shaft

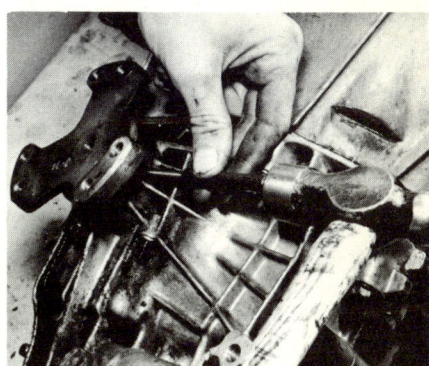

22.10b Locking the differential ring nut by peening

23 Fault diagnosis - clutch

Symptom	Reason/s	Remedy
Judder when taking up drive	Loose engine/gearbox mountings or defective mountings.	Check for tightness. Replace faulty mountings.
	Badly worn friction surfaces or clutch disc contaminated with oil carbon deposit.	Remove engine and replace clutch as required. Rectify any oil leakage.
	Worn splines on the clutch disc or control shaft	Renew disc and or control shaft.
Clutch spin (or failure to disengage so that gears cannot be engaged)	Clutch pedal free movement too great. Clutch disc sticking to pressure plate (usually after standing idle for some time)	Adjust clutch cable. As temporary remedy engage top gear, depress clutch and start engine. When running rev up engine and slip clutch until normal disengagement is possible.
	Damaged or misaligned clutch cover assembly	Replace clutch cover assembly.
Clutch slip (increase in engine speed without corresponding increase in car speed)	Too much clutch pedal free-movement Clutch disc linings worn out or contaminated with oil	Adjust clutch cable. Replace clutch disc. Rectify any oil leak.

24 Fault diagnosis - gearbox

Symptom	Reason/s	Remedy
Ineffective synchromesh. Jumps out of one or more gears (on drive or overrun)	Worn synchro-units Weak lockball springs or worn selector forks or worn gears.	Dismantle and renew. Dismantle and renew.
Noisy, rough, whining and vibration	Worn bearings and gears Crownwheel and bevel pinion out of adjustment	Dismantle and renew. Dismantle and re-adjust.

Note: It is sometimes difficult to decide whether it is worthwhile removing and dismantling the gearbox for a fault which may be nothing more than a minor irritant, considering the amount of work and cost involved. Gearboxes which howl, or where the synchromesh can be 'beaten' by a quick gear change, may continue to perform for a long time in this state. A worn gearbox usually needs a complete rebuild to eliminate noise.

Chapter 5 Semi-automatic gearbox

Contents

Specifications

Torque converter
Control switch contact gap	1.4 ± 0.05
Operating pressure	5.5 to 6.5 bar (80 to 90 psi) at 5000 ± 100 rpm
Oil capacity (including gearbox)	4 litres (7.1 Imp. pints) approx

Gearbox
Number of gears	3 forward, 1 reverse
Ratios:	
1st	2.79 : 1
2nd	1.70 : 1
3rd	1.12 : 1
Reverse	2.50 : 1
Differential unit	Refer to Chapter 4
Oil capacity (including converter)	4 litres (7.1 Imp. pints) approx
Oil change quantity	1.4 litres (2.5 Imp. pints) approx

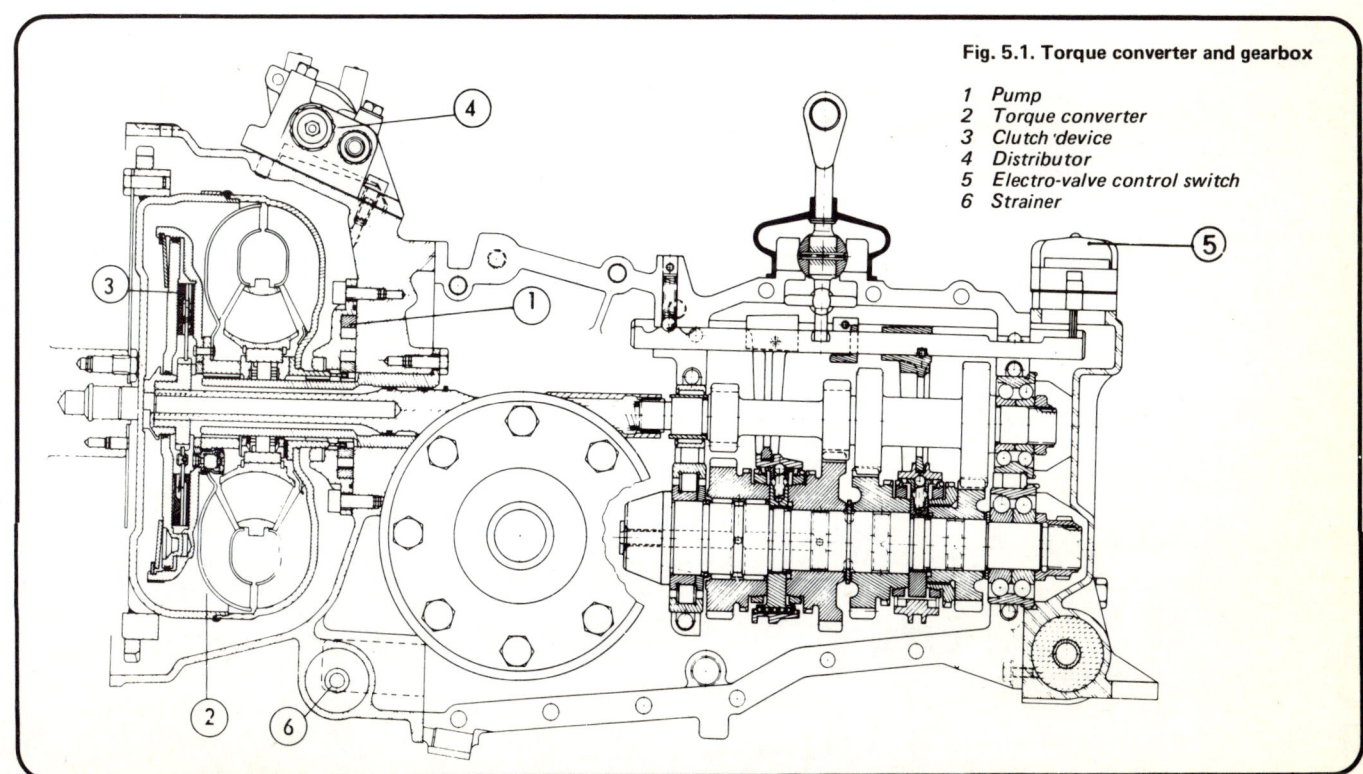

Fig. 5.1. Torque converter and gearbox

1 Pump
2 Torque converter
3 Clutch device
4 Distributor
5 Electro-valve control switch
6 Strainer

1 General description

1   Two types of transmission are available on GS models, a manual transmission with a four speed gearbox, and a semi-automatic transmission with a three speed gearbox. The drive, transmitted to the front wheels through the differential gearing in the gearbox and the driveshafts is very similar on both types. The manual transmission is described in Chapter 4.

2   A wet plate clutch and torque converter transmits the drive from the engine to the gearbox. Engagement and disengagement of the clutch is controlled by a hydraulic valve operated by a solenoid. This electrovalve is controlled in turn by switches operated by the movement of the gearbox selector shafts. The gearbox is a non-automatic type, gear selection is by a floor level gear lever. There is no clutch pedal, the clutch being operated by hydraulic pressure from a pump which is integral with the gearbox. The automatic clutch disengages the drive when a gear selection is being made and the gearing between the three fixed gear ratios is provided through the torque converter.

The oil is pumped from the gearbox through a strainer to the distributor unit where it is directed to operate the clutch, and excess oil is returned to the gearbox via an air cooled, oil cooler.

The clutch and torque converter assembly is a sealed unit and cannot be repaired or overhauled by an owner. If defective it must be replaced as a complete assembly.

2 Oil change - gearbox and torque converter

1   Position the car on level ground, preferably over a pit, or on a lift. Remove the spare wheel. Clean round the filler, level and drain plugs and remove them, draining the oil into a container. Remove the strainer, clean it and replace it, fitted with a new 'O' ring, and tighten it to 1 to 1.5 kg f m (7 to 11 lb f ft). Refit the drain plug and tighten to 3.5 to 4.5 kg f m (26 to 33 lb f ft).

2   Refill the gearbox through the filler plug opening to the oil level plug, approx 1.4 litres (2.5 Imp. pints) with oil of an approved specification. Refit the level plug and the filler plug.

3   Check that the level in the gearbox is correct as follows:

a) *Chock the front wheels and apply the handbrake. Let the engine idle, and engage 3rd gear. Gently move the gear lever to energise the solenoid-operated valve controlling the clutch (it is energised when a faint click is heard). Repeat this operation ten times.*

b) *With the engine still idling and the gear engaged, remove the level plug and the filler plug and top up the oil level of the gearbox. Fit the level and filler plugs. Tighten the level plug to 3.5 to 4.5 kg f m (26 to 33 lb f ft) and the filler plug from 1 to 1.5 kg f m (7 to 11 lb f ft).*

Note: The difference in the oil level between a 'cold' box and a 'hot' box is about 0.2 litres (0.75 Imp. pint). Because of this expansion, when checking the level on a 'hot' box some fluid may run out: do not top-up.

4   Fit the spare wheel.

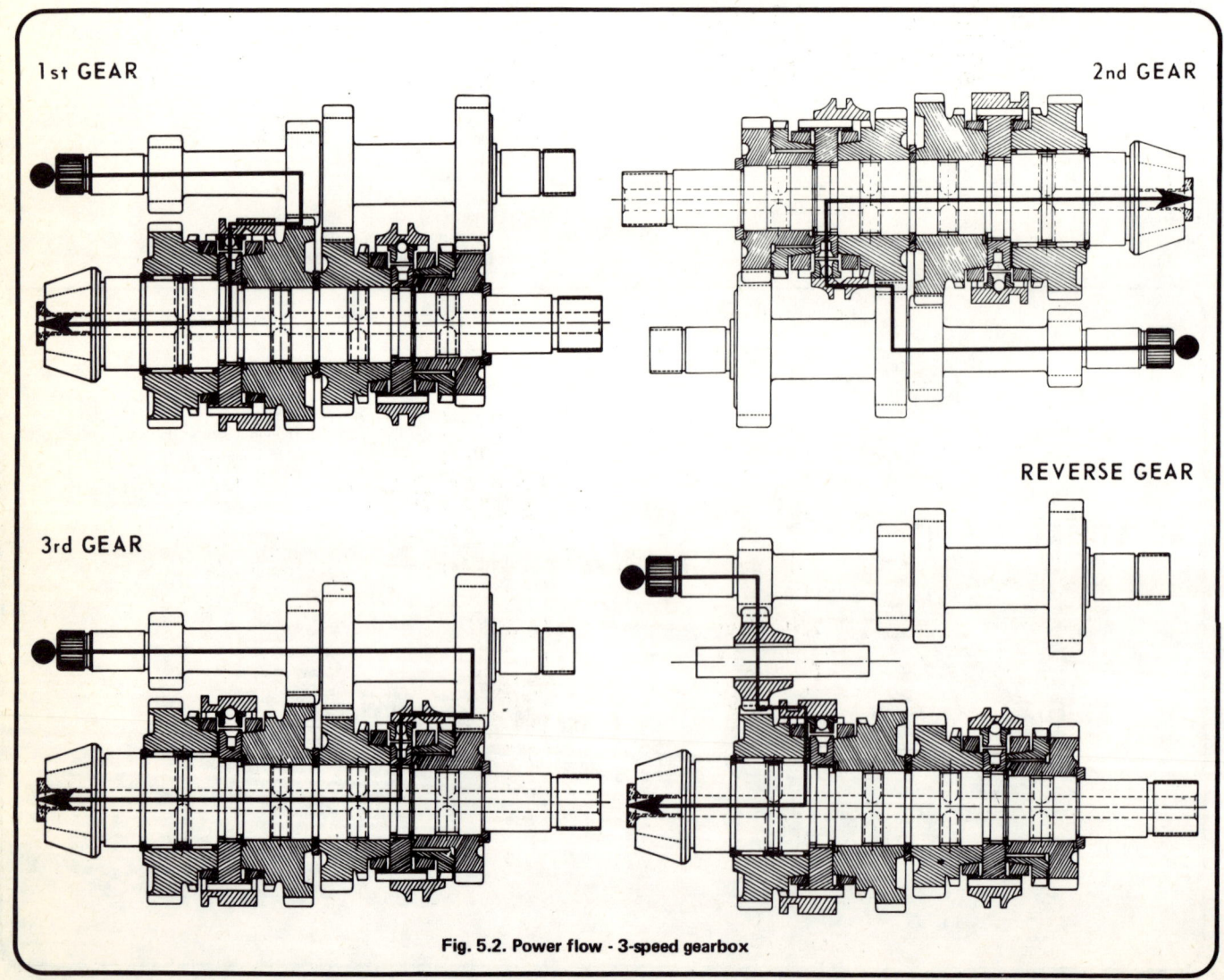

1st GEAR   2nd GEAR   REVERSE GEAR   3rd GEAR

Fig. 5.2. Power flow - 3-speed gearbox

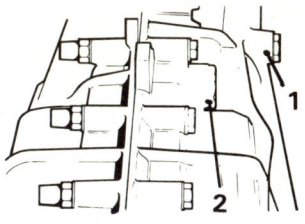

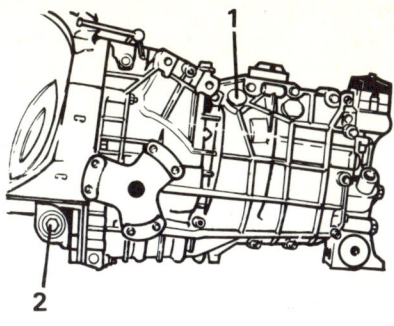

Fig. 5.3. Location of drain and level plugs

1   Drain plug   2   Level plug

Fig. 5.4. Location of filler plug and strainer

1   Filler plug   2   Strainer

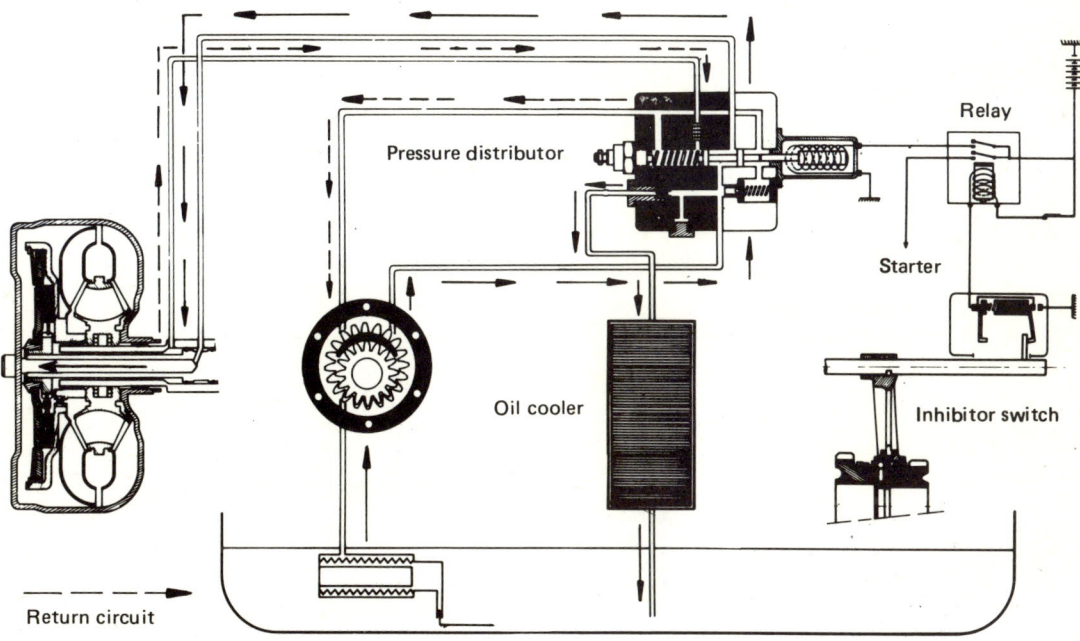

Fig. 5.5. Schematic diagram of torque converter - clutch engaged

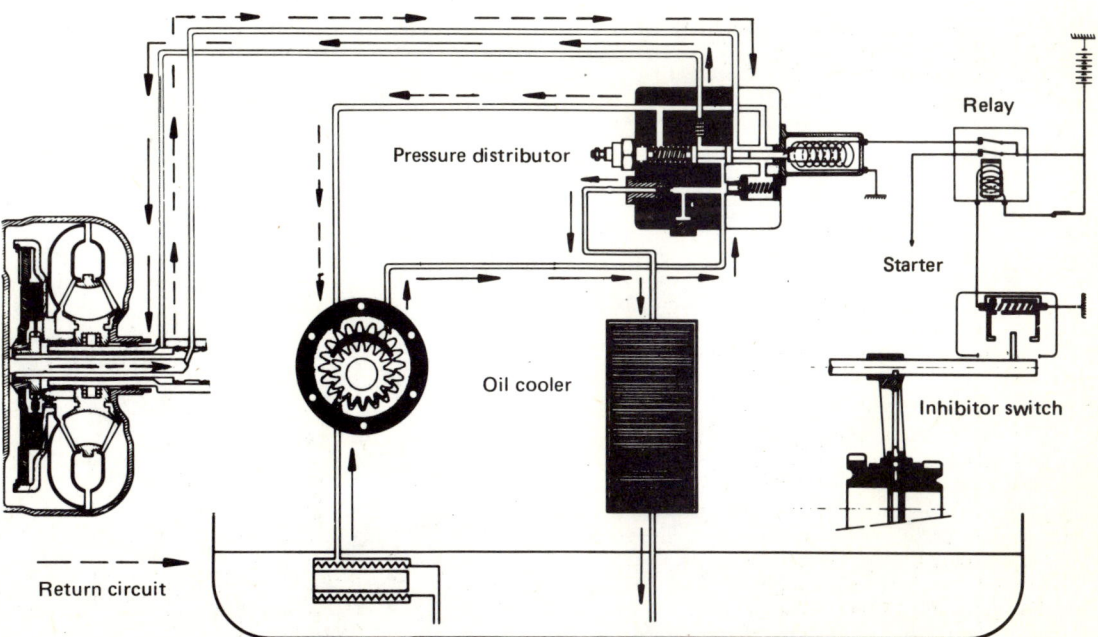

Fig. 5.6. Schematic diagram of torque converter - clutch disengaged

3 Electro-valve switch - checking and adjustment

1 If the clutch is sluggish in operation or it disengages without the gearlever being moved, the cause could be incorrect adjustment of the contact gaps of the electro-valve switch.
2 Open the bonnet. Remove the spare wheel. Disconnect the earth strap from the negative terminal of the battery. Slacken the pressure regulator bleed screw to release the pressure from the hydraulic system. Remove the duct from the left-hand heater box.
3 Refer to Fig. 5.7 and remove the pin and clevis. Free the link rod from the control lever. Remove the screws fixing the gaiter to the console. Pull up the gearlever and remove the retaining and clevis pins. The fixing plate for the gaiter remains in the console, to remove it, the console must be removed. Remove the cover from the electro-valve control switch.
4 The procedure for checking and adjusting the contacts is the same for all four. In neutral, all points should be closed. Select a gear and ensure that it is fully engaged otherwise the check or adjustment would be incorrect. Using a set of feelers, 'A' in Fig. 5.8, check the contact gap, it should be 1.4 $\pm$ 0.05 mm (0.55 $\pm$ 0.002 in). To adjust slacken the securing screw of the fixed contact (3 mm Allen key) and slide the contact in its guide to obtain the correct gap, then moderately tighten the securing screw. Use the same method for the other gears. Refit the switch cover.
5 When replacing the gearlever, fit clips to retain the lower fixing plate and seal in position. Make the clips from two strips of metal 0.5 mm (0.02 in) thick by 10 mm (0.40 in) wide and 40 mm (1.6 in). Fold the strips as shown at 'b' in Fig. 5.9. Working through the console opening position the lower seal and fixing plate under the console, fold the end 'a' of the strip over the metal body of the console so that it holds the plate and seal in position. Replace the gearlever in the reverse of the removal sequence.
6 Check that when the gearlever is in first gear position, that it does not touch the base or the seats. If necessary move the base in its fixing slots.

4 Torque converter oil-feed system - pressure check

1 Drive the car to obtain a gearbox oil temperature of $70^\circ \pm 5^\circ C$.
2 Remove the spare wheel and spare wheel support. Remove the blanking plug from the electro-valve and fit a 6 or 7 mm union as required. Connect a pressure gauge, graduated from 0 to 10 bar (0 to 145 psi) to the union. Fit a workshop tachometer if one is not installed in the car.
3 Run the engine at 5000 $\pm$ 100 rpm and check that the pressure is between 5.5 and 6.5 bar (80 and 94 psi). Run the engine at $850 ^{+50}_{-0}$ rpm and check that the pressure is not less than 4 bar (58 psi).
4 If the pressure is incorrect, and before any other operation, check the gearbox oil level and the state of cleanliness of the suction strainer for the converter feed pump.

5 Gearbox - removal and replacement

1 Remove the engine/gearbox assembly, as described in Chapter 1, Section 5. Separate the gearbox and converter from the engine, as described in Chapter 1, Section 7.
2 Replacing the engine/gearbox assembly is described in Chapter 1, Section 19. Ensure that the converter and driveplate are aligned in the position marked when separating the gearbox from the engine.

6 Torque converter - removal

1 Drain the gearbox oil. With the converter retaining bracket in position (refer to Chapter 1, Section 6, paragraph 5) place the complete assembly in a vertical position with the converter resting on a bench. This prevents the oil from flowing out of the converter.
2 Remove the nuts securing the gearbox casing to the converter housing and lift off the gearbox. Remove the converter retaining bracket and lift off the converter housing leaving the converter on the bench. Remove the control shaft. Do not lost the spring 'a' in Fig. 5.10.

3 Drain the converter by turning it upside down over a suitable receptacle and allow to drain for several hours.
4 Change the starter ring gear if necessary, as described for the flywheel in Chapter 1, Section 11.

7 Torque converter - replacement

1 Place the converter face downwards on the bench. Fill the converter with about 1.5 litres (2.6 Imp. pints) of oil through the hole in the bore. Fill the converter in stages as it takes the oil some time to percolate through the various parts of the converter. The converter must not be completely filled until after the gearbox has been replaced in the car. The true capacity of the converter is about 2.3 litres (4 Imp. pints).
2 Replacement is the reverse of the removal sequence. Check that the two locating dowels are in position on the housing. When engaging the housing on the converter, turn the converter so that the drive pins engage in the notches of the pump gear. Check that the seals and circlip are fitted. Engage the control shaft in the rotor sleeve and in the converter splines and fit them in the end of the shaft.
3 It is essential that the converter retaining bracket is fitted to prevent damage to the driving pins.

8 Gearbox - dismantling (general)

1 The comments in Chapter 4, Section 9, apply equally to the gearbox of the semi-automatic transmission.
2 When removing and fitting the circlips of the bevel pinion shaft, use the method described in Chapter 4, Section 11, paragraph 4, to prevent damage to the special surface treatment of the shaft. Refer to Fig. 4.13.
3 The removal, dismantling and reassembly of the differential unit and output shafts is described in Chapter 4. Adjustment of the crownwheel and bevel pinion, and checking of the backlash, is described in Chapter 4, Sections 20, 21 and 22. Removal and replacement of the brake calipers and discs is described in Chapter 8, Section 4 and 5.

9 Gearbox - dismantling procedure (stage 1)

1 Remove the torque converter, as described in Section 6. Remove the brake calipers and discs. Remove the differential output shafts. Remove the control switch body (4 mm Allen key), the rubber guards and the switch base (4 mm Allen key). Remove the bolts securing the rear cover. Carefully free the cover taking care not to bend the pins which operate the switch unit and remove the rear cover.
2 Refer to Fig. 4.7. Blank off the orifice 'a' with a finger, remove the split pin and collect the blanking disc spring and lockball. Position the gearbox with the left-hand half-casing lowermost and remove the bolts securing the half-casings. Lift off the right-hand half-casing and collect the spring and balljoint guide of the gear selector rod. Remove the balljoint, the plate holding the return spring, the spring and lockball.
3 Remove the primary shaft assembly, the bevel pinion shaft assembly and the differential unit.

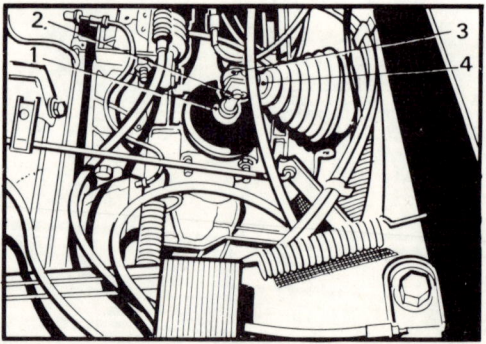

Fig. 5.7. Disconnecting the gearlever

1 Control lever	3 Clevis
2 Pin	4 Link rod

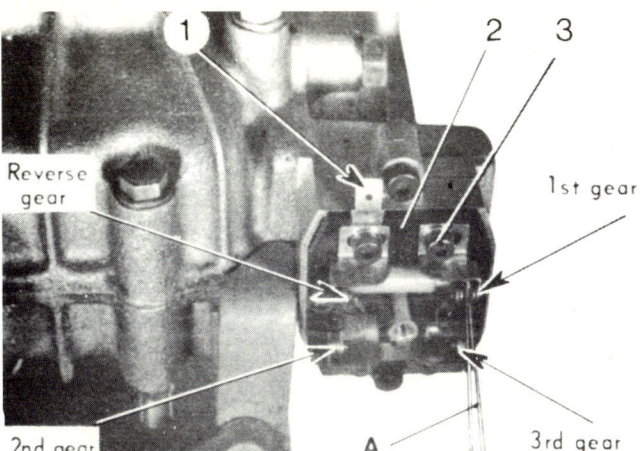

Fig. 5.8. Adjusting the switch contacts

1 Connector   3 Screw
2 Rubber seal

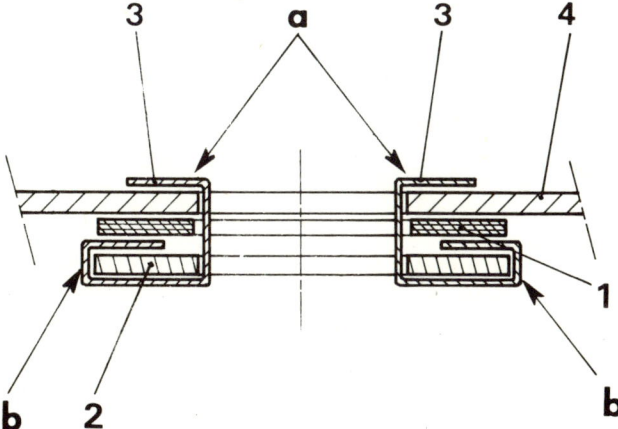

Fig. 5.9. Seal and fixing plate retaining clips

1 Lower seal   3 Clips
2 Lower fixing plate   4 Console

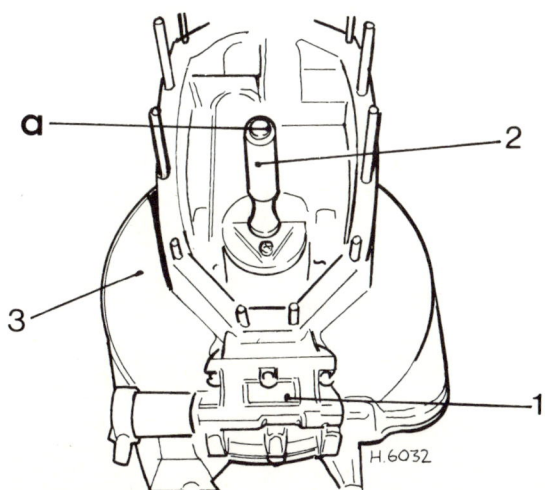

H 6032

Fig. 5.10. Removing the torque converter

1 Distributor assembly   3 Converter housing
2 Control shaft   (a) Spring housing

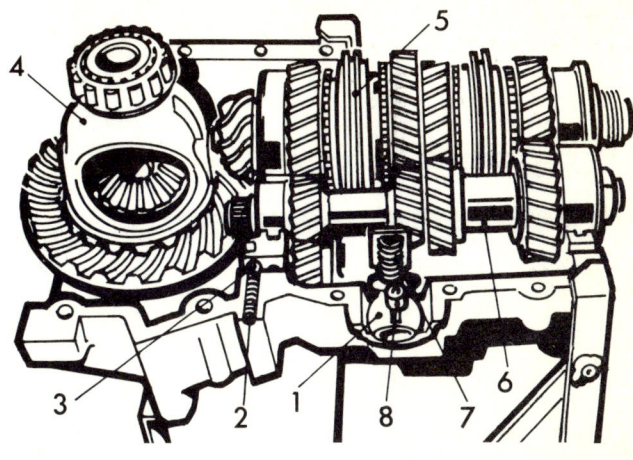

Fig. 5.11. Dismantling the gearbox

1 Balljoint   5 Bevel pinion assembly
2 Spring   6 Primary shaft
3 Lockball   7 Spring holder plate
4 Differential assembly   8 Spring

10 Gearbox - dismantling procedure (stage 2)

1   Dismantle the left-hand half-casing. Remove the pin which retains the reverse idler gearshaft. Drive out the pin holding the spacer on the shaft, (4 mm pin punch). Using a bronze drift, or similar tool, drive out the idler gearshaft. If necessary, remove the differential output shaft seal as described in Chapter 4, Section 11.
2   Dismantle the right-hand half-casing:

a) *Move the 2nd/3rd gearshaft and fork assembly as far as possible to the rear, drive out the pin retaining the fork on the shaft (4 mm pin punch), free the shaft from the rear, remove the fork and the lockball.*
b) *Move the 1st/reverse gearshaft and fork assembly as far as possible to the front and drive out the fork retaining pin (4 mm pin punch). Move the shaft to the rear with a finger over the orifice, 'A' in Fig. 5.13, to avoid losing the lockball, collect the lockball and its spring. Lift out the fork.*
c) *To remove the control lug which operates the reverse gearshaft, move the shaft as far as possible to the rear, so that the lug comes against the casing and drive out the retaining pin. Completely remove the pin by moving the lug to the front and swinging it into the recess below the ball joint socket. Remove the shaft and the control lug. If necessary, remove the pins which operate the control switch (2 mm pin punch).*

3   Dismantle the primary shaft: Remove the needle bearing, (the inner race is not interchangeable). Fit the shaft in a vice equipped with soft jaws and remove the bearing retaining nut and the bearing.
4   Dismantle the bevel pinion shaft assembly:

a) *Fit the bevel pinion assembly in a vice with soft jaws, gripping the reverse gear pinion or the first gear pinion. Lock the bevel pinion by shifting the relevant slider in the appropriate direction.*
b) *Remove the speedometer drive/nut, the bearing, adjusting washer and the 3rd gear pinion and synchro-ring. If the gearbox is to be re-assembled without changing the casing, the bevel pinion or the bearing, identify and retain the adjusting washer to avoid having to adjust the bevel pinion position.*
c) *Remove the circlip retaining the 2nd/3rd synchro-hub. Remove the hub, the 2nd gear synchro ring and the 2nd gear slider. Identify and retain all synchro rings to their pinions.*
d) *Remove the first gear synchro ring, the retaining washer and two half-washers. Remove the 1st gear pinion, its synchro ring and the needle cage.*

e) Remove the circlip retaining the 1st/reverse gear synchro hub, the reverse gear synchro ring, the reverse pinion and the needle cage.

f) If it is necessary to remove the front bearing, remove the retaining circlip, the thrust washer, the bearing and the inner race, using a press and a 50 mm (2 in) diameter tube.

Note: The bevel pinion shaft of semi-automatic transmissions does not have retarding dowels.

5 If necessary, remove the speedometer drive socket, and the drive gear and seals from the rear cover.

6 Dismantle the converter housing:

a) Mark the oil pump in relation to the converter housing. Remove the pump retaining bolts, the pump casing and the pinions. Remove the seals.

b) Remove the oil strainer and 'O' ring seal.

c) If necessary, remove the distributor retaining bolts (6 mm Allen key) and the distributor. Never separate the electro-valve from the distributor, these units cannot be overhauled by an owner, if either is defective, the assembly must be replaced. Do not remove the stator sleeve, if defective, the complete converter housing must be renewed.

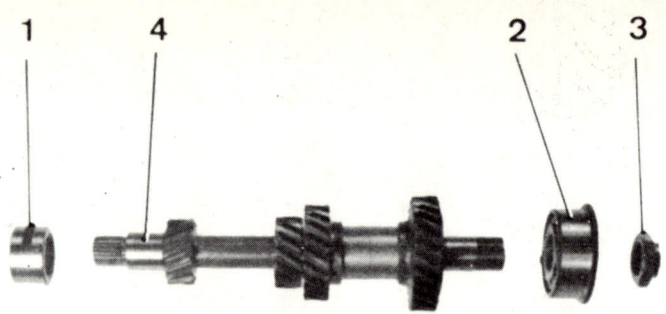

Fig. 5.14. The primary shaft

1 Needle bearing
2 Bearing
3 Nut
4 Inner race

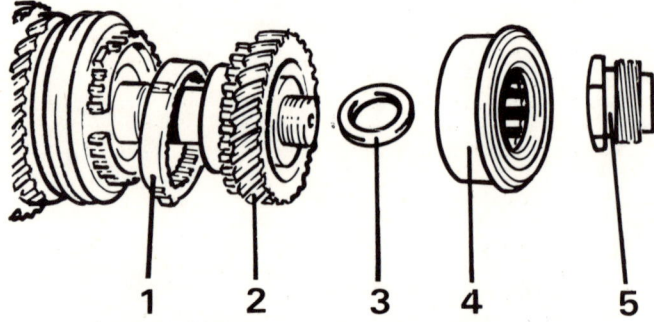

Fig. 5.15. Dismantling the bevel pinion shaft assembly

1 3rd gear synchro-ring
2 3rd gear pinion
3 Adjusting washer
4 Bearing
5 Speedometer drive/nut

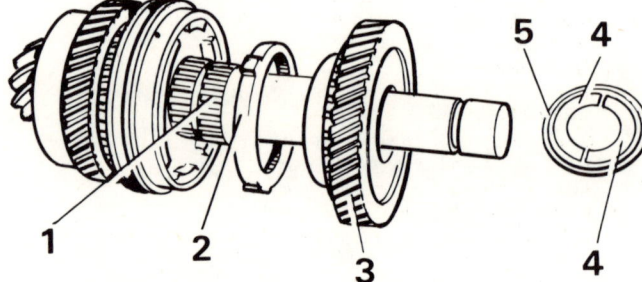

Fig. 5.16. Dismantling the bevel pinion shaft assembly

1 Needle bearing
2 1st gear synchro ring
3 1st gear pinion
4 Half-washers
5 Retaining washer

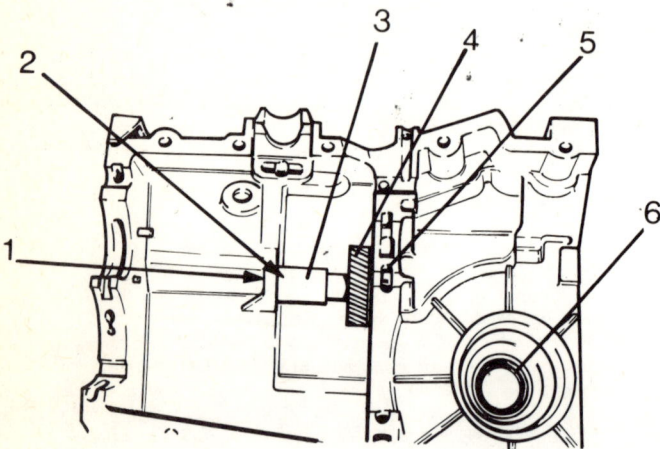

Fig. 5.12. The left-hand half-casing

1 Reverse idler shaft
2 Pin
3 Spacer
4 Reverse idler gear
5 Pin
6 Oil seal

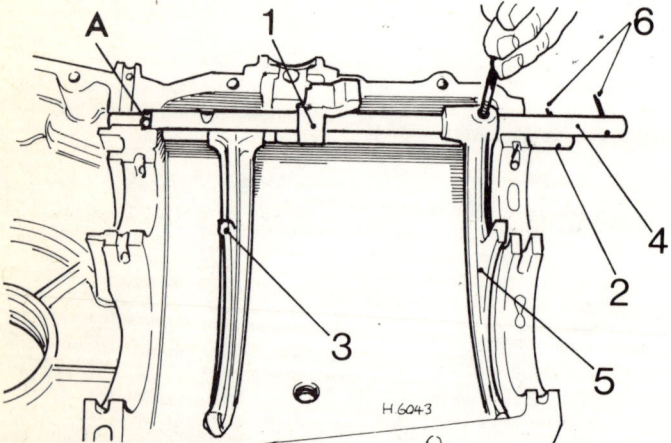

Fig. 5.13. The right-hand half-casing

1 Control lug
2 1st/reverse gear selector shaft
3 1st/reverse gear fork
4 2nd/3rd gear selector shaft
5 2nd/3rd gear fork
6 Control switch operating pins

Fig. 5.17. Dismantling the bevel pinion shaft assembly

1 Circlip
2 Reverse/1st gear synchro-units
3 Reverse gear synchro-ring
4 Reverse gear pinion
5 Needle bearing

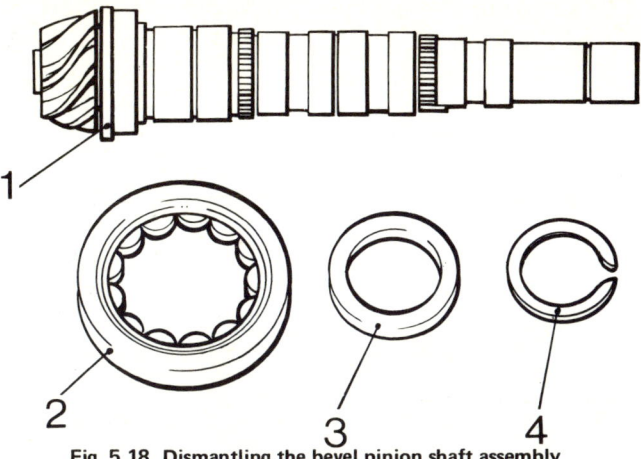

Fig. 5.18. Dismantling the bevel pinion shaft assembly

1	Inner race	3	Thrust washer
2	Roller bearing	4	Circlip

11 Gearbox components - preparation for reassembly

1   Carry out the procedures described in Chapter 4, Sections 1, 2 and 13.

2   Prepare the bevel pinion shaft assembly:

a) *Refer to Figs. 5.15, 5.16, 5.17 and 5.18. Fit the inner race, if it was removed, the roller bearing with the smaller diameter towards the bevel pinion, the thrust washer, with the face without markings towards the bearing, and the circlip.*

b) *Fit the needle cage, the reverse pinion, the reverse gear synchro ring and the reverse/1st gear synchro unit, with the selector fork groove towards the reverse gear pinion. Adjust the axial clearance of the reverse/1st gear synchro hub by selecting a circlip of a thickness which gives a maximum clearance of 0.05 mm (0.002 in) at 'J1' in Fig. 5.19. Fit the selected circlip.*

c) *Fit the needle cage, the 1st gear synchro ring and the 1st gear pinion. Fit the half washers and retaining washer. With the half washers fitted the clearance at 'J2' in Fig. 5.19, must not exceed 0.05 mm (0.002 in). Half washers are supplied in steps of 0.03 mm (0.0012 in) and the two fitted must be of the same thickness.*

d) *Fit the 2nd gear pinion, the 2nd gear synchro ring and the 2nd/3rd gear synchro unit. Adjust the axial clearance of the 2nd/3rd gear synchro unit as described in paragraph (b) above, so that the clearance at 'J3', in Fig. 5.19, does not exceed 0.05 mm (0.002 in). Fit the selected circlip.*

e) *Fit the 3rd gear synchro ring and the 3rd gear pinion. Fit an adjusting washer of known thickness, the bearing with the shoulder towards the rear and the speedometer drive/ nut. Tighten the nut to 10 to 12 kg f m (72 to 80 lb f ft). Do not lock the nut by peening at this stage.*

3   Prepare the primary shaft: Refer to Fig. 5.14. Fit the ball bearing with the shoulder towards the rear. Fit and tighten the nut to 7 to 8.5 kg f m (50 to 62 lb f ft). Lock the nut by peening. Fit the needle bearing.

4   Prepare the control shaft: Oil the seals and fit them on the shaft from the splined end, 'a' in Fig. 5.20. Fit the circlip. The spring will only enter its housing when the shaft is fitted in the converter.

5   Fit the rubber seal and the 'O' ring on the speedometer drive socket. Grease the drive pinion and fit it in the socket. Fit the speedometer drive assembly into the rear cover with the groove of the socket aligned with the hole for the securing screw.

6   Fit the differential shaft seals in each half-casing as described in Chapter 4, Section 8.

7   Prepare the left-hand half-casing: Refer to Fig. 5.12. Preparation of the half-casing is the reverse of the dismantling sequence, described in Section 10. The pin (5) which locks the needle bearing of the primary shaft must stand slightly proud of the surface of this bearing.

8   Prepare the right-hand half-casing: Refer to Fig. 5.13. Preparation of the half-casing is the reverse of the dismantling sequence described in

Section 10. When fitting the pins which operate the control switch unit on the fork shaft, position the split of each pin perpendicular to the longitudinal axis of the fork shaft. The shafts are identified in Fig. 5.21. The projection of the control switch operating pins is given in millimetres. The shaft of the 2nd/3rd gear fork has a single notch at 'd' and two flats at 'a'. The shaft of the reverse/1st gear fork has two notches for the fork locking pins at 'b' and 'c'. The fork gap of the reverse/1st gear fork is greater than that of the 2nd/3rd gear fork.

9   Prepare the converter housing:

a) *Oil the pump pinion, stick the 'O' ring seal in its groove with grease and fit the pump to the casing, align the marks made at removal and fit the retaining bolts. Centre the pump assembly with a mandrel and tighten the bolts to 1.9 kg f fm (13 lb f ft).*

b) *Smear the distributor joint face with Curtylon sealing paste. Fit the distributor on the converter casing with the electro-valve towards the right of the casing. Fit and tighten the retaining bolts to 1.2 to 1.7 kg f m (9 to 12 lb f ft).*

c) *Fit the 'O' ring seal on the strainer and screw the strainer into its housing on the converter casing and tighten it to 1 to 1.5 kg f m (7 to 11 lb f ft).*

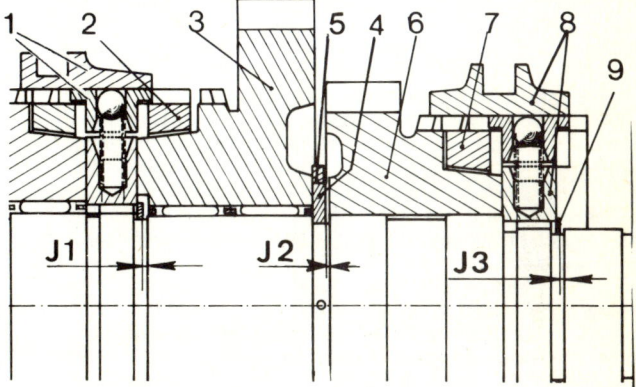

Fig. 5.19. Axial clearance of gears and synchro-hubs

1	1st gear synchro-unit	6	2nd gear pinion
2	1st gear synchro-ring	7	2nd gear synchro-ring
3	1st gear pinion	8	2nd/3rd gear synchro-unit
4	Half-washers	9	Circlip
5	Retaining washer		

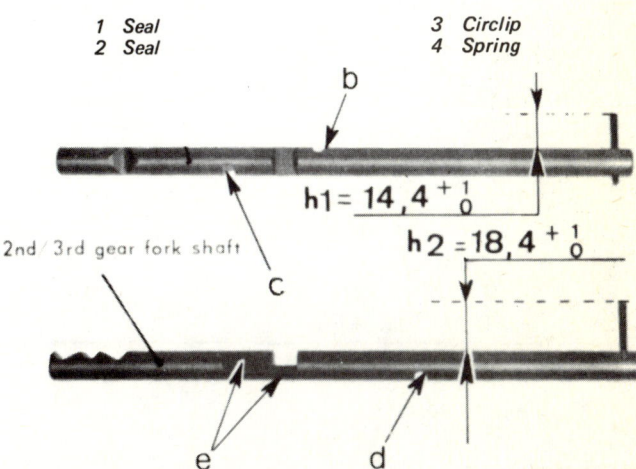

Fig. 5.20. The control shaft

1	Seal	3	Circlip
2	Seal	4	Spring

$$h1 = 14,4 \, ^{+1}_{0}$$

$$h2 = 18,4 \, ^{+1}_{0}$$

2nd/3rd gear fork shaft

Fig. 5.21. Selector fork shafts - identification

12 Gearbox - reassembly procedure

1   If any of the following have been renewed it will be necessary to adjust the position of the crownwheel and pinion, as described in Chapter 4, Sections 19, 20 and 21: the gearbox casing, the crownwheel and pinion, the differential bearings and the differential casing.

2   Fit the differential in the left-hand half-casing. Fit the bevel pinion shaft assembly. Fit the primary shaft assembly, turn the needle bearing so that the end of the locking pin on the reverse gear shaft enters the groove in the bearing.

3   Check the backlash of the crownwheel to pinion, as described in Chapter 4, Section 22, paragraph 2.

4   On the left-hand half-casing fit the spring holder plate with the spring having the thicker diameter wire fitted towards the reverse gear idler pinion. Fit the ball joint with the groove towards the right-hand casing side. Temporarily fit a differential shaft to centre the planet wheels. Position both synchro units in neutral.

5   Grease the spring and balljoint guide and fit them in the right-hand half-casing. Ensure that all locking between the reverse/1st gear shaft and 2nd/3rd gear shaft is in place, and that the forks are in the neutral position.

6   Smear the outer half of the joint faces of the half-casing with Curtylon sealing compound, avoid getting sealing compound inside the casing. Fit the right-hand half-casing on the left-hand half-casing, ensuring that the selector forks engage in the grooves of the synchro units and, at the same time, guide the spring holder plate into its housing in the right-hand casing. Make sure that the balljoint guide enters the groove of the balljoint. Fit the assembly bolts finger tight, final tightening is done after the rear cover is fitted.

7   Smear the joint face of the rear cover with Curtylon sealing compound. Fit the cover on the gearbox casing. Fit and tighten the retaining bolts to 2.5 to 3 kg f m (18 to 21 lb f ft), then slightly slacken the bolts retaining the cover to the right-hand half-casing. Refer to Fig. 4.26 and tighten the half-casing retaining bolts, following the numerical sequence shown. On some casings the bolt (3) may be on the left-hand half-casing. Finally tighten the half-casing bolts to 1 to 1.5 kg f fm (10 to 11 lb f ft). Retighten the slackened rear cover bolts.

8   Fit the 2nd/3rd gear selector shaft lockball, spring and disc, secured with a split pin.

9   Fit the differential shafts and the brake calipers.

10   Smear the seal face of the control switch base plate with Curtylon sealing compound. Fit the plate on the rear cover (4 mm Allen key) with the slot, (a) in Fig. 5.22, towards the front of the gearbox. Fit the rubber seal on the switch and fit the switch on the base plate with the connector towards the right-hand half-casing. Adjust the switch points gap as described in Section 3. Fit the switch cover and the rubber collar.

11   Replace the torque converter, as described in Section 7.

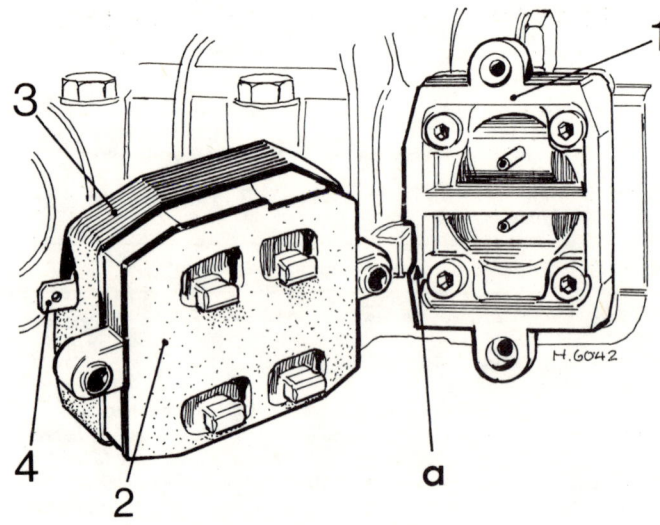

Fig. 5.22. Electro-vaive control switch

1	Baseplate	3	Rubber collar
2	Rubber seal	4	Connector

13 Fault diagnosis - semi-automatic gearbox

Symptom	Reason/s	Remedy
Ineffective synchromesh	Worn synchro-units	Dismantle and renew
Jumps out of gear	Weak lockball springs or worn selector forks	Renew.
	Control switch out of adjustment	Re-adjust contact gaps.
Noisy, rough, whining and vibration	Worn bearings and gears	Dismantle and renew.
	Crownwheel and bevel pinion out of adjustment	Dismantle and re-adjust.
Gear changing difficult	Low oil pressure	See below.
	Electro-valve/distributor defective	Replace.
	Torque converter defective	Replace.
Oil pressure low	Oil strainer blocked	Remove and clean.
	Oil pump defective	Rectify as necessary.
Transmission overheating	Oil cooler ineffective	Check the air duct.
	Torque converter defective	Replace the torque converter assembly.

Chapter 6 Hydraulic system

Contents

Specifications

Hydraulic pump

Type	Single cylinder piston type
Drive	Connecting rod from oil pump
Ratio pump speed/engine speed	1 : 2
Piston diameter	15 mm
Piston stroke	10 ± 0.05 mm
Output under load of 175 bar (2.490 psi)	0.9 cc per rev. at 250 rpm

Pressure regulator

Cut-out pressure	170 ± 5 bar (2418 ± 71 psi)
Cut-in pressure	145 ± 5 bar (2062 ± 71 psi)

Accumulator

Capacity	0.40 litre (24.4 cu in)
Inflation pressure:	
Until 3/1973	40 ± 5 bar (370 ± 71 psi)
From 3/1973	60 + 5 / 10 bar (711 to 925 psi)

Pressure switch range

Until 3/1973	60 to 80 bar (853 to 1138 psi)
From 3/1973	75 to 95 bar (1068 to 1351 psi)

Hydraulic fluid type ... ...

Mineral LHM (green colour)

Reservoir capacity ... ...

3.3 litres (5.8 Imp. pts)

---

1 General description

1 The hydropneumatic suspension and the braking system is pressurized by a common hydraulic system. The hydraulic system is illustrated diagrammatically in Fig. 6.2.

2 Hydraulic fluid is drawn from the hydraulic reservoir, mounted on the right-hand wing valance, and delivered under pressure to the hydraulic pressure regulator mounted on top of the clutch housing. From the pressure regulator, fluid passes to the four-way union. Fitted in the system is a pressure switch, wired to a warning lamp on the instrument panel which lights up when tne hydraulic pressure is too low.

3 From the four-way union, fluid under pressure passes through the front and rear height correctors to their respective suspension cylinders. From the suspension cylinders the low pressure return fluid is returned through pipelines to the hydraulic reservoir.

4 The height correctors maintain the hydropneumatic suspension at the manually selected height by admitting fluid to, and releasing fluid from, the suspension cylinders according to the movement of the front and rear anti-roll bars to which they are connected. Three height positions can be selected by the manual height control. The normal

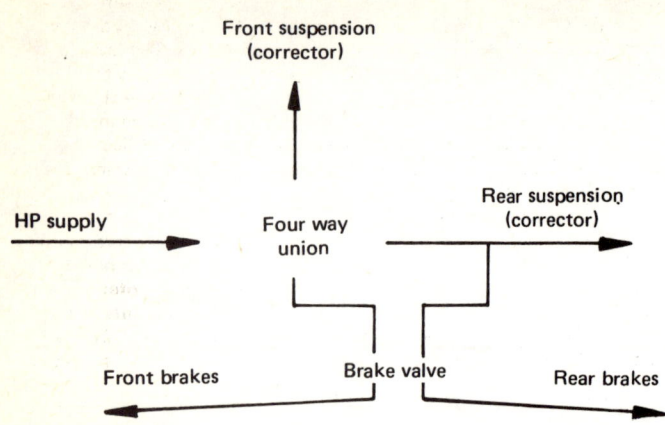

Fig. 6.1. Diagram of operation

driving position is with the lever in the first notch (towards the front), when travelling on good road surfaces. The intermediate position (ground clearance increased), can be used when driving on rough surfaces (very slowly). With the lever in the rear notch the ground clearance is increased to the maximum, 'high position'. This is intended for wheel changing and must not be selected when driving, except in exceptional cases to negotiate particularly difficult surfaces over short distances and at very low speed. As these height positions are obtained by hydraulic pressure they can only be maintained while the engine is running. When the engine is stopped the car sinks down against the bump stops.

5   Hydraulic pressure for the braking system is fed from the four-way union to a connection on the brake control valve for operation of the front brake calipers. The rear brake calipers are operated by hydraulic pressure which is passed to the brake control valve from the rear suspension. This arrangement results in the braking effort being biased in favour of the front brakes, and at the same time, regulates the braking effort on the rear wheels according to the load on the rear suspension - the heavier the load, the greater the pressure in the rear suspension, thus more braking effort.

6   Hydraulic pressure is released from the system by slackening the bleed screw on the pressure regulator. This allows the pressure fluid to bleed off to the reservoir.

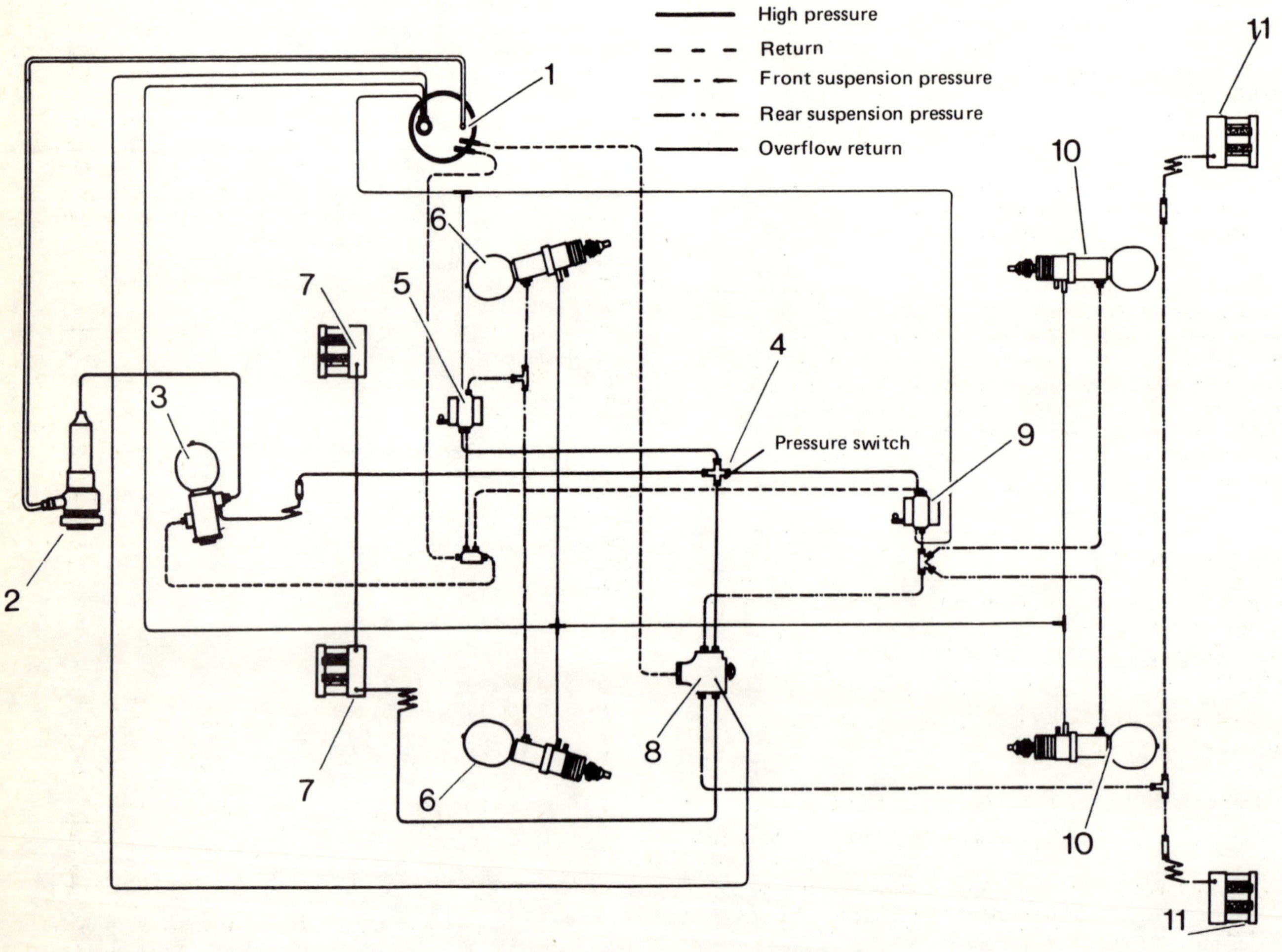

Fig. 6.2. Hydraulic circuit diagram

1 Fluid reservoir	4 Four-way union	7 Front brake calipers	10 Rear suspension cylinders
2 High pressure pump	5 Front height corrector	8 Brake control valve	11 Rear brake calipers
3 Pressure regulator and accumulator	6 Front suspension cylinders	9 Rear height corrector	

2 Hydraulic system and components - precautions

1 Cleanliness is of the utmost importance when working on the hydraulic system and its components. Clean all adjacent areas before disconnecting components, after removal, blank-off all orifices and ensure that components and pipes do not get contaminated.
2 Use only LHM mineral hydraulic fluid in the hydraulic system, the use of any other fluid will ruin the rubber rings and seals. LHM fluid is green in colour. Keep the fluid, carefully sealed, in its original container.
3 Use only genuine spare parts. Components are identified by painting or marking in green. All rubber parts are identified by their white or green colour and are of a special quality for use with LHM fluid.
4 Before starting work on the hydraulic system, the pressure must be released as follows:
  With the engine switched off, place the manual height control lever in the 'high position' (back) and slacken off the hydraulic pressure regulator bleed screw. Wait until the front of the car has reached the low position then place the manual height control lever in the 'normal position' (front) and wait for the rear of the car to stabilize. Select the 'high position' and wait for the car to settle to the low position.

3 Hydraulic system faults - preliminary checks

  In the event of incorrect operation of the hydraulic system, carry out the following checks before dismantling the system:
1 Examine the controls and mechanical linkage to ensure that they are not sticking or are under stress.
2 With the engine idling, slacken the pressure regulator bleed screw one and a half turns, and check that the sound of leakage can be heard.
3 Tighten the bleed screw: cutting-out must occur, this is indicated by less noise from the hydraulic high pressure pump.
4 If cutting-out does not occur check that there is sufficient fluid in the reservoir and that the reservoir filter is clean and in good condition. Check also that there is no leak on the suction side of the pump.

4 Cleaning components and pipelines

1 Hydraulic units must be cleaned with petrol or white spirit and blown through with compressed air. Clean the rubber hoses also with petrol or white spirit and then dry out with compressed air.
2 Always renew all joints and seals at each dismantling.
3 After cleaning, lightly oil all internal parts of components, and block off all orifices.

5 Pipe joints - assembly

1 When connecting pipe joints, lightly oil the seal with LHM fluid, and position it as shown, 'a' in Fig. 6.3.
2 Centre the pipe in the housing by lining it up with the axis of the hole, avoiding all stress. Ensure that the end 'b' of the pipe enters in the small bore 'c'.
3 Start the union nut by hand. Tighten the nut in accordance with the following torque loading:

  3.5 mm pipe
  4.5 mm pipe } – 0.8 to 0.9 kg f m (5.8 to 6.6 lb f ft)
  6.0 mm pipe – 0.9 to 1.1 kg f m (6.6 to 8 lb f ft)

4 Do not overtighten, the design of joint ensures that the sealing action increases with fluid pressure. Overtightening can cause deformation of the pipe and result in leakage.

6 Routine maintenance

1 Every 6000 miles (10,000 km) the hydraulic filter must be cleared. Unclip the filter and remove it from the top of the hydraulic reservoir.
2 Clean the filter in petrol or white spirit and dry it with compressed

air. Refit the filter, check the fluid level and top-up, if necessary.
3 Every 18,000 miles (30,000 km) change the fluid in the hydraulic system. To drain the system place the manual height control lever in the 'normal' position, open the pressure regulator bleed screw then move the manual control lever to the 'high' position. Slacken the clip securing the fluid level sight tube, disconnect the tube and connect it to a length of hose with the other end in a container to collect the fluid. Remove the filter and drain the high pressure pump suction line. Clean the filter as described above.
4 Reconnect the sight tube, fit the filter and prime the high pressure pump with fluid through the pump suction pipe. Fill the reservoir with LHM fluid, run the engine then tighten the pressure regulator bleed screw. Select the 'high' position and top up the reservoir. **Note:** *On later models the fluid level is registered by an indicator mounted on top of the reservoir. The same principle applies, a yellow disc, indicating the fluid level must be maintained between minimum and maximum level marks.*

7 Hydraulic system components - checking (general)

1 The checks must be carried out in the sequence described, if a unit proves to be defective it must be repaired or changed before proceeding with the next check. Units which have been removed from the car can only be tested on a hydraulic test bench and should be taken to a Citroen agent with the appropriate testing equipment.
2 To carry out the checks with the units in position, the equipment illustrated in Fig. 6.5 will be required. The female blanking plug (C) can be made from a two-way union AM-453-37.
3 Before proceeding with the checks, ensure that the filter in the hydraulic reservoir is clean and that the hydraulic fluid is at operating temperature. Drive the car on the road first, if necessary. Check that the fluid level in the reservoir is correct.
4 Release the pressure from the hydraulic system as described in Section 2. Remove the heater distribution box and ducts. Disconnect the supply pipes from the two-way union and connect them to the three-way union, 'B' in Fig. 6.6, fitted with the pressure gauge 'A'. The assembly consisting of the three-way union and the pressure gauge remains in position throughout the checks.

8 Main accumulator - checking

1 From the four-way union disconnect the supply pipes to the front brakes, front suspension and rear suspension. Blank-off the openings with the blanking plugs 'D'.
2 Disconnect the ignition lead to the contact breaker, to prevent the engine from starting. Tighten the pressure regulator bleed screw.
3 Operate the starter motor and check that the needle of the pressure gauge rises gradually and then stabilizes. This value is the inflation pressure of the accumulator and should be between 35 and 45 bar (500 and 640 psi) on models dated until March 1973 and between 50 and 65 bar (715 and 925 psi) on models dated from March 1973. Connect the contact breaker lead.

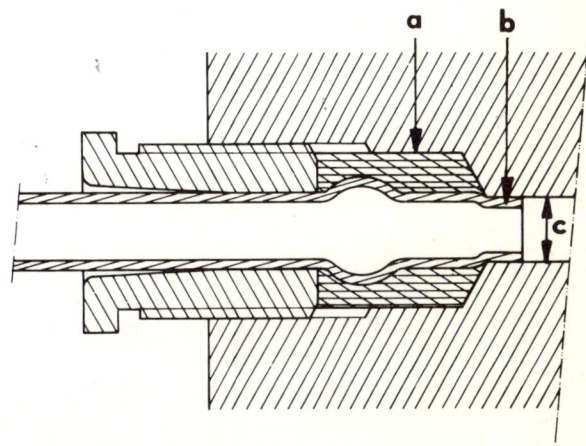

Fig. 6.3. Pipe joint assembly

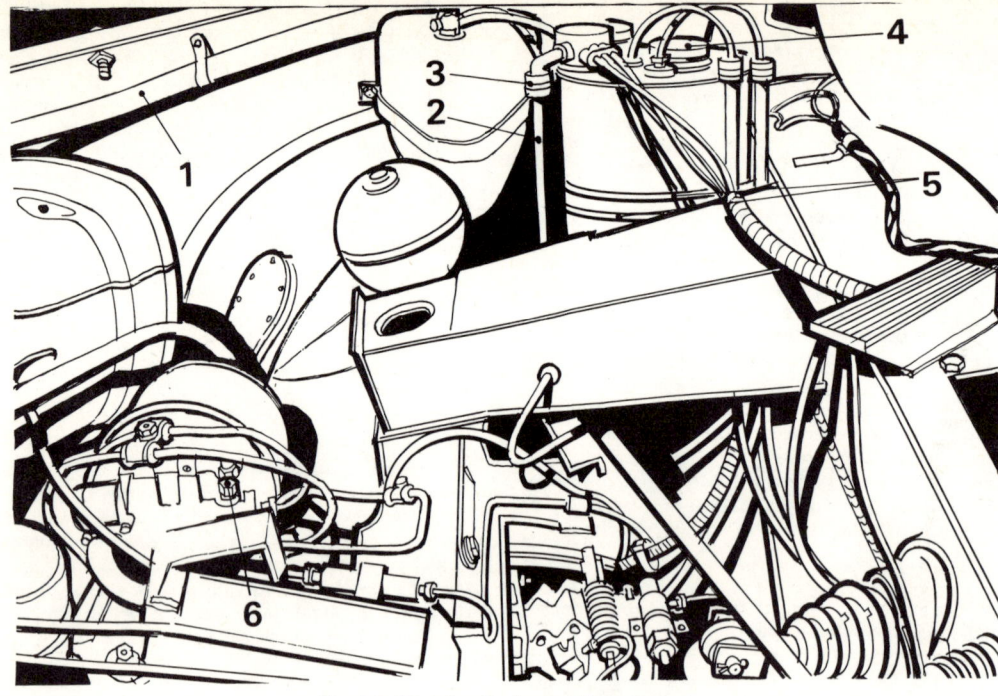

Fig. 6.4. Draining the hydraulic system

1 Pump suction pipe	2 Fluid level sight tube	4 Filter	6 Pressure regulator
	3 Clip	5 Fluid level marks	

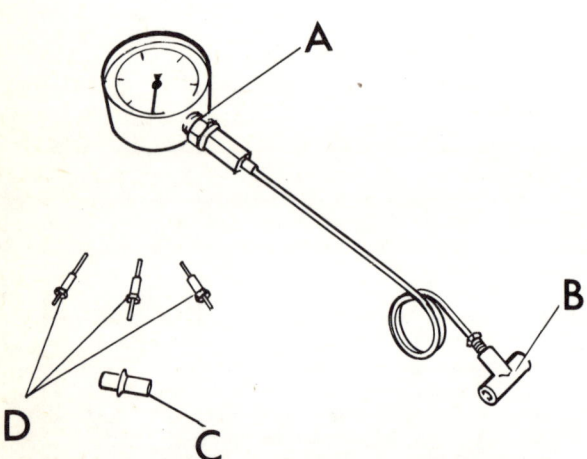

Fig. 6.5. Hydraulic system testing equipment

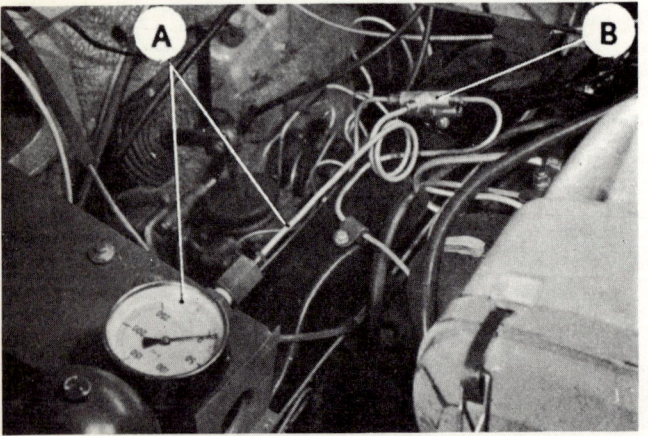

Fig. 6.6. Three-way union and test gauge

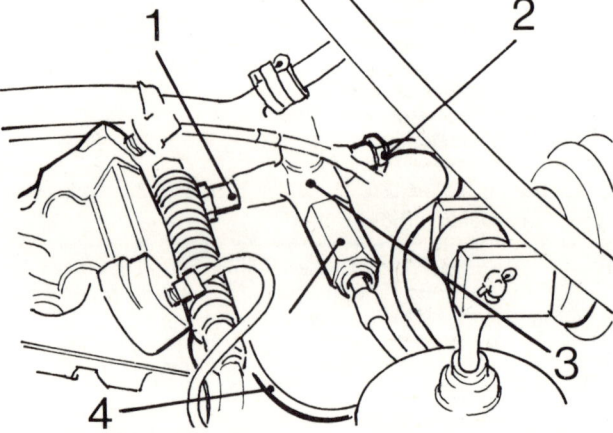

Fig. 6.7. Four-way union connections

1 Front suspension	4 Front brakes
2 Rear suspension	5 Pressure switch
3 Four-way union	

9   Pressure regulator - checking

1   Check the cut-out pressure as follows:

   a) *Start the engine. With the pressure regulator bleed screw closed check that the cut-out pressure is between 165 and 175 bar (2350 and 2490 psi), indicated when the gauge needle stops rising.*

   b) *When the cut-out pressure is reached let the engine run until the pressure stabilizes. Stop the engine and note the pressure drop over a period of three minutes. If the drop is more than 10 bar (140 psi) check the plugs 'D' for leaks and repeat the operation. If the pressure drop is still outside the limit the pressure regulator is defective and must be replaced.*

2   Check the cut-in pressure as follows:

   a) *Start the engine. When cut-out occurs open the pressure regulator bleed screw slightly. The pressure will fall gradually then rise again when the high pressure pump begins to charge.*

b) The minimum reading on the gauge is the cut-in pressure and must be between 140 and 150 bar (1990 and 2130 psi).

3 If the cut-out or cut-in pressure is outside the permitted limits the pressure regulator is defective and must be renewed.

10 Hydraulic brake control unit - checking

1 Slacken the pressure regulator bleed screw. Remove the blanking plug from the front brakes connection of the four-way union and connect the supply pipe for the front brakes.
2 Tighten the pressure regulator bleed screw and start the engine. After cut-out, allow the pressure to stabilize then stop the engine.
3 Note the pressure drop over a period of three minutes. If the pressure drops by more than 10 bar (140 psi) repeat the operation. If the drop is outside the limit, the brake control unit is defective and must be replaced.

11 Pressure switch - checking

1 With the test equipment connected as in Section 10, run the engine to obtain the cut-out pressure. Stop the engine.
2 Operate the brake pedal until the hydraulic pressure warning light is permanently on and note the reading on the pressure gauge. This should be between 60 and 80 bar (850 and 1140 psi). If not, replace the pressure switch.

12 Front suspension - checking

1 Slacken the pressure regulator bleed screw. Remove the blanking plug from the front suspension connection of the four-way union and connect the front suspension supply pipe.
2 Tighten the bleed screw and run the engine. Place the manual height control lever in the 'normal' road position, wait until the front of the car rises and cut-out takes place. Allow the pressure to stabilize and stop the engine. Note the pressure drop over a period of three minutes, if it exceeds 10 bar (140 psi) repeat the operation.
3 If the pressure drop exceeds the permitted limit, this means the front height corrector on one, or both, of the front suspension cylinders are defective. Check these two units by successive elimination, as described in Sections 13 and 14.

13 Front height corrector - checking

1 Remove the three screws and the guard protecting the height corrector. Slacken the pressure regulator bleed screw and place the manual height control lever in the 'high' position.
2 Disconnect the supply pipe to the front suspension cylinders and blank the opening with a blanking plug. Tighten the bleed screw. Place the manual height control lever in the 'normal' position and start the engine.
3 Allow the pressure to stabilize and stop the engine. Note the pressure drop over a period of three minutes, if it exceeds 10 bar (140 psi) repeat the operation.
4 If the pressure drop is outside the permitted limit, the front height corrector is defective and must be replaced. Remove the blanking plug and connect the front suspension supply pipe to the corrector. Refit the corrector guard plate.

14 Front suspension cylinders - checking

1 Slacken the pressure regulator bleed screw. Place the manual height control lever in the 'high' position. Disconnect and remove the supply pipe to the front right hand cylinder.
2 Fit a blanking plug to the opening in the three-way union and repeat the check as described in Section 13. If the front right-hand suspension cylinder is defective it must be replaced. Remove the blanking plug and refit the supply pipe.

3 If, after having checked the front height corrector and the front right-hand suspension cylinder, the drop in pressure still exists then the left-hand suspension cylinder is defective and must be replaced.

15 Rear suspension - checking

1 Slacken the pressure regulator bleed screw and place the manual height control lever in the 'high' position. Remove the blanking plug from the rear suspension connection of the four-way union and connect the supply pipe.
2 Disconnect the supply pipe for the rear brakes at the brake control valve and fit a blanking plug to the pipe opening. Tighten the pressure regulator bleed screw and place the manual control in the 'normal' road position.
3 Carry out the procedure for checking the front suspension, as described in Sections 12, 13 and 14. Renew defective units. Remove the checking equipment and connect the supply pipe for the rear brakes to the brake control valve and reconnect the supply pipes to the two-way union.

16 Brake control valve - simplified check for leakage

1 Slacken the pressure regulator bleed screw and place the manual height control in the 'high' position. Disconnect the rubber, brake return line from the reservoir and attach a transparent plastic tube to the end and support it vertically.
2 Tighten the bleed screw, select 'normal' road position on the manual height control and start the engine. When the car has settled, depress the brake pedal until fluid appears in the plastic tube. Release the brake pedal and check that the fluid level in the plastic tube remains virtually constant. If it does not, replace the brake control unit, as described in Chapter 8, Section 14.

17 Hydraulic pump - general

1 The hydraulic pump is mounted at the front of the engine behind the fan cowl. It is a piston type pump and is driven by a connecting rod from an eccentric on the engine oil pump.
2 Removal of the pump on earlier models required the removal of the fan cowl, on later models access is provided by an aperture in the fan cowl.
3 Removal of the pump is described in Chapter 1, Section 10 and replacement in Chapter 1, Section 18. After fitting the pump always prime it by removing the suction pipe from the reservoir and filling it with LHM fluid.

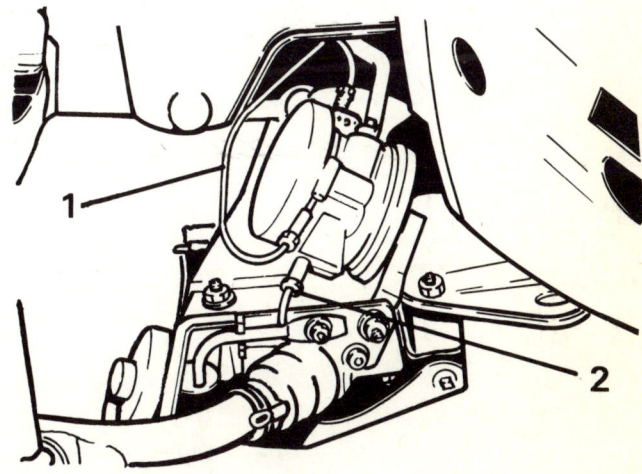

Fig. 6.8. Front height corrector

1 Supply pipe to front suspension

2 Blanking plug

18 Pressure regulator and accumulater - general

1   The pressure regulator and accumulator supplies and maintains a supply of hydraulic fluid pressure of between 140 and 175 bar (1190 and 2490 psi), the minimum cut-in pressure and the maximum cut-out pressure respectively.
2   Checking the pressure regulator and accumulator for leakage, inflation pressure and cut-out and cut-in pressures are described in Sections 8 and 9. No overhaul procedures are described; if the unit is defective it should be renewed.
3   Removal and replacement is as follows:

   a) *Release the hydraulic pressure from the system, as described in Section 2. Disconnect the earth strap from the negative terminal of the battery. Note the pipe connections and disconnect them from the pressure regulator and accumulator. Remove the securing bolts and lift off the pressure regulator.*
   b) *Replacement is the reversal of removal, always fit new seals to the pipe connections.*

19 Pressure switch - general

1   The pressure switch is fitted at the four-way union and is wired into a warning light on the instrument panel. When the pressure in the hydraulic system is below the following pressure range the warning light is illuminated:

   Models upto March 1973 — 60 to 80 bar (853 to 1138 psi).
   Models from March 1973 — 75 to 95 bar (1068 to 1351 psi).

2   When the engine is stopped (no pressure in the hydraulic system) and the ignition switched-on, the instrument panel warning light should be on, if not, check the bulb and wiring. It is important that the warning light is working correctly as it indicates when the pressure in the brake system is below the safety level.
3   The pressure switch is removed by disconnecting the wiring and unscrewing the switch from the four-way union. When replacing the switch tighten it to a torque of 1.1 to 1.2 kg f m (8 to 9 lb f ft).

20 Front height corrector - removal and replacement

1   Jack-up and support the front of the car. Release the hydraulic pressure from the system, as described in Section 2. Remove the right-hand roadwheel. Remove the height corrector guard plate and the anti-roll bar bearing guard plate from the right-hand side. Disconnect the pipes from the corrector.
2   Remove the anti-roll bar right-hand bearing bolts and the corrector support retaining bolt. Remove the corrector with its support.
3   Replacement is the reverse of the removal sequence. Carry out the anti-roll bar adjustment as described in Chapter 7, Section 9. Start the engine, tighten the pressure regulator bleed screw and check for leaks. Lower the car and check the suspension heights as described in Section 25.

21 Rear height corrector - removal and replacement

1   Release the pressure from the hydraulic system, as described in Section 2. Disconnect the pipes from the height corrector.
2   Set the manual control to 'normal' position and disconnect the ball joint. Mark the position of the corrector, remove the retaining bolts and the corrector.
3   Replacement is the reverse of the removal sequence. Start the engine, tighten the pressure regulator bleed screw and check for leaks. Check the suspension heights, as described in Section 25.

22 Front suspension cylinder - removal and replacement

1   Position the car as described in Chapter 7, Section 4, for the removal of a suspension arm, and disengage the ball and socket from the suspension arm. Disconnect the pipes from the cylinder.

2   With a strap wrench remove the spheres. Remove the cylinder retaining bolts, turn it 90º, raise the suspension arm and remove the cylinder.
3   There is no repair instruction for the cylinders; defective cylinders must be replaced.
4   Replacement is the reverse of the removal sequence. When assembly is complete, start the engine, tighten the pressure regulator bleed screw and check for leaks. Check the suspension heights as described in Section 25.

23 Rear suspension cylinder - removal and replacement

1   Position the car as described in Chapter 10, Section 3, for the removal of a suspension arm, and disconnect the ball and socket from the suspension arm. Disconnect the pipes from the cylinder.
2   Remove the retaining collar. Jack-up the suspension arm fully and remove the suspension cylinder and sphere.
3   Replacement is the reverse of the removal sequence. When assembly is complete, start the engine, tighten the pressure regulator bleed screw and check for leaks. Check the suspension heights, as described in Section 25.

24 Suspension heights - presetting

1   Presetting the heights enables an approximate adjustment to be made. It should be carried out whenever major components of the suspension are replaced.
2   Support the car, front and rear, as described for the removal of the suspension arms in Chapters 7 and 10. Remove the guard plate from the front corrector and the inspection panel in the floor of the boot. Slacken the bolt securing the clamp of the front automatic control rod. Slacken the screws securing the rear corrector, slide them to the centre of their slots and tighten the screws.
3   Set the manual control lever to the 'normal' road position. Relieve the stress on the corrector slide valves as necessary by displacing the sector and slackening the plastic fork end (old type control) or bush nut of the control rod.
4   With a jack and a cross beam placed under the suspension arms, raise the arms until the beam is up against the axle unit. In this position the lever 'A' of the front wishbones is halfway between the travel stops (Fig. 6.10), ie 'J1' = 'J2' $\pm$ 2 mm (0.08 in) and the rear suspension arms on both sides are at an equal distance from the travel stops, ie 'J1' = 'J2' $\pm$ 2 mm (0.08 in) in Fig. 6.11.
5   Ensure that the slide valves of the front and rear correctors are at the neutral position. Tighten the clamps of the front and rear automatic control rods, taking care not to jam the ball joint of the front corrector tie rod in its fork, and at the rear not to touch the edge of the hole with the rod of the automatic control rod. Tighten the clamps to 0.8-0.9 kg f m (6 to 6.5 lb f ft).
6   Fit the roadwheels, lower the car and run the engine. Tighten the pressure regulator bleed screw. Adjust the suspension heights as described in Section 26.

25 Suspension heights - checking

1   Place the manual control lever in the 'normal' road position and allow the engine to idle. Check the suspension heights with the car on level ground and the tyres at the correct pressure.
2   Lift the front of the car, by hand, as high as possible. When released, the car will drop, then rise again, and settle. Measure the distance between the lower point of the centre of the anti-roll bar, 'a' in Fig. 6.12, and the ground.
3   Push the front of the car down by hand as far as possible and then release it. The car will rise, drop again and then settle. Measure the front height again. Calculate the average of the two measurements, it should be between 179 and 199mm (7 and 7.8in).
4   Measure the rear suspension height in the same manner. The height is measured between the centre of the rear flanged edge of the sub-frame, 'b' in Fig. 6.13, and the ground. It should be between 262 and 282mm (10.3 and 11.1in). If the heights are not within the specified range, adjust the suspension heights as described in Section 26.

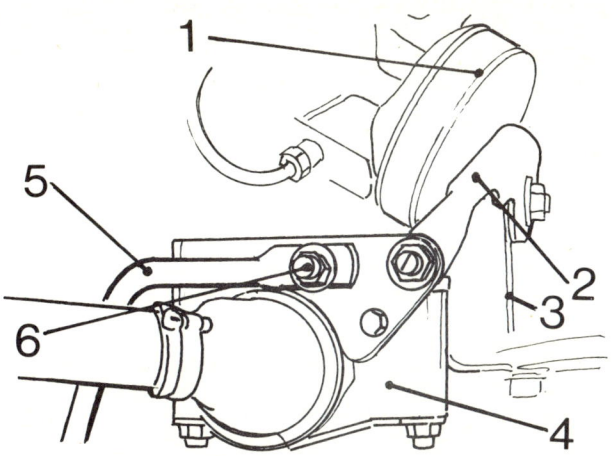

Fig. 6.9. Front height corrector removal

1 Corrector   4 Anti-roll bar bearing
2 Support   5 Manual control
3 Lever   6 Nut

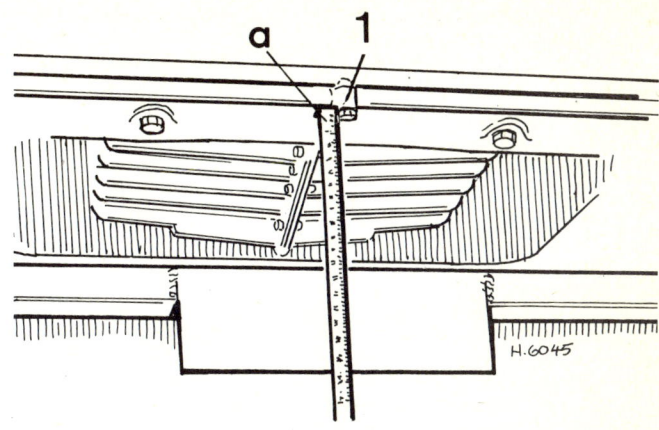

Fig. 6.12. Measuring the front suspension height

1 Clamp

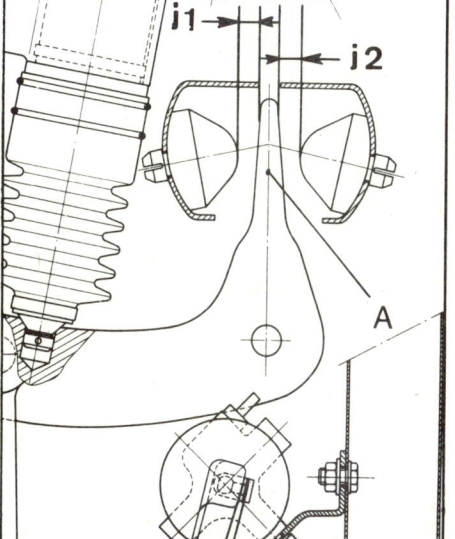

Fig. 6.10. Presetting the front suspension height

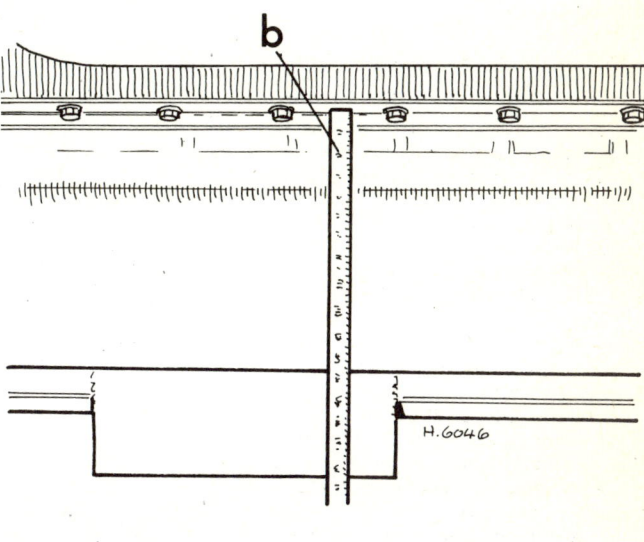

Fig. 6.13. Measuring the rear suspension height

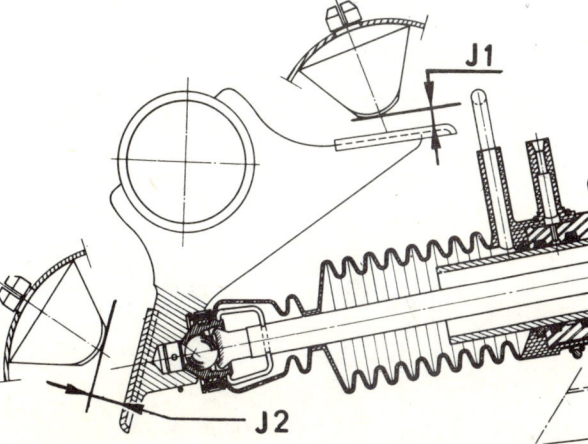

Fig. 6.11. Presetting the rear suspension height

26 Suspension height - adjustment

1 The suspension height adjustment can be made without presetting, if the heights of the car only require slight alteration.

2 Remove the front corrector guard plate and the inspection panel on the floor of the boot. Set the manual control lever to the 'normal' road position. Start the engine and allow it to idle.

3 Disconnect the manual control from the front and rear correctors. At the front, slightly slacken the clamp bolt, '1' in Fig. 6.12, and adjust the clamp to obtain a front height of 189mm (7.4in). Tighten the clamp bolt to 1.3 to 1.5 kg f m (9 to 10 lb f ft). At the rear, slacken the screws securing the corrector and adjust the position of the corrector to obtain a rear suspension height of 272mm (10.7in). Retighten the corrector securing screws.

4 Adjust the manual height control linkage, as described in Section 27, so that the linkage can be connected without altering the corrector to a higher or lower height setting. After connecting the manual height control linkage check the suspension heights, as described in Section 25.

27 Manual height control - adjustment

1 On models produced until March 1973 refer to Fig. 6.14 and proceed as follows:

a) Remove the inspection panel on the floor of the boot to give access to the rear corrector. Set the manual control lever to the 'normal' road position. Underneath the front axle check that the pin of the front fork is in the centre of the slot. If not, slacken the sector plate securing screws and move the sector to achieve this position. If this adjustment cannot be obtained position the sector plate in the centre and tighten the securing screws. Slacken the control rod clamp and adjust its length until the pin of the fork is in the middle of the slot. Tighten the clamp.

b) Check that the pin of the rear fork is in the centre of the slot. If not, slacken the plastic fork screw and adjust to obtain this position. Tighten the fork screw.

c) Operate the manual control and return to the 'normal' road position. Check the adjustment. Refit the inspection panel in the boot.

2 On models produced since March 1973 refer to Fig. 6.17 and proceed as follows:

a) Remove the guard plate from the front corrector and the inspection panel in the floor of the boot. Set the manual control lever to the 'normal' road position.

b) On the front corrector control check that the lever '2' in Fig. 6.15 is not pressing on the adjusting screw. Allow a clearance of approximately 5mm (0.2in). On the rear corrector control the clearance 'J1' and 'J2' must be as nearly equal as possible on each side of the fork.

c) Move the manual height control lever to the intermediate position and check that the height increases by 30 to 40mm (1.2 to 1.6in). If necessary, adjust at the fork and/or the adjusting screw to obtain this condition.

d) Move the manual control lever to the 'normal' road position and check the suspension heights as described in Section 25. Refit the front corrector guard plate and the inspection panel in the floor of the boot.

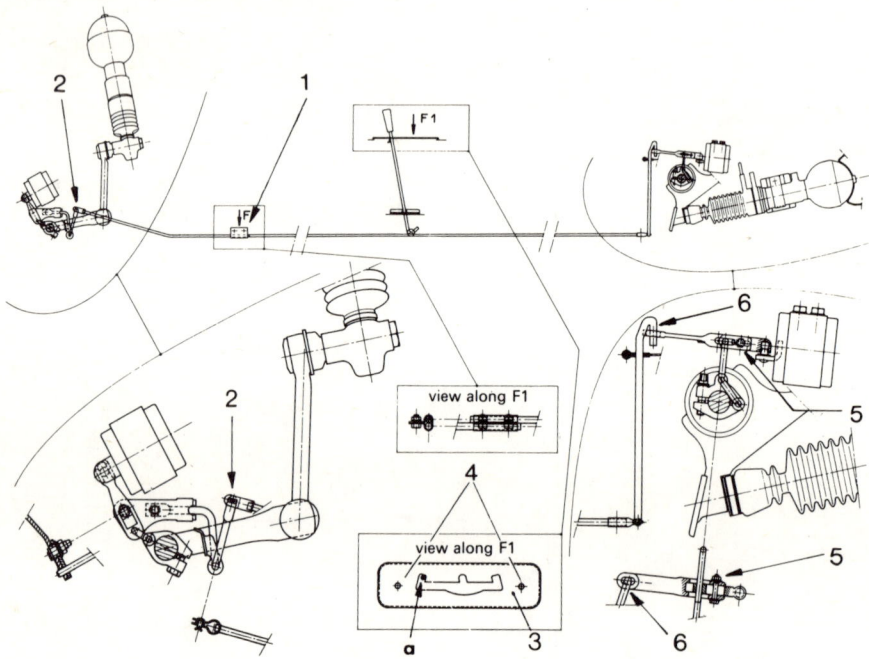

Fig. 6.14. Manual height control (before March 1972)

1 Clamp	3 Sector plate	5 Fork screw	(a) Control lever 'normal'
2 Front fork	4 Securing screws	6 Slot	position

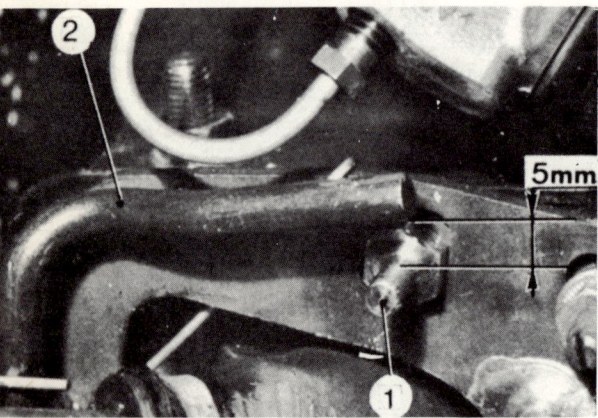

Fig. 6.15. Manual control adjustment

1 Adjusting screw   2 Lever

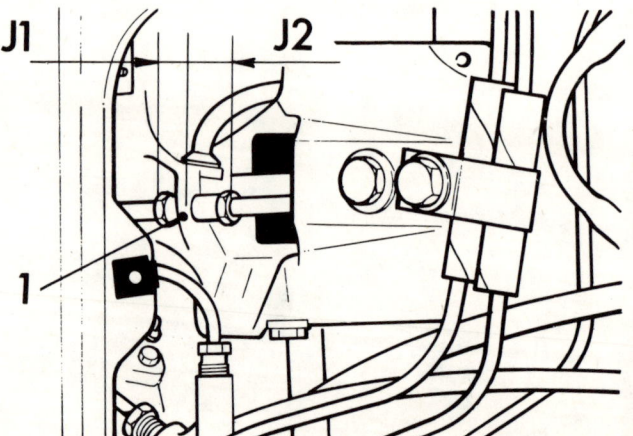

Fig. 6.16. Manual control linkage

1 Fork

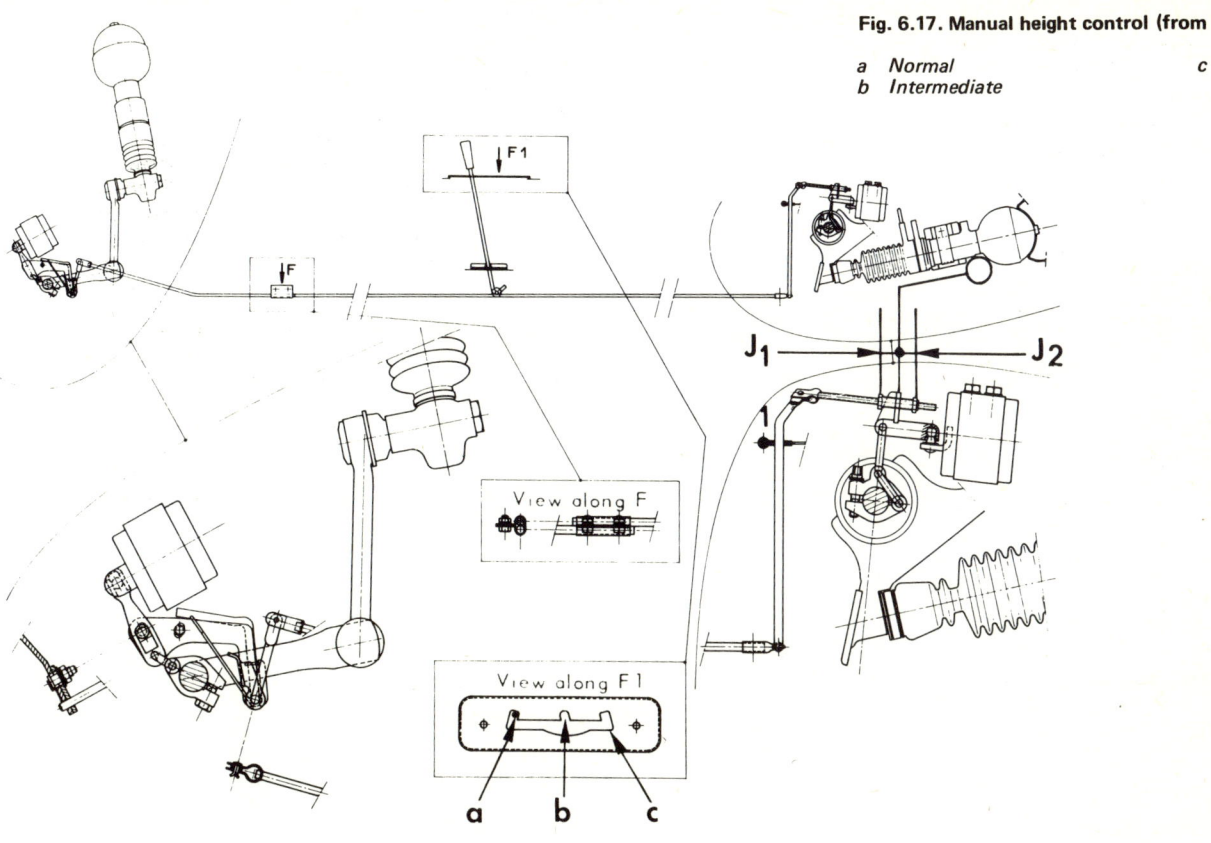

Fig. 6.17. Manual height control (from March 1972)

a Normal   c High
b Intermediate

28 Fault diagnosis - hydraulic system

Before diagnosing faults from the following chart, check that the hydraulic reservoir is filled to the correct level, that the pressure regulator bleed screw is tightened and that there are no visual leaks in the system, with the engine running.

Symptom	Reason/s	Remedy
No hydraulic pressure	Reservoir filter blocked	Clean the filter.
	Suction pipe from pump leaking	Tighten connection or renew pipe.
	High pressure pump defective	Replace pump.
	Pressure regulator defective	Replace pressure regulator.
Hydraulic pressure too low	Partially blocked reservoir filter	Clean the filter.
	High pressure pump defective	Replace the pump.
	Pressure regulator cut-out setting too low	Replace pressure regulator.
Hydraulic pressure too high	Pressure regulator not cutting-out	Replace pressure regulator.
Suspension not maintaining the car at selected height	Suspension cylinder defective	Replace defective cylinder.
	Manual control linkage worn or sticking	Dismantle and replace as necessary.
	Presetting of height incorrect	Carry out presetting procedure.
	Height corrector defective	Replace the corrector.
	Height adjustment incorrect	Re-adjust the suspension height.
	Clamp loose on anti-roll bar	Re-adjust the height and ensure clamp is tightened.
Car fails to rise when the engine is started	Reservoir filter blocked	Clean the filter.
	Pump suction pipe leakage	Tighten connections or renew pipe.
	Pump defective	Replace the pump.
	Pressure regulator defective	Replace the pressure regulator.
	Defective suspension cylinder	Replace.
	Defective height corrector	Replace.
	Clamp loose on anti-roll bar	Re-adjust suspension height.
Vibration and rattles	Steering defective	Check the steering system.
	Suspension ball and sockets worn	Renew as necessary.
	Rear axle unit flexible mountings defective	Replace the rear flexible mountings.
	Loose components or piping	Check and rectify as necessary.

Chapter 7 Front axle and suspension

Contents

Specifications

Suspension

Type	Independent, double wishbone
Springing	Hydropneumatic cylinders
Damping	Integral with hydropneumatic cylinders
Anti-roll bar	21 mm diameter
Suspension height (normal)	189 ± 10 mm (7.44 ± 0.4 in)
Suspension cylinder spheres:	
Inflation pressure:	
Until February 1973	$50 \pm \frac{5}{10}$ bar ($710 \pm \frac{70}{140}$ psi)
From February 1973	$55 \pm \frac{5}{10}$ bar ($780 \pm \frac{70}{140}$ psi)

Driveshafts

Driveshafts	Ball-type constant velocity joint at wheel end. In-axial joint at gearbox end.

1 General description

1 The front axle which is a subframe bolted to the bodyframe, carries the engine and transmission, the anti-roll bar, upper and lower suspension arms and swivel assemblies, the steering system and the suspension cylinders.
2 The height of the suspension can be selected manually to provide three different settings. Stop and bump buffers are fitted for the upper suspension arms. The wheel hubs run on ball bearings which are secured by ring nuts. The driveshafts are bolted to the differential output shafts, with the brake discs between them, and splined to the hubs.
3 The anti-roll bar is connected by ball jointed connecting rods to the upper suspension arms. Connected to the anti-roll bar is the height corrector which maintains the hydropneumatic suspension at the manually selected height.

2 Maintenance - general

Although there is no routine maintenance prescribed for the front axle and suspension system, visual and manual inspection of moving parts should be made periodically for wear or damage. Check the rubber bellows and the suspension arm bushes for splitting or deterioration. Damaged rubber bellows allow the ingress of dirt and grit which can result in expensive repairs. On all models from November 1972 the rubber bellows type dust shields protecting the suspension ball joints contain 7cc (0.42 cu. in) of LHM fluid, it is therefore most important that they are maintained in good condition.

3 Suspension balls - lubrication

1 Jack-up and support the front of the car with the roadwheels hanging free. Release the pressure from the hydraulic system, as described in Chapter 6, Section 2. Remove the front wheels and thoroughly clean the working area.
2 Remove the pin securing the socket into the arm, and the thimble clip. Disengage the protective thimble and push the dust shield back along the pushrod.
3 Remove the clip and disengage the socket securing pin, Fig. 7.2, from the pushrod. Remove the ball and socket.
4 Thoroughly clean the pushrod and the ball and socket, smear the socket with multi-purpose grease and insert the ball into its socket.
5 Reassembly is the reverse of the disassembly sequence.

4 Upper suspension arm - removal and replacement

1 Jack-up and support the front of the car. Release the pressure from the hydraulic system, as described in Chapter 6, Section 2, and remove the roadwheel. If a right-hand suspension arm is being removed remove the height corrector guard plate.

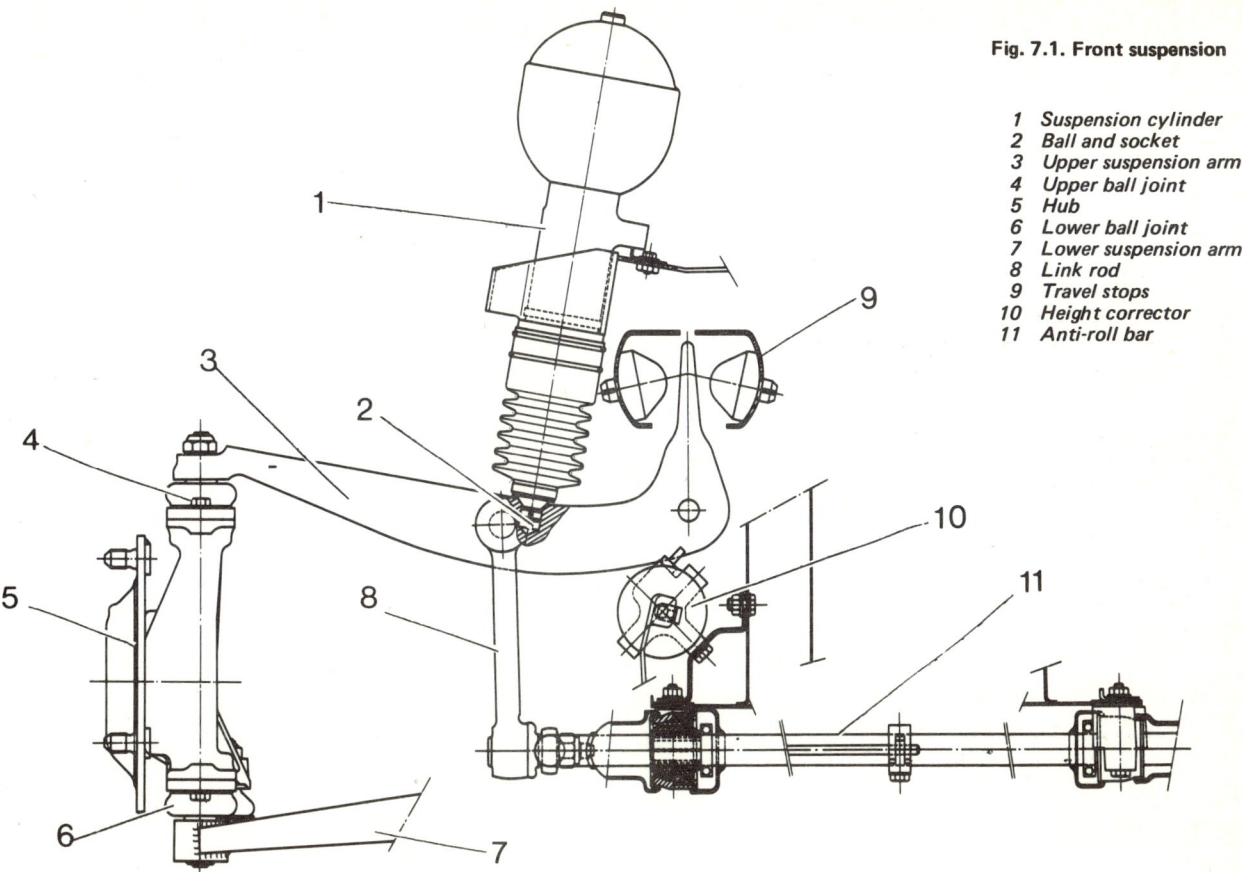

Fig. 7.1. Front suspension

1 Suspension cylinder
2 Ball and socket
3 Upper suspension arm
4 Upper ball joint
5 Hub
6 Lower ball joint
7 Lower suspension arm
8 Link rod
9 Travel stops
10 Height corrector
11 Anti-roll bar

2   To disconnect the anti-roll bar, slacken the castellated nut by a few threads and tap it sharply to free the ball joint, remove the nut and disconnect the link rod. Remove the pin securing the socket into the arm.

3   Slacken the nut, securing the upper ball joint, by a few threads and using a suitable extractor, release the ball joint. Remove the nut.

4   Remove the pivot pin nut, drive out the pivot pin and remove the suspension arm, shim and protective caps.

5   Replacement is the reverse of the removal sequence. The right and left-hand arms are different. The boss 'a' in Fig. 7.4 must face forward when the arm is fitted on the car. Check the ball joint seals, if defective replace the ball joints. Check the movement of the suspension arm, there should be no endplay, if necessary, adjust with different thickness of shim. Always fit new NYLSTOP nuts after each dismantling. Tighten the pivot pin nut to 5.9 to 6.5 kg f m (43 to 47 lb f ft). Tighten the castellated nut to 2.5 to 3 kg f m (18 to 22 lb f ft) and the upper ball joint nut to 2.7 to 3 kg f m (20 to 22 lb f ft).

5   Lower suspension arm - removal and replacement

1   Carry out the procedure described in Section 4, paragraph 1.

2   Slacken the lower ball joint nut by a few threads and using a suitable extractor, release the lower ball joint from the suspension arm. Remove the nut and disconnect the joint.

3   Slide back the steering trackrod rubber bellows, as described in Chapter 9, to give access to the lower suspension arm pivot pin. Remove the pivot pin nut and the pivot pin, if necessary bend the wheel arch slightly. Remove the lower arm.

4   Examine the rubber seal of the ball joint, if it is in poor condition replace the ball joint assembly. Examine the fluidbloc bushes and replace, if necessary, as described in Section 6.

5   Replacement of the suspension arm is the reversal of the removal sequence. Always fit new NYLSTOP nuts after each dismantling. Tighten the pivot pin nut to 8 to 9 kg f m (58 to 84 lb f ft) and the ball joint nut to 2.7 to 3 kg f m (20 to 22 lb f ft).

6   Lower suspension arm bushes - removal and replacement

1   Remove the lower suspension arm, as described in Section 5.

2   Use of an 8mm expanding pin (Rawlpin or similar type) as shown in Fig. 7.5 simplifies the removal of the bushes. Fit the expanding pin with a threaded rod and a nut. Insert the pin in the bush and tighten the nut to open the two legs of the pin until they grip the bush. Pull on the rod while rotating the bush until the bush is withdrawn. Discard the bush. Remove the other bush.

3   Clean the bore of the arm and grease the metal cups and the thrust face of the fluidbloc bushes with a multi-purpose grease. Fit the bushes in the bore and tap them home with a mallet.

7   Anti-roll bar - removal

1   The anti-roll bar must be mounted with an axial preload of 35 to 40 kg (77 to 88 lb) on the clamp bearings. To set this preloading the Citroen tool 2067-T is required, if this tool is not available to the owner this work will have to be left to your local agent.

2   Jack-up, and support, the front of the car. Release the pressure from the hydraulic system as described in Chapter 6, Section 2. Remove the roadwheels. Remove the height corrector guard plate.

3   Remove the castellated nuts and disconnect the connecting rods from the upper suspension arms. Remove the plates protecting the anti-roll bar bearings. Disconnect the automatic height control rod from the anti-roll bar, by removing the clamp bolt, and leave the automatic control system in position on the suspension unit.

4   Remove the bolts holding the anti-roll bar bearings and remove the assembly of bar and bearings. Take care not to lose the plastic shells of the automatic control rod, located in the right-hand bearing. If necessary, using a suitable extractor remove the connecting rods from the anti-roll bar. Dismantle and clean the anti-roll bar. Renew bearings and dust shields, as necessary.

8 Anti-roll bar - assembly and replacement

1   Refer to Fig. 7.7 and fit the inner dust shields. Fit the clamps positioned so that 'a' = 93mm (3.66in) and the heads of the clamp bolts face forward and the clamps are perpendicular to the bar. Fit the bearing. Note that the bearings are different, the right-hand bearing has a housing for the plastic bearing of the automatic height control rod. Fit the outer dust shields. Fit the connecting rods, note the rods are different, and tighten the ball joint nuts to 5.5 to 7 kg f m (40 to 50 lb f ft).

2   Place a cross bar supported by a jack under the lower suspension arm ball joints and raise the bar until it bears against the axle-frame. Offer up the anti-roll bar and couple the connecting rods to the upper suspension arms. Tighten the ball joint nuts to 2.5 to 3 kg f m (18 to 22 lb f ft).

3   Grease the nylon shells and fit them in the bearings. On the right-hand side fit the plastic shells on the automatic height control rod.

4   Raise the anti-roll bar until it is possible to fit the retaining bolts and nuts. Engage the nuts by a few threads, check that the automatic control rod bearing is in its housing and continue to raise the bar by its centre until one of the bearings comes into contact with the axle frame. If the other bearing does not make contact with the frame, insert shims between this bearing and the frame until it can be secured without any stress on the anti-roll bar. Tighten the retaining nuts to 1 to 2.1 kg f m (13 to 15 lb f ft).

5   Preload the bearings as described in Section 9. Preset the height control, as described in Chapter 6, Section 24.

6   Remove the jack and crossbar. Fit the corrector and bearing guard plates, and the roadwheels. Lower the car, run the engine and tighten the pressure regulator bleed screw. Check the heights, as described in Chapter 6, Section 25.

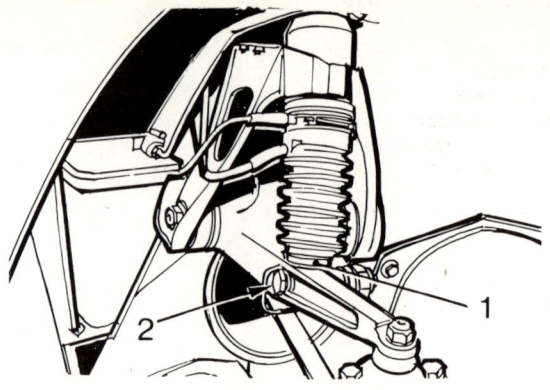

Fig. 7.2. Suspension ball lubrication

1   Clip   2   Securing pin

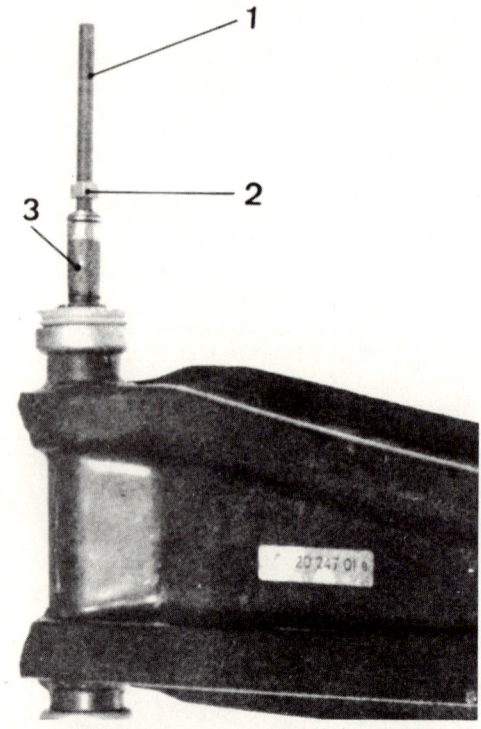

Fig. 7.5. Removing suspension arm bush

1   Threaded rod   3   Pin
2   Nut

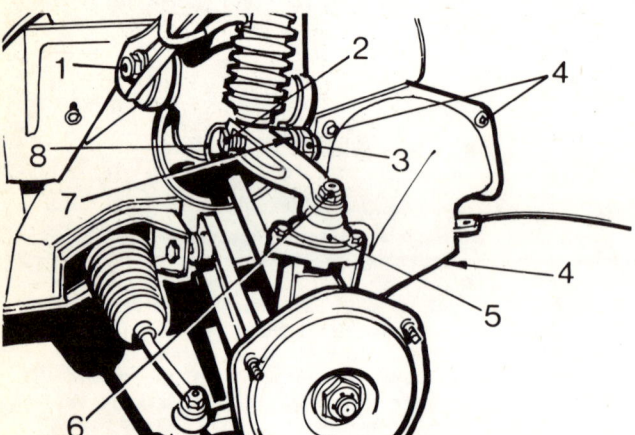

Fig. 7.3. Upper suspension arm removal

1   Pivot pin nut   5   Ball joint seal
2   Castellated nut   6   Nut
3   Ball joint   7   Link rod seal
4   Corrector guard bolts   8   Pin

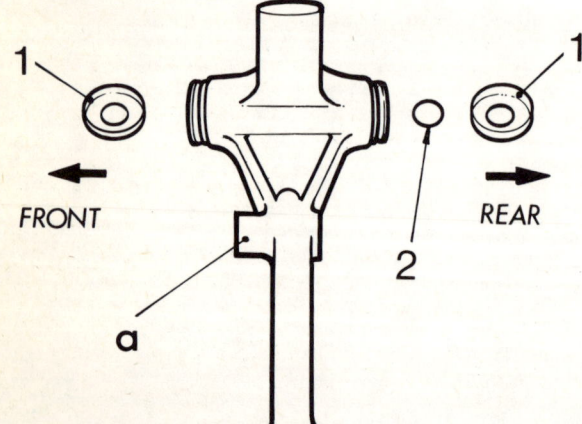

Fig. 7.4. Upper suspension arm

1   Protective caps   2   Shim

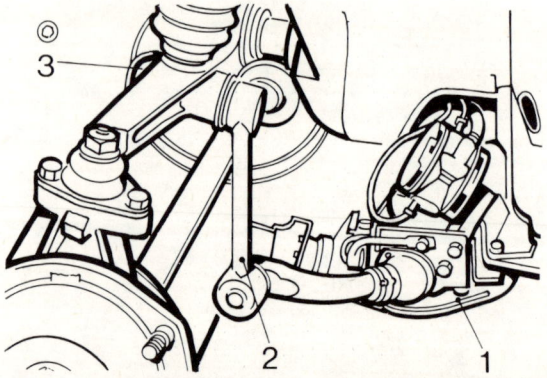

Fig. 7.6. Removing the anti-roll bar

1   Corrector guard plate   3   Nut
2   Connecting rod

9 Anti-roll bar - adjustment

Note: Citroen tool 2067-T is required to preload the clamp bearings.
1 Place the car on a lift or over a pit. Remove the bearing protective plates and disengage the lower part of the inner dust shields.
2 Slacken one bolt of the left-hand clamp. Compress the springs of tool 2067-T by screwing in the nut '4' in Fig. 7.9. Position the tool so that the forked ends are located on the two stop clamps, completely unscrew the nut '4' so that the tool exerts the correct preload on the two bearings of 35 to 40 kg (77 to 88 lb). Tighten the clamp bolt to 1 to 1.1 kg f m (7 to 8 lb f ft) and remove the tool 2067-T.
3 Fit the dust shields and the bearing protective plates. If the plates touch the anti-roll bar fit a plain washer between the plate and the axle frame at the front securing points.

10 Driveshaft - removal and replacement

1 Remove the wheel disc. Remove the split pin and slacken the retaining nut. Jack-up and support the front of the car. Release the pressure from the hydraulic system, as described in Chapter 6, Section 2. Remove the roadwheel. Remove the retaining nut.
2 Remove the nuts securing the driveshaft to the output shaft. Disconnect the lower suspension arm and the steering linkage from the hub carrier, as described in Section 6 and Chapter 9, respectively. Swing the hub outwards, without disengaging the swivels of the inner universal joint, and withdraw the driveshaft splines from the hub and remove the shaft.
3 Replacement is the reversal of the removal sequence. Tighten the retaining nut to 35 to 40 kg f m (252 to 288 lb f ft).

11 Hub - removal and replacement

1 Disconnect the driveshaft from the hub, as described in Section 10. Disconnect the steering tie-rod from the steering arm, as described in Chapter 9. Disconnect the upper and lower suspension arm, as described in Sections 4 and 5.
2 Push back on the end of the driveshafts, so that the inner universal joint does not separate, disengage the splines from the hub and remove the hub.
3 Replacement is the reversal of the removal sequence.

12 Hub - dismantling and reassembly

1 Remove the inner seal. Using a 4mm drill clear the peening, locking the ring nut. Remove the ring nut (Citroen supply special tools for this, 3321-T and 3320-T). Using an extractor (Citroen tool 1893-T) remove the hub. Remove the outer seal and the hub bearing.
2 Examine the bearing and seals and renew as necessary. Smear the bearing with grease and using a suitable mandrel and a press, fit the bearing with the projecting part, (B in Fig. 7.10), of the ball race facing outwards. Fit the inner race. Fit the ring nut and tighten it to 40 to 50 kg f m (290 to 360 lb f ft). Lock the ring by peening it in two places.
3 Fit the outer seal, leaving a clearance between it and the ball race, 'A' in Fig. 7.10. Grease the inner lip of the seal and the bearing. Using a suitable mandrel and a press, bearing on the inner race, fit the hub. Fit the inner seal and press it fully home into the housing.

13 Front axle unit - removal

1 Removal of the front axle unit is a major operation and the owner should ensure that adequate facilities and assistance is available before undertaking the task. When stripping down the unit after removal and when preparing a unit for refitting, reference should be made to the relevant Chapters in the manual for removal and replacement procedures of the various components.
2 Remove the engine/gearbox assembly, as described in Chapter 1. Remove the bolt securing the Cardan shaft to the pinion of the steering box. On each side remove the plates between the chassis and axle unit, and the plates protecting the suspension spheres. Using a strap wrench

remove the spheres from the suspension cylinders and blank off the cylinders.
3 Remove the bolts holding the four-way union and the union for the overflow return pipes. Disconnect the supply union from the height corrector and the overflow return pipes from the suspension cylinders and remove them from the clips. Remove the bolts holding the anti-roll

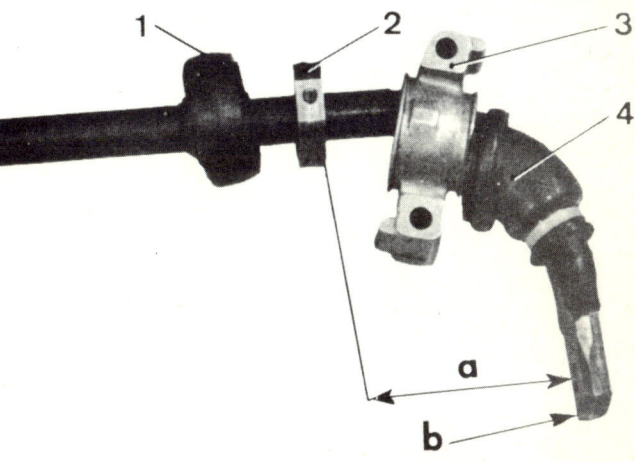

Fig. 7.7. Anti-roll bar bearing assembly

1 *Inner dust shield*	4 *Outer dust shield*
2 *Clamp*	(b) *Machined surface*
3 *Bearing*	

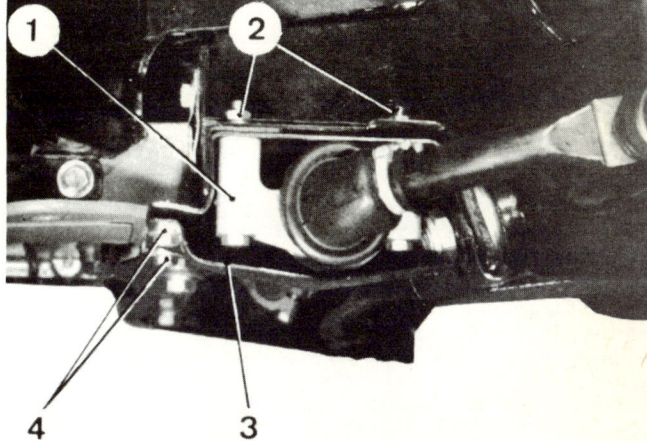

Fig. 7.8. Anti-roll bar adjustment

1 *Bearing*	3 *Guard plate*
2 *Nuts*	4 *Front securing point*

Fig. 7.9. Preloading the anti-roll bar

1 *Dustshields*	3 *Stop clamp*
2 *Stop clamp screw*	4 *Nut*

bar right-hand bearing and the linkage rod from the manual height control. Remove the driveshafts.

4   Place a jack and a crossbeam under the axle unit to support it while removing the retaining bolts. Lift up the carpet under the pedals and at each side remove the rear retaining bolts, refer to Fig. 7.11. Remove the two front retaining bolts. Free the hydraulic pipes from their brackets.

5   Make a careful check to ensure that all pipes and components have been disconnected. Hold the height corrector so that it will not get damaged, lower the jack and remove the unit. Collect the shims fitted between the chassis and the lower unit mounting '1' in Fig. 7.11.

14 Front axle unit - replacement

1   Replacement is the reverse of the removal sequence. When replacing and connecting components refer to the relevant Chapter for procedure and adjustments.

2   Refer to Fig. 7.11 and fit the mounting bolts. Fit bolts '2' and '4' and tighten bolt '2' to 2 kg f m (14 lb f ft). Fit bolt '3' and tighten the bolts '4', '2' and '3' (in that order) to 4.5 to 5 kg f m (33 to 36 lb f ft). Fit shims at bolt '1' between the chassis and axle unit to give a maximum clearance of 0.5mm (0.020in) and tighten the bolts to 9 to 10 kg f m (65 to 72 lb f ft).

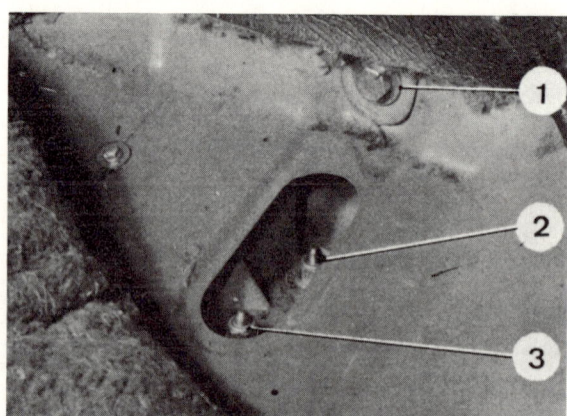

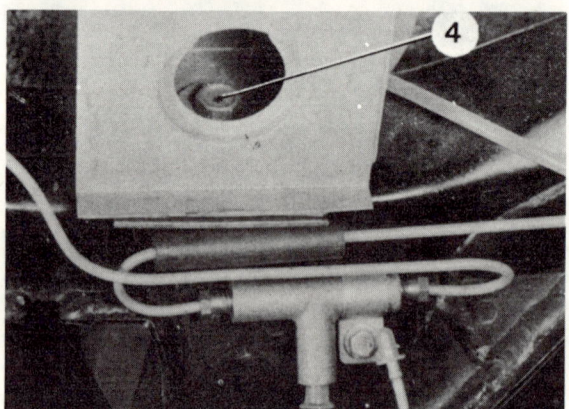

Fig. 7.11. Axle unit retaining bolts

1 Rear bolt		3 Rear bolt	
2 Rear bolt		4 Front bolt	

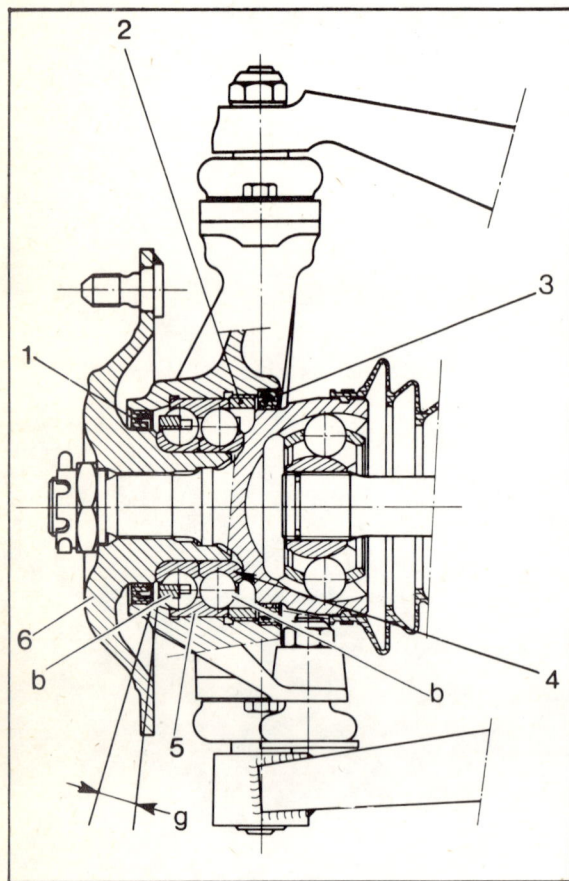

Fig. 7.10. Front hub assembly

1 Outer seal		4 Inner race	
2 Ring nut		5 Outer race	
3 Inner seal		6 Hub	

15 Fault diagnosis - front axle and suspension

Before diagnosing faults from the following chart, check that any irregularities are not caused by:

1   *Defective steering*
2   *Incorrect tyre pressures*
3   *Incorrect 'mix' of tyres*
4   *Incorrect wheel alignment*

Symptom	Reason/s	Remedy
Vibration and rattles	Worn suspension arm ball joints	Renew as necessary.
	Worn suspension arm pivot pin and/or bearing	Renew.
	Suspension cylinder loose	Tighten cylinder retaining bolts.
	Suspension cylinder ball and socket worn	Replace cylinder.
	Pipe securing clips and brackets loose	Tighten as necessary.
	Axle unit securing bolts and nuts loose	Tighten as necessary.
	Hub bearings worn	Renew bearings.
Suspension bottoming	Fault in hydraulic system	Check through the hydraulic system.
	Defective suspension cylinder/s	Replace as necessary.
	Suspension heights set incorrectly	Re-adjust the suspension heights.

Chapter 8 Braking system

Contents

Specifications

Type

Front and rear brakes	Hydraulically operated disc brakes
Parking brake	Mechanically operated, acting on front discs

Footbrakes

	Front	Rear
Disc diameter	270 mm (10.6 in)	178 mm (7 in)
Disc thickness (G10 engines until September 1972)	7 mm (0.28 in)	6 mm (0.24 in)
Disc thickness (all types from September 1972)	9 mm (0.35 in)	6 mm (0.23 in)
Minimum thickness after wear	4 mm (0.16 in)	4 mm (0.16 in)
Maximum run-out of disc	0.2 mm (0.008 in)	0.2 mm (0.008 in)
Thickness of pad (without wear leads)	8.55 mm (0.34 in)	7.55 mm (0.30 in)
Thickness of pads (with wear leads)	12 mm (0.47 in)	12 mm (0.47 in)

Handbrake

Thickness of pad	3.65 mm (0.14 in)

1 General description

1 The dual circuit braking system, with disc brakes fitted to all four wheels is hydraulically operated from the main hydraulic system. The front brakes are supplied from the hydraulic pressure regulator and the rear brakes are supplied from the rear suspension system. This arrangement favours the front brakes and imposes a braking effort limitation on the rear axle in relation to the load. The braking action is applied through the brake pedal operating a hydraulic control valve which allows pressure to the braking system.

2 The front discs are mounted inboard of the front wheel driveshafts and are secured between the differential output shafts and driveshafts. The two-piston type calipers are mounted on the gearbox. The friction pads fitted in each caliper are renewable. As the brake pads wear, they are automatically adjusted and when the wear limit of the pad is reached a wire in the pad lining contacts the disc, and a warning light on the instrument panel lights up. On earlier models which are not fitted with a pad wear warning device, the pads must be checked visually at regular intervals.

3 The rear brake discs are bolted to the inner face of the wheel hubs. The calipers are mounted on the rear suspension arms. Brake adjustment is automatic but unlike the front brakes there is no warning light, therefore the pad thickness must be checked visually at regular intervals.

4 The handbrake is applied through a "spade handle" control and flexible cables operating the calipers (separate from the main front brakes) which forces the friction pads against the brake disc.

2 Routine maintenance

1 Visually check the thickness of the brake friction pad linings every 10,000 km (6,000 miles). When replacing pads always fit new pads to both calipers on each axle.

2 Every 10,000 km (6,000 miles) adjust the parking brake as described in Section 15.

3 Every 40,000 km (24,000 miles) check that the thickness of the brake discs is not less than 4 mm (0.16 in) and variation in thickness does not exceed 0.02 mm (0.008 in).

3 Brake pads (front brakes) - renewal

1 Remove the spare wheel and the heater distributor box with its ducting. Disconnect the wear detector leads (if fitted).

2 On cars fitted with old type calipers (Fig. 8.1) push on the ends 'a' of the pads with the hand, to push back the pistons, in the direction of the arrows. Pull on the end 'b' of the pad retaining spring and with

a wire hook pull the pad forward to release it. Remove the other pad in the same way. Do not depress the brake pedal until the new pads are fitted. Fit the pads into the caliper by pushing it as far as possible to the rear so that the spigots engage in their corresponding slots. Lock the pads by raising the ends so that the spring arms engage in the pad arm notches. Connect the wear detector leads (if fitted).

3   On cars fitted with new type calipers, Fig. 8.2, push the pad at 'c' with a screwdriver and remove the pin. Hold the pad by the wear detector lead and push out the spindle. Remove the spindle and the spring. Remove the pads from above.

Note: Do not depress the brake pedal until the new pads are fitted.

4   Press the caliper pistons back into their bores with a suitable blunt tool. Fit the inner pad first. Hold the pad with a hook inserted in the hole 'd' of the pad. Fit the spring. Insert the spindle into the brake caliper and into the upper hole of the pad after interposing the spring below the spindle. Repeat the same operation for the other pad. Push home the spindle and fit the pin. Connect the wear detector leads.

5   Operate the brake pedal a few times to settle the brake pads and ensure that the pedal travel remains normal.

6   Fit the heater distributor box, ducting and spare wheel.

4   Caliper (front brakes) - removal

1   Place the manual height control in 'high' position and slacken the pressure regulator bleed screw. Disconnect the earth strap from the negative terminal of the battery. Remove the spare wheel. If the right-hand caliper is being removed it is necessary to remove the heater distributor box and ducting.

2   Disconnect the hydraulic connection pipe and, if a left-hand caliper, disconnect the feed pipe and release it from its support bracket. Slacken the caliper attaching bolts, remove the rear bolt, swing the caliper upwards and refit the bolt. Fit a nut to the bolt and tighten to retain the two halves of the caliper together.

3   Remove the locknuts and nuts of the handbrake cable, withdraw the cable and collect the spring.

4   Remove the front attaching bolt and lift out the caliper. If it is the old type caliper collect the shim, located between the caliper and the gearbox, used for positioning the caliper in relation to the brake disc.

5   Calipers (front brakes) - replacement

1   Check that the contact faces of the caliper and gearbox are clean and smooth. Scrape off any burrs.

2   With the two halves of the caliper held together by the rear attaching bolt and nut, offer up the complete caliper, fitted with the handbrake pads, and in the case of the old type caliper, the original shim removed. Fit the front attaching bolt, finger-tight. Remove the nut from the rear attaching bolt, swing the caliper into position and fit the rear bolt. Check that the shim is in position (old type caliper) and tighten the bolts to 4.5 to 5 kg f m (33 to 36 lb f ft) on old type calipers and to 6 kg f m (43 lb f ft) on new type.

3   Fit the main brake pads, as described in Section 3.

4   Adjust the clearance of the handbrake pads, as described in Section 15. Connect up and adjust the handbrake cable, as described in Section 15.

5   Connect up the feed pipe and connection pipe. Fit new seals and tighten the unions to 0.8 to 0.9 kg f m (5.8 to 6.5 lb f ft).

6   Bleed the front brakes, as described in Section 18.

7   Fit the heater distributor box and ducting. Fit the spare wheel and connect the earth strap to the negative terminal of the battery.

6   Disc (front brakes) - removal and replacement

1   Remove the caliper, as described in Section 4, but do not disconnect the parking brake cable. Disconnect the driveshaft inner universal joint from the differential output shaft, as described in Chapter 7, Section 10.

2   Using a suitable stud extractor, remove the six studs from the differential output shaft flange and remove the disc from above.

3   Check that the thickness of the discs is not less than 4 mm (0.16 in) and that variation in thickness round the disc does not exceed 0.02 mm (0.008 in). Check that maximum run-out of the disc does not exceed 0.2 mm (0.008 in) when fitted.

4   Replacement is the reverse of the removal sequence.

3.1 Brake pad rear detector leads disconnected

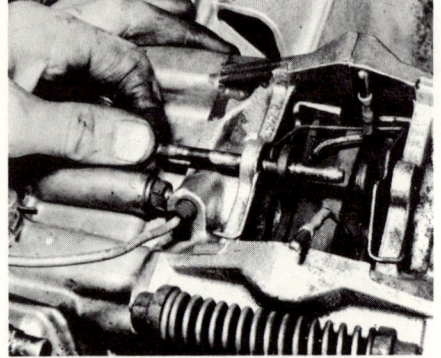
3.3a Removing the pad retaining spindle and clip

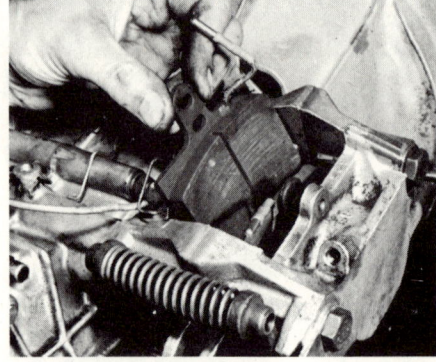
3.3b Removing a brake pad

4.2 Disconnecting the hydraulic pipe

4.2a Removing the caliper retaining bolts

6.4 Fitting the studs in the differential shafts

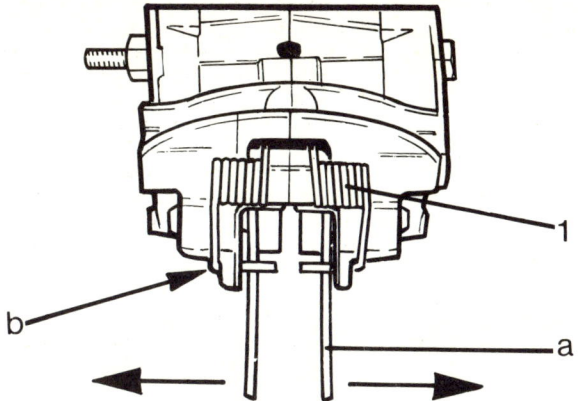

Fig. 8.1. Old type caliper

1 Pad retaining spring

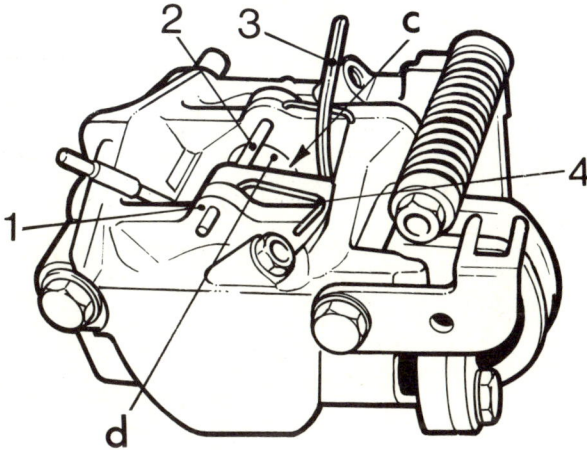

Fig. 8.2. New type caliper

1	*Pin*	*3*	*Wear lead*
2	*Spindle*	*4*	*Spring*

7 Calipers (front brakes) - renovation

1   Remove the calipers, as described in Section 4, and remove the brake pads, as described in Section 3. Separate the two halves of the caliper.
2   Apply a controlled supply of compressed air to the hydraulic pipe connections and carefully blow the pistons from their bores.
3   Examine the pistons and bores for scoring, corrosion or damage. Renew any defective parts and reassemble with new seals.
4   Replace the pads and refit the caliper, as described in Sections 3 and 4.

8 Brake pads (rear brakes) - renewal

1   Jack-up the rear of the car and remove the wheels.
Note: All four pads should be renewed at the same time.
2   Unscrew the nut and withdraw the central locating bolt (or remove the split pin on later models). Remove the pad shield and pads. Do not depress the brake pedal until the pads have been refitted.
3   Using a suitable blunt tool press the pistons into their bores. Fit the new pads and the pad shield. Fit the locating bolt (or slot pin).
4   When all four pads have been refitted, depress the brake pedal several times to settle the pads and to ensure that the brake pedal travel is normal.

9 Calipers (rear brakes) - removal

1   Jack-up and support the rear of the car. Slacken the pressure regulator bleed screw to release the pressure from the hydraulic

system. Remove the roadwheel.
2   Disconnect the hydraulic feed pipe. Slacken both retaining nuts and remove the nut and bolt on the bleed screwside. Swing the caliper upwards, refit the bolt and tighten the nut to retain both halves of the caliper together. Remove the other nut and bolt and remove the caliper.

10 Calipers (rear brakes) - replacement

1   Replacement is the reverse of the removal sequence. Tighten the nuts of the retaining bolts to 3.6 to 4 kg f m (26 to 29 lb f ft). Fit a new seal in the feed pipe connection and tighten to 0.8 to 0.9 kg f m (6 to 6.5 lb f ft).
2   Start the engine. Tighten the pressure regulator bleed screw. Place the manual height control to 'high' position and, if necessary, move the rear suspension arms to cause the pressure to rise. Bleed the brakes as described in Section 19. Check for leaks.
3   Fit the roadwheel and lower the car to the ground.

11 Disc (rear brakes) - removal and replacement

1   Removal and replacement of the rear disc is described in Chapter 11, Sections 7 and 8.
2   Check the condition of the disc, as described in Section 6.

12 Calipers (rear brakes) - renovation

Renovation of the rear calipers is the same as described for the front calipers in Section 7.

13 Brake pedal and stoplamp switch adjustment

1   Refer to Fig. 8.4. The clearance 'J' between the brake and the control valve must be maintained between 0.1 and 0.5 mm (0.004 and 0.020 in). Adjustment is by slackening the locknut and turning the stop screw as required, then tightening the locknut.
2   To check the operation of the brake pedal set the manual height control to the normal road position, slacken the pressure regulator bleed screw then select the 'high' position. Operate the pedal three or four times, to move the control slide valve to the end of its stroke, and ensure that the pedal returns freely and is maintained against its stop by the return spring.
3   The stoplamp switch contacts are kept open, when the brake pedal is against its stop, by the contact plate. When the pedal is operated the stoplamp must light up as soon as the pedal contacts the control valve. Adjust as necessary by bending the switch support plate to achieve this condition.

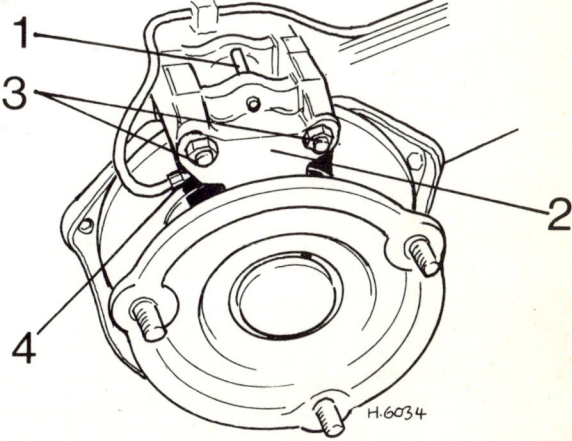

Fig. 8.3. Rear brake caliper removal

1	*Locating bolt (split pin on later models)*	*3*	*Retaining nuts and bolts*
2	*Caliper*	*4*	*Feed pipe*

14 Control valve - removal and replacement

1   Jack-up and support the front of the car. Remove the right-hand roadwheel. Remove the spare wheel.
2   Slacken the hydraulic pressure regulator bleed valve and move the manual height control to the 'high' position to release the pressure from the hydraulic system.
3   Remove the control valve guard plate. Note the pipe connections and disconnect the pipes from the control valve. Remove the retaining bolts and the control valve.
4   Replacement is the reverse of the removal sequence. Tighten the retaining bolts to 1.7 to 1.8 kg f m (12 to 13 lb f ft). Check the adjustment of the brake pedal, as described in Section 13. Bleed the brakes as described in Sections 18 and 19.

15 Handbrake - adjustment

1   Jack-up and support the front of the car on stands. Remove the spare wheel. Release the handbrake. Remove the heater distributor box and flexible ducts.
2   Refer to Fig. 8.6. On each brake unit slacken the locknuts and back-off the nuts for adjusting the handbrake cables.
3   Slacken the screw securing the eccentric adjusters and set the eccentrics to the position which gives the maximum clearance. Ensure that the arms are against their stops at 'a'.
4   Turn the eccentrics in the direction of the arrows until a clearance of 0.1 mm (0.004 in) is obtained between the pad backplates and the heel 'b' of each arm. The use of a mirror helps when checking this clearance. Ensure this clearance is adjusted at the point of maximum disc run-out.
5   When the clearance has been set, tighten the screw securing the eccentric to 4 kg f m (29 lb f ft). Re-check the clearance between the pad backplate and the heel of the arm.
6   Check that each end of the cables is located in the cable sheath ends. Screw on the adjusting nut until it contacts the arm (pull on the cable to facilitate this operation). Screw on the nuts alternately so that the length of thread protruding through the adjusting nuts is the same on both sides to within 5 mm (0.20 in). Tighten the locknuts to 1.5 kg f m (11 lb f ft).
7   Operate the handbrake handle several times, ensuring that the adjustment does not alter and that the handle locks in position when the brake is applied.
8   Replace the heater distributor box and ducting and the spare wheel. Lower the car to the ground.

16 Handbrake pads - removal and replacement

1   For even braking, the four pads must always be renewed at the same time.
2   If old type calipers are fitted remove them, as described in Section 4, and remove the pads.
3   Slacken the screws locking the eccentric adjusters and turn the eccentrics to the position giving the maximum clearance at the pads (direction of arrows in Fig. 8.7). Fit the pads and check that the anti-noise springs are correctly positioned.
4   Fit the calipers as described in Section 5. Adjust the pad clearance and brake cable, as described in Section 15.
5   If new type calipers are fitted, partly remove and swing the caliper upwards as described in Section 4. Position the eccentrics to give maximum clearance (turn them in direction of arrows in Fig. 8.8), hold the pad spring and remove the pads.
6   To replace, lift the spring and fit the pad to its support. Replace the brake caliper as described in Section 5. Adjust the pad clearance and brake cable, as described in Section 15.

17 Bleeding the hydraulic braking system - general

1   When any part of the system has been dismantled or after changing

the fluid in the hydraulic system the brakes will have to be bled to remove any air from the braking system. While bleeding the rear brakes ensure that the fluid in the hydraulic reservoir does not fall below the minimum level.
2   Bleeding the brakes is a two man job, as the brake pedal has to be held depressed during the bleeding operation.

18 Bleeding the front brakes

Note: This operation must be carried out without pressure to prevent emulsifying the fluid with air, which could later result in the formation of air bubbles in the system.
1   With the engine stopped, slacken the hydraulic pressure regulator bleed screw. Select the 'normal road' position on the manual height control.
2   Clean round the bleed screw and remove the protective cap from the right-hand brake unit. Connect a transparent bleed tube to the bleed screw with the other end into the hydraulic reservoir.
3   Depress the brake pedal and slacken the brake unit bleed screw. Keep the pedal depressed and start the engine.
4   Tighten the hydraulic pressure regulator bleed screw and allow fluid to flow through the bleed tube, into the reservoir, until the bleed tube is free from air bubbles, then tighten the brake unit bleed screw.
5   Release the brake pedal and remove the bleed tube. Push down hard on the brake pedal and check that the brake unit bleed screw is not leaking. Stop the engine and replace the rubber protective cap over the brake unit bleed screw.

19 Bleeding the rear brakes

1   Select the 'high' position on the manual height control, run the engine, then place a support immediately beneath the rear seats. Set the manual height control to the 'normal road' position, slacken the hydraulic pressure regulator bleed screw, move the manual height control to the 'high' position and wait for the car to sink down.
2   Jack-up the car, place it on stands and remove the rear wheels. With the aid of a jack, lift one rear suspension arm (the rear height corrector will then be in the 'inlet' position).
3   Clean round the brake unit bleed screws, remove the rubber protective caps and connect a transparent bleed tube to each bleed screw with the other end placed in a clean container. Open the brake bleed screws and push the pedal hard down.
4   Keeping the brake pedal depressed, tighten the hydraulic pressure regulator bleed screw and start the engine. Allow fluid to flow through the bleed tubes until they are free from air bubbles, then tighten the brake bleed screws. Release the brake pedal.
Note: The pressure will now build up in the hydraulic system and the suspension arms will assume the 'high' position.
5   Remove the jack from the suspension arm. Remove the bleed tubes, depress the brake pedal and check the brake bleed screws for leaks. Fit the rubber caps.
6   Stop the engine. Fit the roadwheels, remove the supports and lower the car to the ground.

20 Control valve - renovation

1   Remove the control valve as described in Section 14. Remove the operating pad, the retaining ring and withdraw the boot. Remove the circlip, the piston, the spring and the collar. From the other end of the valve remove the circlip and the plug seal. Collect the spring and the other piston.
2   Examine the parts and renew as necessary. Always fit a new 'O' ring at every dismantling. If a piston is defective, both pistons and the body must be renewed, as they are supplied as a matched set.
3   Lightly oil the parts with LHM fluid and reassemble in the reverse of the removal sequence. Replace the control valve, as described in Section 14, and bleed the brakes, as described in Sections 18 and 19.

a
2
3
4
1
5
6

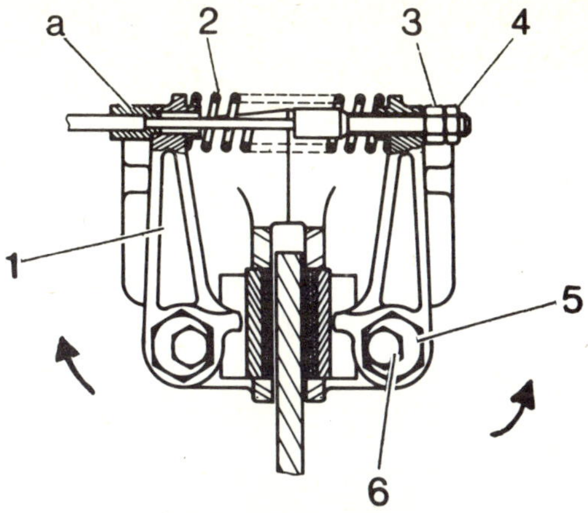

Fig. 8.6. Handbrake adjustment

1 Arm
2 Spring
3 Adjusting nut
4 Locknut
5 Eccentric adjuster
6 Lockscrew

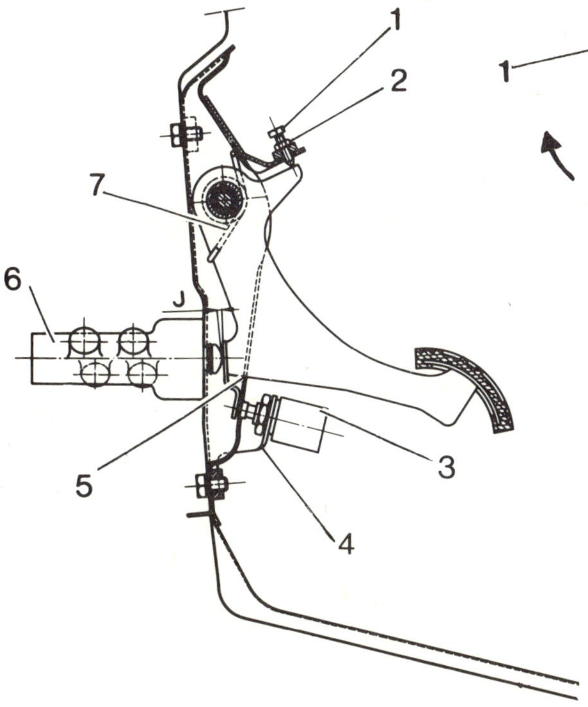

1
2
7
6
J
5
3
4

Fig. 8.4. Brake pedal adjustment

1 Stopscrew
2 Locknut
3 Stoplamp switch
4 Support plate
5 Contact plate
6 Control valve
7 Return spring

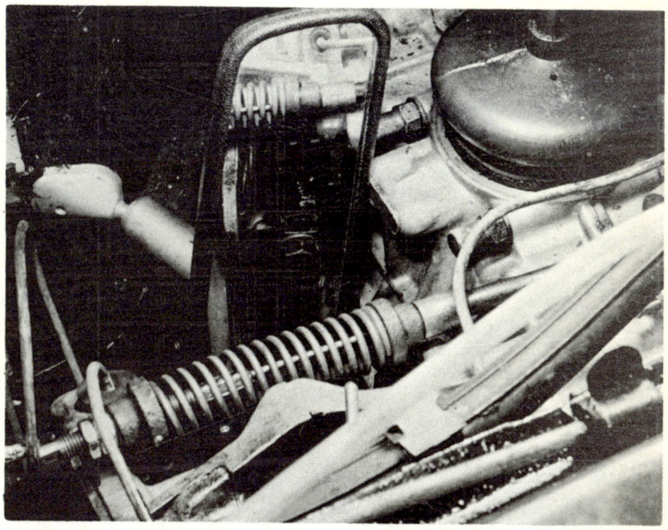

15.4 Adjusting the handbrake eccentrics with the help of a mirror

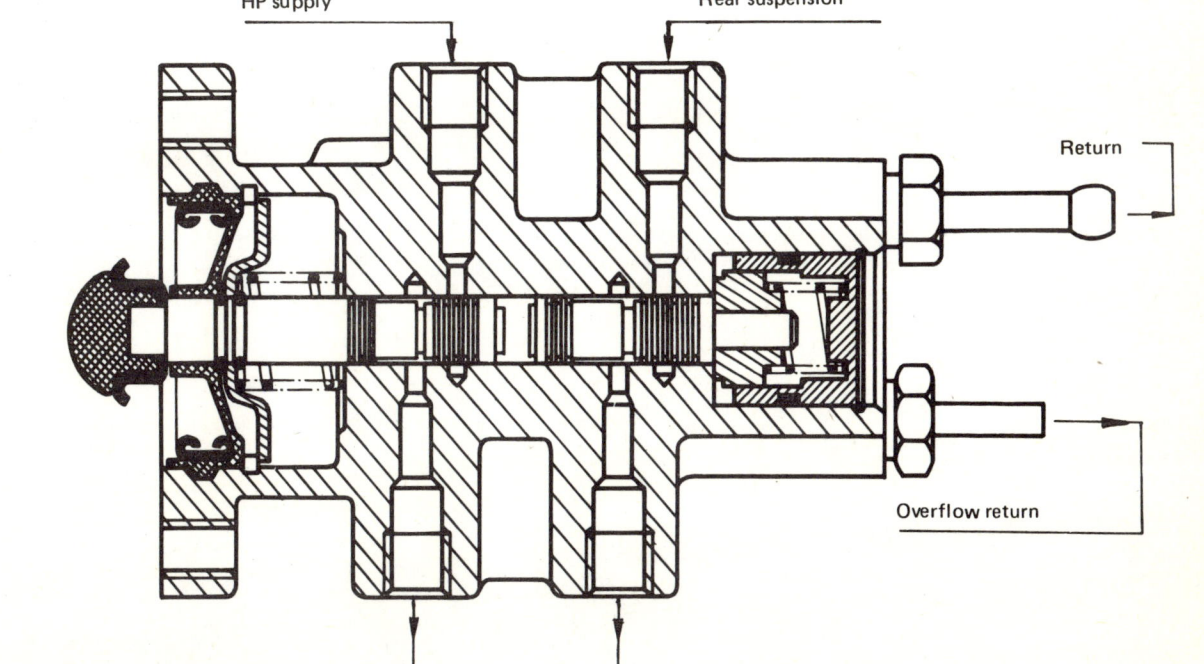

HP supply
Rear suspension
Return
Overflow return
Front brakes
Rear brakes

Fig. 8.5. Brake control valve

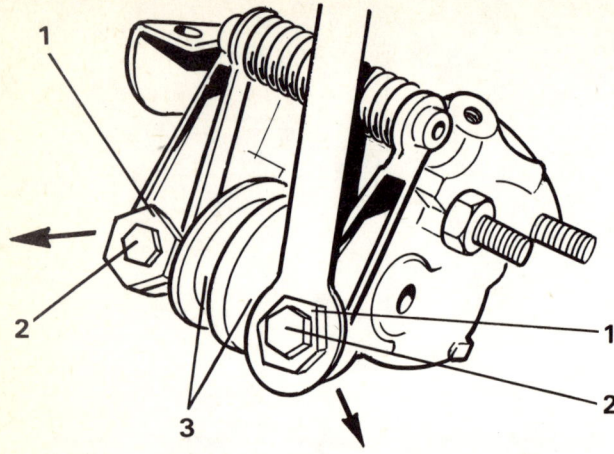

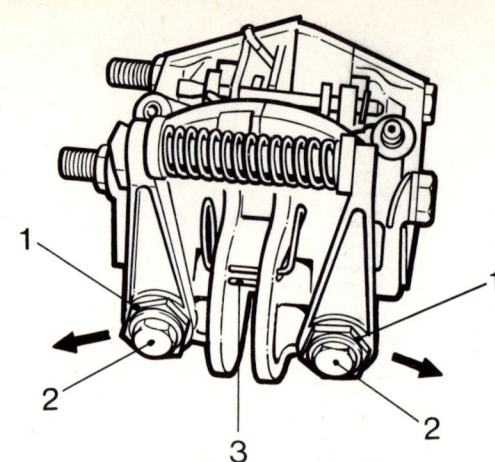

Fig. 8.7. Handbrake pad replacement (old type caliper)

    1 Eccentric adjusters   *3 Pads*
    2 Lockscrews

Fig. 8.8. Handbrake pad replacement (new type caliper)

    1 Eccentric adjusters   *3 Spring*
    2 Lockscrew

21 Fault diagnosis - braking system

Before diagnosing faults from the following chart, check that any braking irregularities are not caused by:
    1 Uneven or incorrect tyre pressures
    2 Incorrect 'mix' of radial and crossply tyres
    3 Wear in the steering mechanism
    4 Defects in the suspension
    5 Misalignment of the bodyframe

Symptom	Reason/s	Remedy
Stopping ability poor	Brake pads and/or discs badly worn or scored	Dismantle, check and renew as required.
	Brake control valve faulty	Remove, dismantle and renew parts as necessary.
	Brake caliper seals defective	Dismantle and renew.
	Leak in the hydraulic system	Identify and rectify.
	Air in the hydraulic system	Bleed the system.
	Low main hydraulic system pressure	Check the main hydraulic system, Chapter.
Uneven braking, brakes grabbing or pulling to one side	Brake pads contaminated with oil	Renew brake pads, identify and rectify source of oil
	Brake disc distorted	Check and replace if necessary.
	Piston seized in a brake caliper	Dismantle and renew.
Parking brake inefficient	Worn brake pads	Renew brake-pads.
	Brake adjustment incorrect	Re-adjust.

Chapter 9 Steering, wheels and tyres

Contents

Specifications

Steering
Type	Rack and pinion
Lock angle	48° 36' (not adjustable)
Ratio	1 : 19
Turning radius:	
Between walls (approx.)	5.10 m (17 ft 0.2 in)
Between kerbs (approx)	4.70 m (15 ft 9.6 in)
Steering wheel turns (lock-to-lock)	3.8
Wheel alignment	0 to 2 mm (0 to 0.07 in) toe-in
Camber angle	1° positive to 1° negative
Castor angle	$1° 15' \begin{smallmatrix} +\ 1° 25' \\ -\ 1° 15' \end{smallmatrix}$

Wheels
Type	Vent disc, 3 stud fixing 4½J x 15
Size	4½J x 15 in

Tyres
Size	145 - 15 ZX (tubeless)

Pressures (all models)
Front	1.8 kg/sq cm (26 psi)
Rear	1.9 kg/sq cm (28 psi)

1 General description

1 The rack and pinion type steering unit is mounted on the front axle unit. A steering arm is connected to each end of the rack by a tie-rod which is adjustable for setting the wheel alignment. Camber and castor angles are not adjustable: if they are suspect consult your Citroen agent.

2 When removing the steering, it is necessary to remove the steering column as the wheel is integral with the steering column shaft and cannot be removed separately. When the roadwheels are in the straight-ahead position the spoke of the steering wheel is positioned 30° below the horizontal towards the outside of the car.

3 The drive from the steering column to the steering unit is transmitted through a Cardan shaft, the universal joints of which are not identical, so care must be taken to ensure that it is fitted correctly.

4 Rubber bellows type dust covers are fitted over the axial joints between each end of the steering rack and the tie-rods.

2 Maintenance

1 No routine maintenance, as such, is required for the steering mechanism, but a visual examination should be made periodically to check the condition of the rubber bellows. They should be checked for cracking and general deterioration of the rubber. Defective bellows will allow the ingress of dirt and water and could lead to failure of the steering unit.

2 If there is any sign of excessive free-movement in the steering, check the tie-rod ball joints for wear. If the ball joints are worn, the complete tie-rod must be renewed as the balljoints are integral with the tie-rods. Check the wheel alignment periodically, as described in Section 6. Incorrect wheel alignment can ruin tyres very quickly.

3 Steering unit - removal

1 Raise and support the front of the car. Remove the front wheels.

2 Move the rubber bellows back and unlock the tabwashers. Unscrew the tie-rod ball joints, while holding the rack to prevent it turning. Remove the plastic sheath from the rack.

3 Before removing the Cardan shaft, mark the position of the ends so that it can be refitted correctly, as both ends are not identical. Slacken the nut holding the lower universal joint and remove the bolt holding the upper universal joint. Free the steering column from the support tube and remove the Cardan shaft.

4   Remove the two bolts securing the steering unit to the front axle unit, and remove the control rod from the front height corrector (mark the position of the collar on the rod). The height settings are not altered by removing the control rod of the height corrector.
5   Remove the steering unit from the car.

4   Steering unit - replacement

1   Fit the steering unit into its recess on the front axle unit. Fit the securing bolts, with washers under the heads, and torque tighten to 3.6 to 4 kg f m (26 to 29 lb f ft).
2   Place the Cardan shaft in position with the universal joints located as marked at removal. Engage the lower universal joint with the pinion.
3   Adjust the position of the rack so that an equal amount protrudes from each side of the casing and fit the steering column into the support tube. Insert the nylon washer.
4   Position the spoke of the steering wheel at the four o'clock position and connect the steering column to the upper universal joint of the Cardan shaft. Fit the securing bolt and nut. Always fit a new Nylstop nut whenever the bolt is removed. Tighten the nut to 1.3 to 1.4 kg f m (9.5 to 10 lb f ft).
5   Fit the lower universal joint of the shaft to the pinion so as to give a clearance of 1 to 1.5 mm (0.040 to 0.060 in) between the nylon washer and the support tube (Fig. 9.3). Fit the clamping bolt and new nut. tighten to 1.3 to 1.4 kg f m (9.5 to 10 lb f ft).
6   Fit the plastic sheaths on the housing. Fit the stop washer and tabwasher, and screw the tie-rod ball joints fully home on the rack. Hold the rack from turning and torque tighten the ball joints to 3.6 to 4 kg f m (26 to 29 lb f ft). Bend the tab of the tabwasher back onto the flat of the ball joint.
7   Connect the control rod to the front height connector, if necessary, operate the height control to adjust to the marks made when the collar was removed.
8   Fit the front wheels and lower the car to the ground.
9   Check the toe-in of the front wheels, as described in Section 6.
10 Fit the rubber bellows over the plastic sheaths and adjust them so that, with the wheels in the straight-ahead position, their length is 155 ± 3 mm (6.10 ± 0.12 in), 'a' in Fig. 9.4.

5   Tie-rods - removal and replacement

1   Movement is transmitted from the rack of the steering unit to each wheel by a tie-rod which is secured, at its outer end, by a ball joint to the steering arm on the front hub. If the tie-rods are bent, or the ball joints are worn, the wheels will be out of alignment or have excessive free-movement independent of the steering unit, this will result in inaccurate steering and abnormal tyre wear.
2   Disconnect the tie-rods from the steering rack, as described in Section 3.
3   Remove the nut holding the tie-rod ball joint in the steering arm, and using a suitable extractor, remove the ball joint. If an extractor is not available, try holding a hammer to one side of the steering arm eye and striking the opposite side a sharp blow with a hammer, this will usually free the joint.
4   Replacement is the reversal of the removal sequence. Always fit a new tabwasher. When screwing the tie-rod swivel joint onto the steering rack prevent the rack from turning while tightening the joint to 3.6 to 4 kg f m (26 to 29 lb f ft). Tighten the nuts securing the ball joints to the steering arms to 1.8 to 2 kg f m (13 to 14.5 lb f ft).
5   Check the wheel alignment, and adjust as necessary, refer to Section 6.
6   Replace the rubber bellows, as described in Section 4.

6   Wheel alignment - checking and adjustment

1   The alignment of the front wheels does not normally alter unless the steering linkage or front suspension has been subject to abnormal stress or the tie-rods have been disturbed or renewed.
2   Before checking the wheel alignment the front and rear heights of the car must be correctly adjusted (refer to the relevant Chapters) and the tyre pressures must be correct.

3   Position the car on level ground with the wheels in the straight-ahead position, steering wheel spoke at the 4 o'clock position, and the manual height control set to the 'normal' road position.
4   With the engine running measure the toe-in of the front wheels using a wheel alignment gauge, of which there are various types available, and check that the toe-in is between 0 and 2 mm (0 and 0.080 in).
5   If adjustment of the toe-in is necessary, proceed as follows:

   a) *Slide the rubber bellows back to uncover the tie-rod ball joints and slacken the locknuts.*
   b) *Turn the ball joint ends a fraction of a turn at a time to obtain the correct adjustment. Make sure both ends are turned an equal amount. One complete turn of each ball joint end alters the adjustment by approximately 4 mm (0.16 in).*

6   Tighten the locknuts to a torque of 3.6 to 4 kg f m (26 to 29 lb f ft) and re-check the alignment. Check that the length of the threaded portion visible on the left and right-hand tie-rods ('b' in Fig. 9.5), is the same to within 2 mm (0.08 in).
7   Refit the rubber bellows, as described in Section 4.

7   Steering wheel and column - removal and replacement

1   Disconnect the Cardan shaft from the steering column assembly, as described in Section 3.
2   Disconnect the earth strap from the negative terminal of the battery. Disconnect the speedometer drive. Loosen the shelf and disconnect the wiring.
3   Remove the dashboard screws and withdraw the dashboard sufficiently to allow for the removal of the steering column upper securing bracket. Remove the screws holding the lower bracket and withdraw the steering wheel and column assembly.
4   Replacement of the assembly is the reversal of the removal procedure. Ensure that the steering shaft position is adjusted, as described in Section 4.

8   Wheels and tyres - general

1   To provide equal, and minimum wear from all the tyres, they should be rotated on the car at intervals of 6,000 miles (10,000 km) to the following pattern:

   Spare to right-hand front
   Right-hand front to left-hand rear
   Left-hand rear to left-hand front
   Left-hand front to right-hand rear
   Right-hand rear to spare

   Wheels should be rebalanced when this is done. If two tyres only are being renewed, the new pair should always be fitted to the front wheels, as these are the most important from the safety aspect of steering and braking.
2   Never mix tyres of radial and crossply construction on the same car, as the basic design differences can cause unusual and, in certain conditions, very dangerous handling and braking characteristics. If an emergency should force the use of two different types, make sure the radials are on the rear wheels and drive particularly carefully. If three of the five wheels are fitted with radial tyres, make sure that no more than two radials are in use on the car (and these at the rear). Rationalise the tyres at the earliest possible opportunity.
3   Wheels are not normally subject to servicing problems, but when tyres are renewed or changed the wheels should be balanced to reduce vibration and wear. If a wheel is suspected of damage, caused by hitting the kerb or a pothole which could distort it out of true, change it and have it checked for balance and true running at the earliest opportunity.
4   When fitting the wheels, do not overtighten the nuts. The maximum possible manual torque applied by the manufacturers wheel brace is adequate. It also prevents difficulties when the same wheel brace has to be used for removal of the wheels!

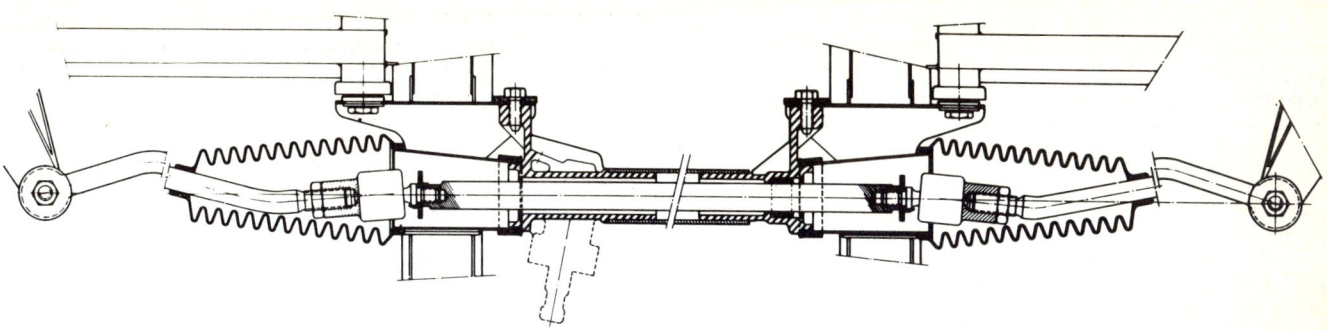

Fig. 9.1. Cross-section of the steering rack housing

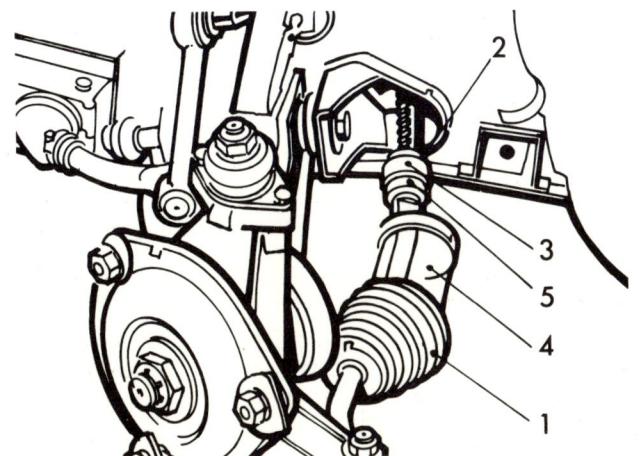

Fig. 9.2. Tie-rod to steering rack ball joint

1   *Rubber bellows*
2   *Stop washer*
3   *Tabwasher*
4   *Plastic sheath*
5   *Ball joint*

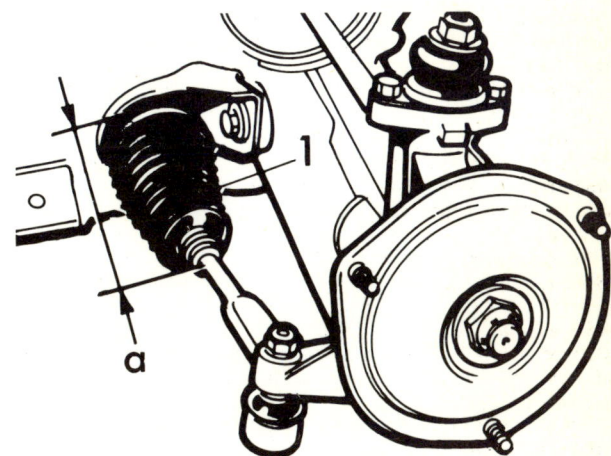

Fig. 9.4. Rubber bellows measurement

1   *Rubber bellows*

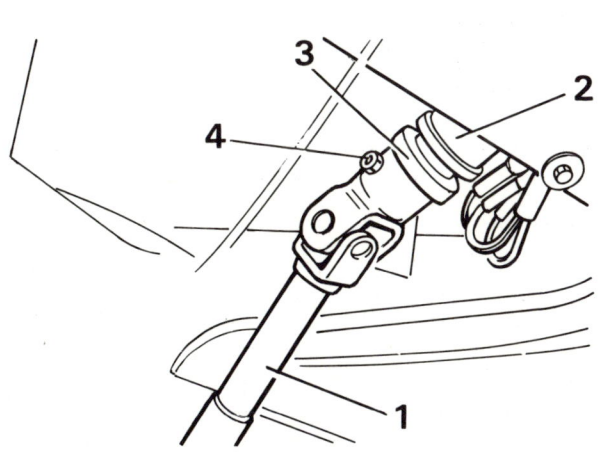

Fig. 9.3. Cardan shaft and support tube

1   *Cardan shaft*
2   *Support tube*
3   *Nylon washer*
4   *Upper universal clamping bolt*

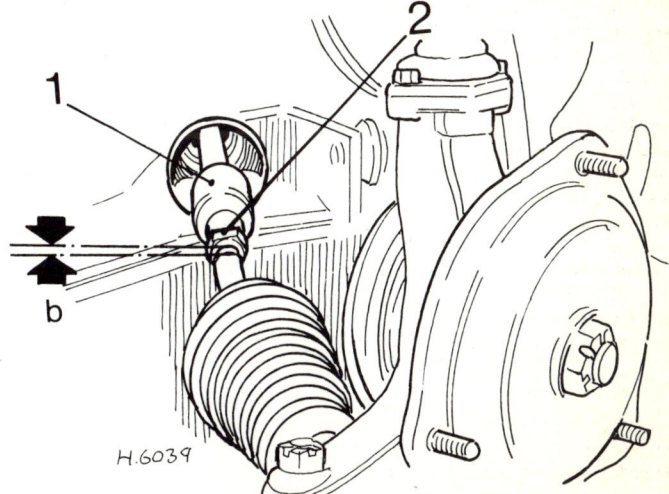

Fig. 9.5. Tie-rod adjustment

1   *Ball joint*
2   *Locknut*

9   Fault diagnosis - steering, wheels and tyres

Symptom	Reason/s	Remedy
Excessive free movement in steering wheel	Wear in steering linkage, gear and Cardan shaft joints	Check condition of all joints and steering gear. Renew as required.
Wander	As above Wheels out of alignment Uneven tyre pressure Worn suspension arm pivot bushes	As above. Check alignment. Check pressures. Renew pivot bushes.
Steering stiff and heavy	Ball joints seized Incorrect wheel alignment	Renew. Check wheel alignment.
Wheel wobble and vibration	Roadwheels out of balance Wheels out of alignment Worn wheel bearings Worn ball joints	Balance wheels. Check alignment. Renew bearings. Renew tie-rods

Chapter 10 Electrical system

Contents

Specifications

Battery

Type	Steco 71901 or Fulmen AS209W
Voltage	12
Capacity	40 amp/hour
Earth	Negative

Alternator

Ducellier	7540A and B three phase 7562A single phase
Paris-Rhone	A11M7 single phase A11R1 three phase

Regulator

Type	Ducellier 8366A or Paris-Rhone AYC 213

Starter motor

Type	Paris-Rhone D8E 103 Ducellier 6208B until March 1972 Ducellier 6217 from March 1972 Ducellier 6217B from November 1972

Windscreen wipers ... ...   Electric motor - 2 speed

Fuses ... ...   8 (6 of 16 amp and 2 of 10 amp)

Lights

Headlamps	SEV Marchal 80/90 watt
Bulbs:	

Lamp	Watt
Head	45/40
Direction indicator	21
Stop	21
Reversing	21
Front side	5
Tail	5
Number plate	5
Interior	12
Boot	12
Speedometer	4

Tachometer and clock	...	...	...	...	...	...	...	2
Battery indicator and fuel gauge	...	...	...	...	...	...	...	2
Warning lights:								
Engine oil pressure ...	...	...	...	...	...	...	...	2
Brake pressure	...	...	...	...	...	...	...	2
Sidelamps ...	...	...	...	...	...	...	...	2
Headlamps ...	...	...	...	...	...	...	...	2
Direction indicators ...	...	...	...	...	...	...	...	2
Engine oil temperature	...	...	...	...	...	...	...	2
and brake pad wear ...	...	...	...	...	...	...	...	2
Heated rear window	...	...	...	...	...	...	...	2
Converter oil temperature ...	...	...	...	...	...	...	...	2

1 General description

The electrical system of all models covered by this manual is of the 12 volt type and the major components comprise, a 12 volt battery, of which the negative terminal is earthed, an alternator which is mounted on top of the engine at the front and is belt driven from the fan mounted on the front of the crankshaft, and a starter motor which is fitted on the rear left-hand side of the engine.

The battery supplies the power required to operate the starter motor, which places a heavy demand on it. The battery also provides the current for the ignition, lighting and other electrically operated equipment when the current being consumed exceeds the output of the alternator. It is kept fully charged by the alternator, the output of which is controlled by the regulator mounted on the side of the battery.

Do not connect a charging unit to the battery and never carry out any electrical welding repairs on the car unless both the negative and positive leads are disconnected from the battery, as serious damage can be caused to the electrical systems.

2 Battery - removal and replacement

1 The battery is housed in the engine compartment at the rear, left-hand side.
2 Disconnect the negative terminal first and then the positive terminal (screw or clamp).
3 Remove the regulator mounted in front of the battery by pulling it vertically to slide it out of its holder.
4 Unscrew the retaining nut and remove the clamp. Slide the battery towards the left to free it, and lift it out.
5 Before fitting the battery, make sure that both terminal posts and clamps are clean and free from corrosion, then smear them with petroleum jelly (not grease) to prevent corrosion.
6 Replacement is the direct reversal of removal. Before connecting the negative lead ensure that there is no flow of current. This is established by briefly touching the negative terminal with the lead end: any sparking indicates a short circuit which must be corrected first.

3 Battery - maintenance and inspection

1 Normal weekly battery maintenance consists of checking the electrolyte level of each cell to ensure that the separators are covered by 6.35 mm (0.25in) of electrolyte. If the level has fallen, top up the battery using distilled water only. Do not overfill. If any electrolyte is spilled, the spillage must be wiped away immediately as electrolyte attacks and corrodes very quickly, any metal with which it comes in contact.
2 As well as keeping the terminals clean and covered with petroleum jelly, the top of the battery, and especially the top of the cells, should be kept clean and dry. This helps prevent corrosion and ensures that the battery does not become partially discharged by leakage through dampness and dirt.
3 Once every three months, remove the battery and inspect the battery tray and battery leads for corrosion (white fluffy deposits on the metal which are brittle to touch). If any corrosion is found, clean off the deposits with ammonia. Paint over the clean metal with an anti-rust/anti-acid paint.

4 At the same time inspect the battery for cracks. If a crack is found, clean and plug it with one of the proprietary compounds marketed by firms, such as Holts, for this purpose. If leakage through the crack has been excessive then it will be necessary to refill the appropriate cell with fresh electrolyte as detailed in Section 4. Cracks are frequently caused in the top of the battery cases by topping-up with distilled water in the middle of winter after instead of BEFORE a run. This gives the water no chance to mix with the electrolyte and so the former freezes and splits the battery case.
5 If topping-up the battery becomes excessive and the case has been inspected for cracks that could cause leakage, but none are found, the battery is being over-charged and the voltage regulator will have to be checked.
6 With the battery on the bench at the three monthly check, measure the specific gravity with a hydrometer to determine the state of charge and condition of the electrolyte. There should be very little variation between the different cells and if a variation in excess of 0.025 is present it will be due to either:

   a) *Loss of electrolyte from the battery at some time caused by spillage or a leak, resulting in a drop in the specific gravity of the electrolyte when the deficiency was replaced with distilled water instead of fresh electrolyte.*

   b) *An internal short-circuit caused by buckling of the plates or a similar malady pointing to the likelihood of total battery failure in the near future.*

7 The specific gravity of the electrolyte for fully charged conditions at the electrolyte temperature indicated, is listed in Table A. The specific gravity of a fully discharged battery at different temperatures of the electrolyte is given in Table B.

TABLE A

Specific gravity - battery fully charged
1.268 at 38°C (100°F) electrolyte temperature
1.272 at 32°C (90°F) electrolyte temperature
1.276 at 27°C (80°F) electrolyte temperature
1.280 at 21°C (70°F) electrolyte temperature
1.284 at 16°C (60°F) electrolyte temperature
1.288 at 10°C (50°F) electrolyte temperature
1.292 at 4°C (40°F) electrolyte temperature
1.296 at -1.5°C (30°F) electrolyte temperature

TABLE B

Specific gravity - battery fully discharged
1.098 at 38°C (100°F) electrolyte temperature
1.102 at 32°C (90°F) electrolyte temperature
1.106 at 27°C (80°F) electrolyte temperature
1.110 at 21°C (70°F) electrolyte temperature
1.114 at 16°C (60°F) electrolyte temperature
1.118 at 10°C (50°F) electrolyte temperature
1.122 at 4°C (40°F) electrolyte temperature
1.126 at -1.5°C (30°F) electrolyte temperature

4 Battery - electrolyte replenishment

1 If the battery is in a fully charged state and one of the cells maintains a specific gravity reading which is 0.025 or more lower than the

others, and a check of each cell has been made with a voltage meter to check for short circuits (a four to seven seconds test should give a steady reading of between 1.2 and 1.8 volts), then it is likely that electrolyte has been lost from the cell with the low reading.

2   If a significant quantity of electrolyte has been lost through spillage it will not suffice to merely refill with distilled water. Top-up the cell with electrolyte which is a mixture of sulphuric acid and water in the ratio of 2 parts acid to 5 parts water and the ready mixed solution should be obtained from battery specialists or large garages. The 'normal' solution can be added if the battery is in a fully charged state. If the battery is in a low state of charge, use the normal solution, charge the battery then empty out the electrolyte. Swill the battery out with clean water then refill with a new charge of electrolyte.

5   Battery - charging

1   In winter when a heavy demand is placed on the battery, such as when starting from cold, and much electrical equipment is continually in use, it is a good idea to occasionally have the battery fully charged from an external source at a rate of 3.5 to 4 amps.

2   Continue to charge the battery at this rate until no further rise in specific gravity is noted over a four hour period.

3   Alternatively, a trickle charger, charging at the rate of 1.5 amps can be safely used overnight.

4   Special rapid 'boost' charges which are claimed to restore the power of the battery in 1 to 2 hours are most dangerous unless they are thermostatically controlled as they can cause serious damage to the battery plates through overheating.

5   While charging the battery ensure that the temperature of the electrolyte never exceeds 37.8°C (100°F).

Caution: *If the battery is being charged from an external power source whilst the battery is fitted in the car, both battery leads must be disconnected to prevent damage to the electrical circuits.*

6   Alternator - general description

1   The use of alternators for generating the current required to operate car electrical systems is now more commonplace. Their main advantage over the dynamo type generator is that they provide a higher output for lower revolutions and are lighter in weight/output ratio.

2   The alternator generates alternating current and this current is rectified by diodes into direct current which is the current needed for battery storage.

3   The regulator, which controls the voltage output, is a transistorized unit and is permanently sealed. It requires no attention and will last indefinitely providing all wiring connections are correctly made, refer to Fig. 10.1.

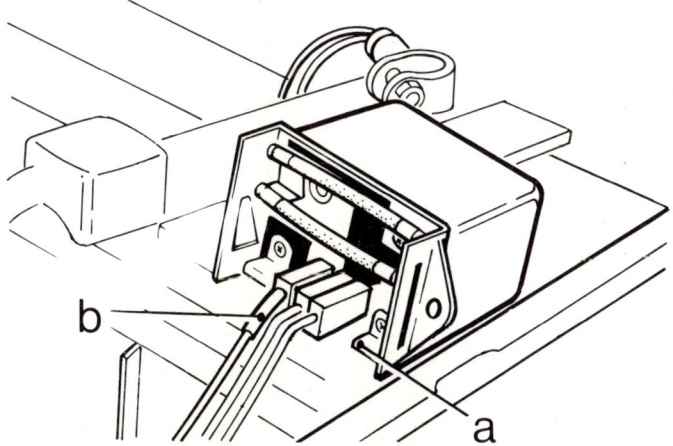

Fig. 10.1. Alternator regulator connections

(a) Positive terminal   *(b) Yellow lead*

7   Alternator - safety precautions

1   If there are indications that the charging system is malfunctioning in any way, care must be taken to diagnose faults properly, otherwise damage of a serious and expensive nature may occur to parts which are in fact quite serviceable.

2   The following basic requirements must be observed at all times:

   a) *All alternator systems use a negative earth. Even the simple mistake of connecting a battery the wrong way round could burn out the alternator diodes in a few seconds.*

   b) *Before disconnecting any wires in the system the engine and ignition circuits should be switched off. This will minimise accidental short circuits.*

   c) *The alternator must never be run with the output wire disconnected.*

   d) *Always disconnect the battery from the car's electrical system if an external charging source is being used.*

   e) *Do not use test wire connections that could move accidentally and short circuit against nearby terminals. Short circuits will not blow fuses - they will blow diodes or transistors.*

   f) *Always disconnect the battery cables and alternator output leads before carrying out any electric welding work on the car.*

   g) *Never lever on the alternator body when adjusting its drive belt. The casing is easily fractured.*

8   Alternator - removal and replacement

1   Disconnect the earth lead from the negative terminal of the battery. Remove the front grille as described in Chapter 1.

2   Make a note of the connections and disconnect the three leads from the alternator.

3   Remove the adjusting arm bolt, slacken the pivot bolt and remove the drivebelt from the pulley. Remove the pivot bolt and the alternator.

4   Replacement of the alternator is the reverse of the removal sequence. Adjust the drivebelt tension by pivoting the alternator upwards on the pivot bolt, then tightening the adjusting arm bolt and the pivot bolt. When correctly tensioned a 10mm (0.4in) deflection of the belt should be possible.

9   Alternator - fault diagnosis

Special equipment is required for the testing of the alternator and the regulator. If a fault develops it is recommended that checks are made by a service station equipped for this work.

10 Starter motor - testing in the car

1   If the starter motor fails to operate then check the condition of the battery by switching on the headlamps. If they glow brightly for several seconds and then gradually dim, the battery is in an uncharged condition.

2   If the headlamps continue to glow brightly and it is obvious that the battery is in good condition, then check the tightness of the battery connections, particularly the earth lead from the battery terminal to its connection on the bodyframe. Check all connections from battery to solenoid switch and cable to starter for cleanliness and tightness.

3   If the starter motor still fails to turn check the solenoid by putting a voltmeter or bulb across the main cable connections on the starter side of the solenoid and earth. When the switch is operated there should be a reading or lighted bulb, if not the solenoid switch is faulty. If it is established that the solenoid is not faulty and 12 volts are getting to the starter then the fault must be in the starter motor.

11 Starter motor - removal and replacement

1   Disconnect the battery earth strap from the negative terminal of the battery. Take note of the connections and disconnect the wiring

from the starter motor.

2   Remove the six screws securing the left-hand upper cooling duct, disengage the two sealing rings and remove the upper cooling duct.

3   Remove the left-hand induction pipe assembly and blank off the open orifices in the cylinder heads and intake manifold, and carburettor assembly.

4   Remove the starter motor retaining bolts and draw the starter motor forward and remove it.

5   Replacement is the reverse of the removal sequence. Tighten the retaining bolts to 1.8 kg f m (13 lb f ft).

12 Starter motor (Ducellier) - dismantling and reassembly

1   Disconnect the field coil supply lead. Remove the three nuts securing the bearing endplate and remove the rear cover. Remove the plastic cover.

2   Drive out the fork hinge pin. Hold the drive gear and remove the bolt and washer from the commutator end of the shaft. Remove the bearing endplate and release the positive brush and its guide.

3   Remove the yoke from the two assembly rods. Remove the solenoid securing nuts and the solenoid. Remove the pinion fork and the armature.

4   Dismantle the solenoid by holding the solenoid core by the two flats, (a) in Fig. 10.2, and removing the two studs, the bolts, the spring with its washer, the adjustment sleeve and its nut.

5   From the armature assembly remove the celeron washer, the steel washer, the thrust bearing snap ring, the thrust bearing and the driving gear.

6   If necessary, unsolder the positive brush from the yoke and the negative brush from the bearing endplate.

7   Clean all the parts, take care that the cleaning fluid does not get on to the field coils or armature windings. Examine all the parts carefully, if the armature commutator is scored slightly it can be cleaned-up with fine glass paper (never use emery cloth as the carborundum particles will become embedded in the copper surfaces). If necessary undercut the mica insulation using an old hacksaw blade ground to suit. If the commutator is badly worn it will require skimming on a lathe and should be left to an electrical engineer. The minimum diameter of the commutator after machining must not be less than 30mm (1.181in). Check the length of the brushes, the minimum wear length is 7mm (0.275in), and ensure that they slide freely in the brush holders.

8   Using an ohmmeter connected between the solenoid supply terminal (flat blade) and the terminal marked DEM, check that the insulation resistance of the pull-in coil is approximately 0.24 ohms. With the ohmmeter connected between the solenoid supply terminal and the solenoid body check that the resistance of the hold-in coil is 1.08 ohms. Replace a solenoid which does not satisfy these conditions.

9   If the armature or field coil windings are suspect this is a job best left to an electrical engineer with the necessary test equipment.

10 Assembly is the reversal of the removal sequence. When assembling the armature, lightly oil the steel washer, the celeron washer and the splines with a very thin oil. Preset the adjusting sleeve halfway along its travel in the nut, (18) in Fig. 10.2.

11 Adjust the travel of the drive pinion as described in Section 13 and fit the plastic cover.

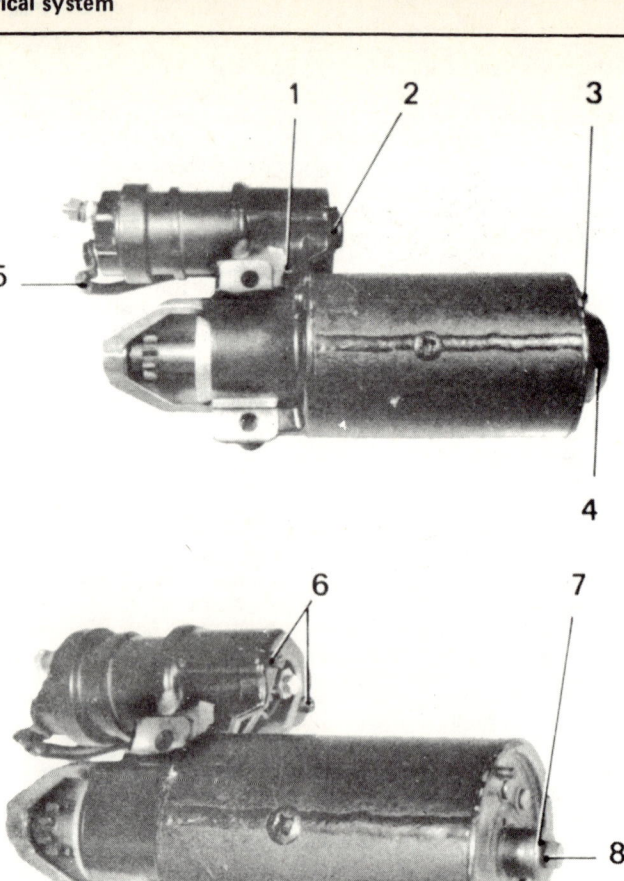

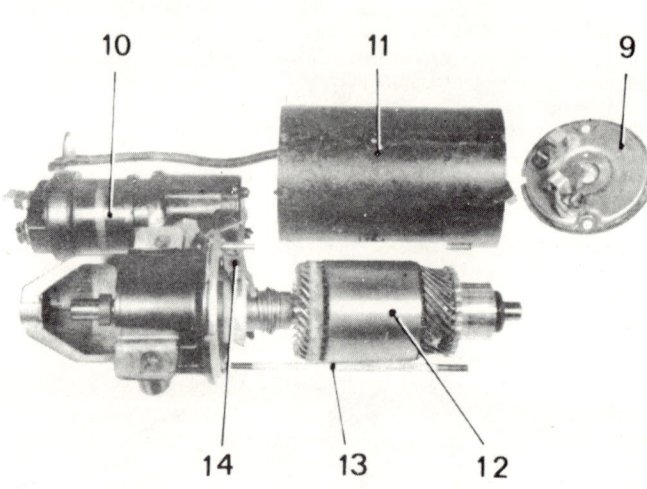

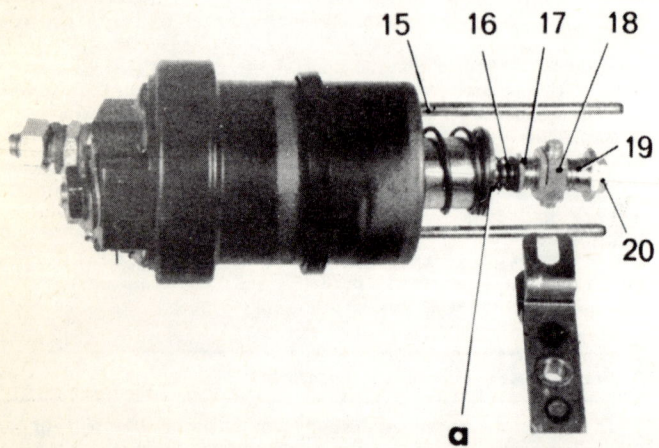

Fig. 10.2. Ducellier starter motor - dismantling

1 Fork pin	8 Bolt	15 Studs
2 Plastic cover	9 Bearing endplate	16 Spring
3 Endplate nuts	10 Solenoid	17 Washer
4 Rear cover	11 Yoke	18 Nut
5 Supply lead	12 Armature	19 Adjustment sleeve
6 Nuts	13 Assembly rods	20 Bolt
7 Steel washer	14 Pinion fork	

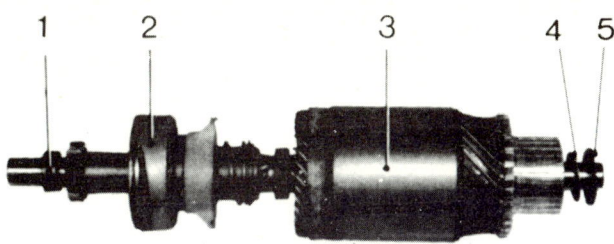

Fig. 10.3. Armature assembly

1 Thrust bearing
2 Driving gear
3 Armature
4 Steel washer
5 Celeron washer

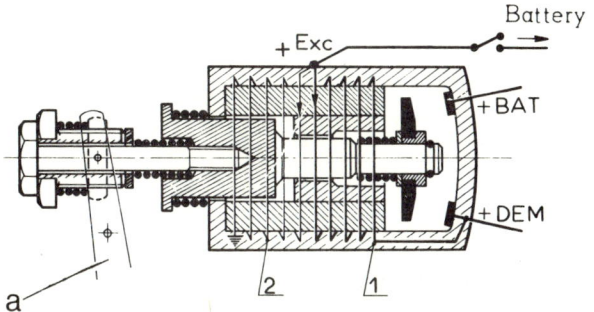

Fig. 10.4. Starter motor solenoid

1 Pull-in coil
2 Hold-in coil
A Pinion fork

13 Starter motor (Ducellier) - adjustment of drive pinion

1 Remove the plastic cover. Energise the solenoid by connecting the positive terminal of a 12 volt battery to the flat blade connector on the solenoid and the battery negative to the terminal marked DEM. This will engage the drive pinion.
2 With the pinion in the engaged position measure dimension (a) in Fig. 10.5. This should not exceed 37.5mm (1.47in).
3 Disconnect the supply from the battery and measure the dimension (b) (drive pinion in its free position). Dimension (b) must be between 47.3 and 48.5mm (1.86 and 1.91in).
4 Adjustment is by altering the position of the adjusting sleeve on the solenoid. If the dimensions specified cannot be obtained by adjustment of the sleeve the starter must be dismantled.
5 Fit the plastic cover.

14 Starter motor (Paris-Rhone) - dismantling and reassembly

1 Disconnect the field coil cable from the solenoid. Remove the three retaining nuts, the clamp plate, the fibre seal and the solenoid.
2 Remove the plastic cap. Drive out the hinge pin of the operating lever and its support.
3 Remove the two assembly bolts. Partly separate the endplate, commutator end from the yoke and lift the positive brush from its guide. Remove the driving end starter bearing, the operating lever, the endplate, armature and starter drive assembly and the starter drive.
4 Remove the endplate from the armature by removing the retaining bolt, the thrust washer and the friction washer. Release the endplate, the bakelite coated washer, the steel washer, the flexible washer and the second steel washer.
5 If necessary, unsolder the negative brush from the endplate and the positive brush from the yoke.
6 Cleaning, examination and servicing is the same as described for Ducellier starter motors as described in Section 12 except that the commutator diameter must not be less than 35mm (1.378in) and the resistance of the solenoid pull-in coil and hold-in coil should be 3 ohms and 1 ohm respectively.
7 Assembly is the reversal of the removal sequence. When fitting the assembly bolts fit the bolt with the insulating tape between the two brush holders. Tighten the bolts to 0.8 to 1.1 kg f m (6 to 8 lb f ft).
8 Adjust the travel of the drive pinion as described in Section 15.

15 Starter motor (Paris-Rhone) - adjustment of drive pinion

The check and adjusting procedure is the same as for the Ducellier starter motor except that dimension (a) is 38.3mm (1.51in) maximum and dimension (b) is between 47.4 and 48mm (1.86 and 1.89in), obtained by adjusting the sleeve, Fig. 10.6, after having removed the solenoid securing flange.

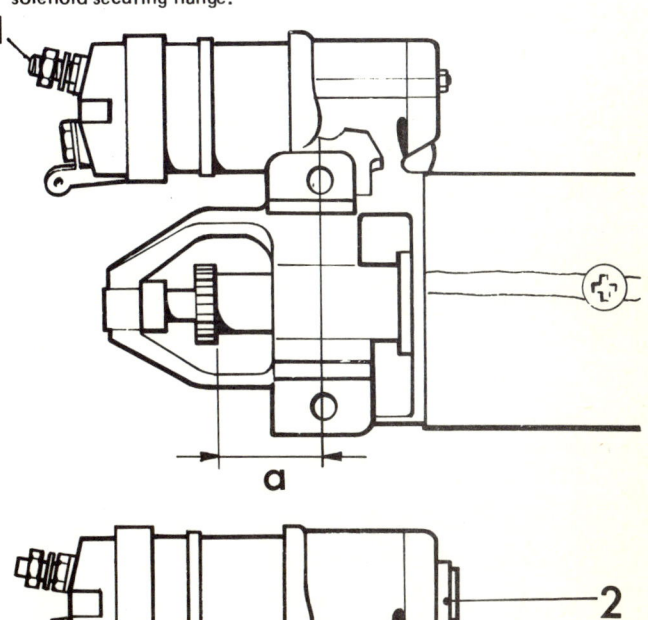

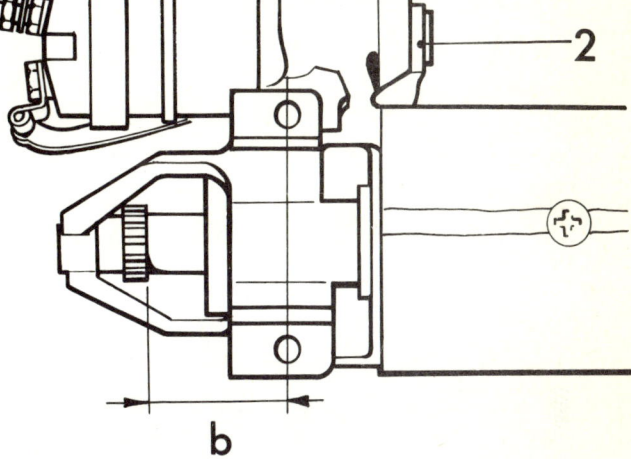

Fig. 10.5. Ducellier starter motor - drive pinion adjustment

1 DEM terminal
2 Plastic cover

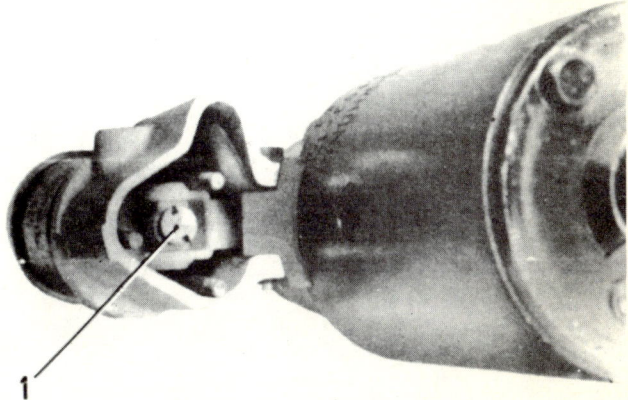

Fig. 10.6. Paris-Rhone starter motor - drive pinion adjustment

1 Adjusting sleeve

16 Fuses - general

1   There are two fuse boxes, each containing four fuses, mounted on the inner valance of the left-hand front wing, adjacent to the battery box. The front box contains fuses 1 to 4 and fuses 6 to 9 are in the rear box.
2   The circuits they protect (some accessories are optional and may not be fitted) are as follows:

Front box
(a) Yellow marking (10A) - Front and rear LH sidelamps - Number plate light - Clock light - Tachometer light - Battery indicator light - Fuel gauge light - Side and tail lamps warning light - Speedometer light.
(b) Green marking (16A) - Direction indicators - Fresh air blower - Rear window heating - Regulator - Cigarette lighter - Clock - Radio - Reversing lamps.
(c) Red marking (16A) - Battery charging indicator - Fuel gauge - Windscreen wipers - Windscreen washers - Oil pressure warning light - Hydraulic pressure warning light - Torque converter oil temperature warning light - Engine oil temperature and brake pad wear warning light - Stop lamps - Boot lighting - Interior light - Torque converter clutch relay - Heater blower.
(d) Blue marking (10A) - Front and rear RH sidelamps.

Rear box 2
(a) Green marking (16A) - Headlamp dipped beam, LH.
(b) Red marking (16A) - Headlamp dipped beam, RH.
(c) Yellow marking (16A) - Headlamp main beam, LH.
(d) White marking (16A) - Headlamp main beam, RH.

3   The following are not protected by fuses:

Horn - Starter solenoid - Torque converter clutch solenoid - Coil - Tachometer - Feed for headlamp flasher - Main beam warning light.

4   If the car is fitted with supplementary heating, a 16A fuse (mauve) will be found inside the rear box.
5   Always replace fuses with the correct type. When a fuse blows, check the circuits on that fuse, trace and rectify the fault before replacing the fuse. The circuits are all included in the wiring diagrams Fig. 10.14 and

17 Headlamp - adjustment

The headlamps can only be adjusted correctly using beam alignment equipment and this work should be left to a service station so equipped. The headlamp beam adjusters are shown in Fig. 10.7.

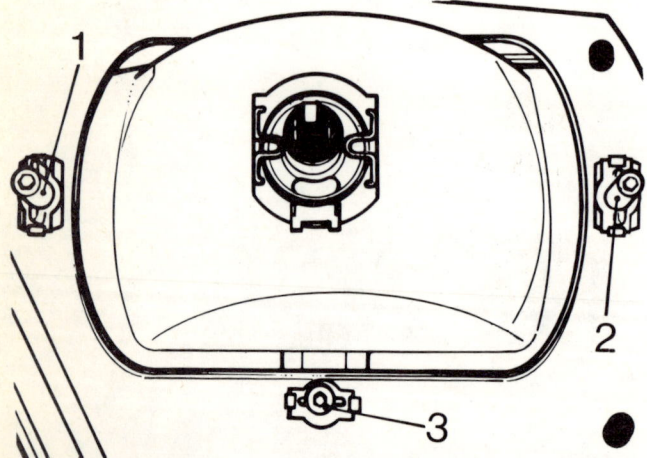

Fig. 10.7. Headlamp adjusters

1 Horizontal adjuster   3 Vertical adjuster
2 Horizontal adjuster

18 Heating system - general

1   Warm air is drawn through the heating ducts and the heater box by the electrically driven fan motor.
2   If the fan does not operate check that the fuse is not blown and that the wiring and connections are in good condition. If the motor is defective it should be removed for exchange or repair by an auto-electrician.

19 Fan motor - removal and replacement

1   Disconnect the battery earth strap and remove the spare wheel.
2   Remove the rubber collar between the heater box and the fan. Note the connections and disconnect the wiring from the motor. Remove the securing screws and the motor assembly.
3   Replacement is the reversal of the removal sequence.

20 Windscreen wiper motor and mechanism - fault diagnosis

1   If the wipers fail to operate first check that current is reaching the motor. This can be done by switching on and using a voltmeter or 12 volt bulb and two wires between the positive terminal on the motor and earth.
2   If no current is reaching the motor check if there is any at the switch. If there is then a break has occurred in the wiring between switch and motor.
3   If there is no current at the switch go back to the ignition switch and so isolate the area of fault.
4   If current is reaching the motor but the wipers do not operate, switch on and give the wiper arm a push - they or the motor could be jammed. Switch off immediately if the wipers do not operate, as damage to the motor may occur. If the wipers do operate the reason for them jamming is most likely to be due to wear in the linkage of the wiper mechanism or the motor.
5   If the wipers run too slowly it will be due to something restricting the free operation of the linkage or a fault in the motor.
6   At this stage remove the motor, this is a fairly easy task, and have it checked out by an auto-electrician before going on to the removal of the wiper linkage mechanism as this is a much more involved task.

21 Windscreen wiper motor - removal and replacement

1   Disconnect the battery earth strap. Remove the bonnet as described in Chapter 1.
2   Remove the seal and ventilation panel, Fig. 10.8. Remove the crank arm retaining nut and the crank arm, Fig. 10.9.
3   Remove the support plate retaining bolts and the bolts which secure the motor to the support plate.
4   Note the connections, disconnect the wiring and remove the motor.
5   Replacement is the reverse of the removal sequences. Tighten the support plate retaining bolts to 0.35 to 0.4 kg f m (2.5 to 3 lb f ft) and the motor securing bolts to 0.5 kg f m (3.6 lb f ft). The crank arm must be fitted with the motor in the 'automatic stop' position. To ensure this, connect up the battery, switch on the ignition for about 5 seconds and then switch off again. Now fit the crank arm on the motor spindle and in alignment with the connecting rod as shown in Fig. 10.9. Tighten the crank arm retaining nut to 0.45 to 0.5 kg f m (3.2 to 3.6 lb f ft). Check the operation of the windscreen wipers.

22 Windscreen wiper mechanism - removal and replacement

1   Remove the battery earth strap and the bonnet. Remove the seal and ventilation panel.
2   Remove the nut securing the crank arm to the motor spindle and lift off the arm. Remove the wiper arms.
3   Disconnect the choke cable from the carburettor, the heater flap operating cable, the parking brake handle from the operating lever, the gear lever from the selector fork operating lever and the speedometer cable from the speedometer.

4   Refer to Fig. 10.10 and remove the instrument panel as follows:

  a) *Remove the cover by pushing it forward and removing it from the back. Disconnect the leads from the switch (or switches according to model).*
  b) *Remove the two fixing bolts and remove the panel from the dashboard by pulling downwards on the right-hand and then on the left-hand side, press lightly at (a) on the dashboard to assist the removal.*
  c) *Disconnect the connector or connectors (according to model) of the different leads on the panel and remove the panel.*

5   Remove the dashboard as follows:

  a) *Remove the parking brake handle and the knobs controlling the heater and demister (pull them out).*
  b) *Disconnect the electrical plugs.*
  c) *Remove the steering wheel as described in Chapter 9.*
  d) *Remove the seven screws holding the dashboard, Fig. 10.11, and remove the dashboard.*

6   Remove the shelf by removing the six retaining screws, refer to Fig. 10.12.
7   Remove the bolts securing the duct and the bolts securing the console, pull the console a little way to the rear.
8   Remove the bolt holding the pipe and free it. Remove the bolts holding the windscreen wiper bearings on the dashboard. Remove the nut, cap washer and seal from each spindle. Remove the mechanism from the dashboard.
9   Examine the mechanism and wiper bearing for wear or damage and replace as necessary.
10 Replacement is the reverse of the removal sequence. Ensure the crank arm is replaced as described in Section 22. When replacing the windscreen wiper arms position them as shown in Fig. 10.13 so that; 'A' = 60 $\pm$ 10mm (2.40 $\pm$ 0.4in) and 'B' = 35 $\pm$ 10mm (1.40 $\pm$ 0.4in). Tighten the retaining nuts to 0.9 kg f m (6.5 lb f ft).

---

23 Instruments and instrument panel bulbs - general

---

1   Access to the instruments and warning or light bulbs necessitates the removal of the instrument panel as described in Section 22.
2   If a warning lamp or light bulb fails check the relevant fuse before removing the instrument panel.
3   If the speedometer fails to register check the cable drive from the gearbox before removing the instrument.
4   If the fuel tank contents gauge fails to register, check the fuse first. If the fuse is all right remove the transmitter cover as described in Chapter 2. Short circuit the transmitter leads and switch on the ignition briefly. A reading on the gauge indicates that the gauge is serviceable. Check the wiring and connections to the transmitter at the tank, if necessary remove the transmitter for checking as described in Chapter 2.

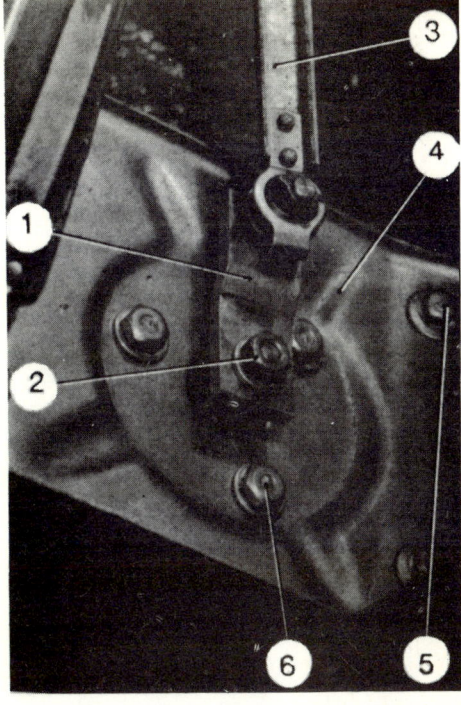

Fig. 10.9. Windscreen wiper motor removal

1 Crank arm
2 Retaining nut
3 Connecting rod

4 Support plate
5 Support plate retaining bolts
6 Windscreen wiper motor securing bolts

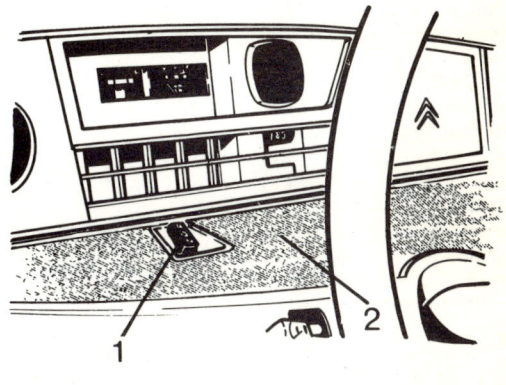

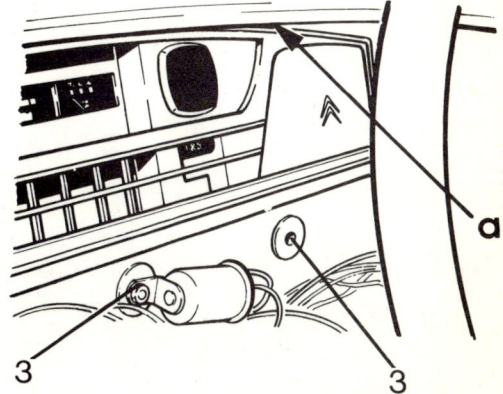

Fig. 10.10. Removing the instrument panel

1 Switch
2 Cover

3 Fixing bolts

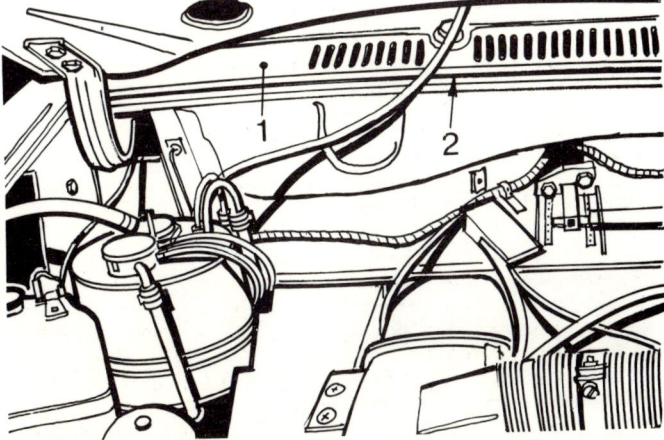

Fig. 10.8. Ventilation panel removal

1 Panel

2 Seal

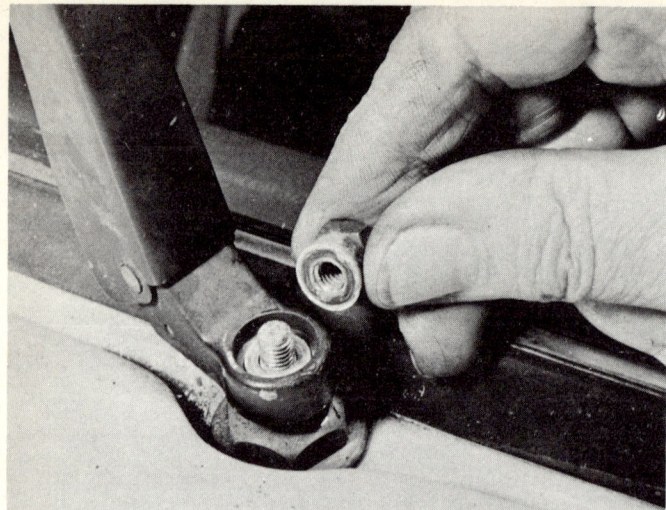

22.10a Fitting the windscreen wiper arm and retaining nut

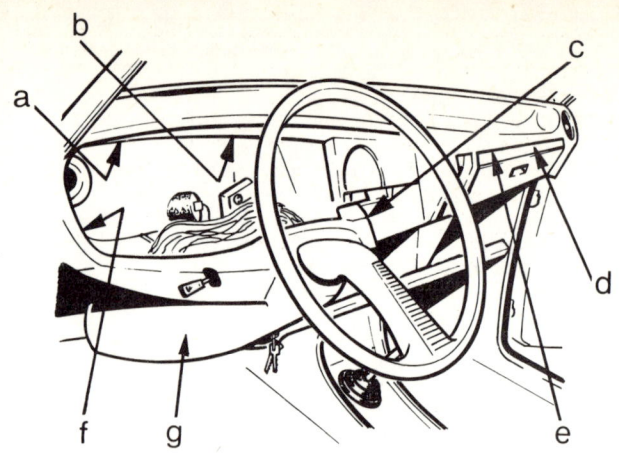

Fig. 10.11. Dashboard securing screws

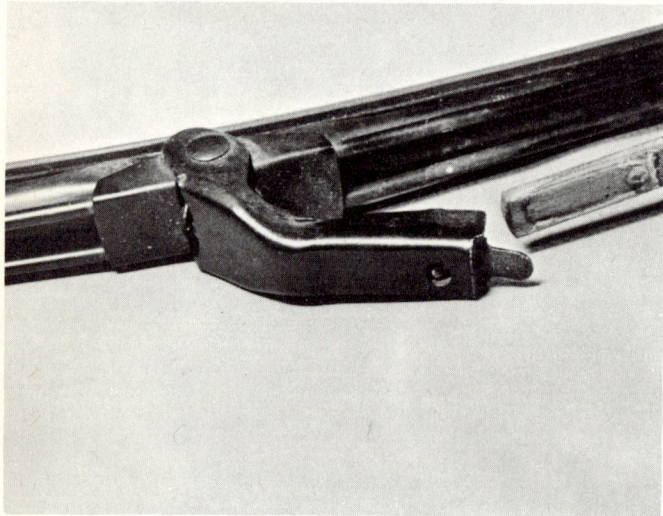

22.10b Fitting the windscreen wiper blade

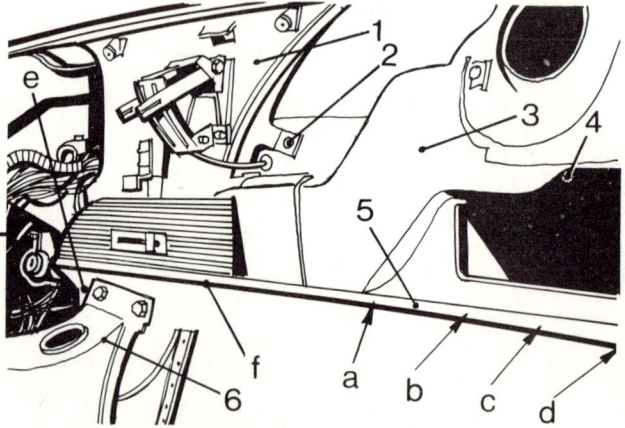

Fig. 10.12. Shelf removal

1	Pipe	4	Bolts
2	Bolt	5	Shelf
3	Duct	6	Console
(a - f)	Retaining screws		

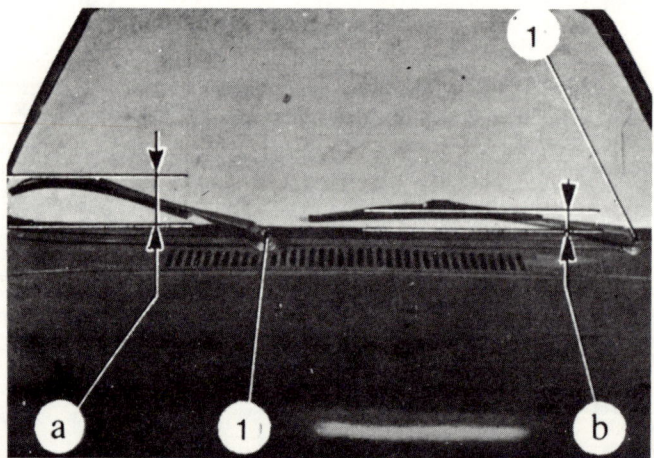

Fig. 10.13. Windscreen wiper arm adjustment

1 Arm retaining nuts

24 Bulb - renewal

1   Before replacing a headlamp bulb always check the relevant fuse. If both front and rear right-hand sidelights fail at the same time, check the fuse as most likely cause of failure.

2   To replace a European-Dip type bulb, swing the springs retaining the bulb flange clear. Pull back the black plastic connector to withdraw it from the reflector. Remove the bulb, pulling it by its flange, from the connector carrying the feed leads. Fit the new bulb into the connector, then fit the unit into the reflector by rotating it until the flange locator fits into the slot. Swing the retaining springs back into place.

3   To replace a quartz-halogen bulb, withdraw the bulb holder unit by turning it, it will come out automatically. (On some designs a restrainer has to be depressed.) Disconnect the bulb from the feed lead. When fitting the new bulb hold it by the metal part taking care not to touch the glass with your fingers, as this will shorten the life of the bulb and reduce its light output. If it is inadvertently touched by the fingers it should be wiped clean immediately with a clean cloth dipped in spirit.

4   Side and tail-lamp, direction indicator, stop and reversing lamp bulb. Remove the two screws securing the front side-lamp transparent cover. The tail-lamp cover is secured with three screws.

5   Number plate lamp, remove the two screws securing the protector.

6   Interior lamp, hinge down the cover about the front, then disengage it or pivot the cover by means of the slot at the rear, then disengage it from the front, according to type fitted.

25 Heated rear window - general

If the rear window is not being heated check the fuse. If the fuse and the wiring to the window is in order, a failure of the wiring in the window is indicated. In this case it is advisable to take the car to a Citroen agent who can test it and if necessary repair a break in the wiring.

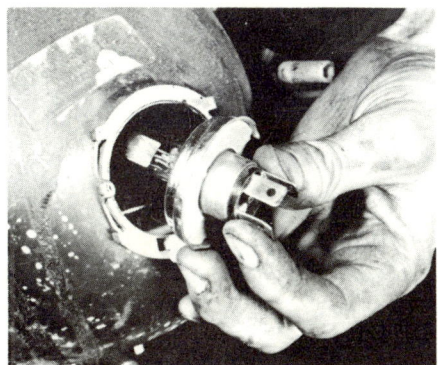

24.2 Replacing a headlamp bulb

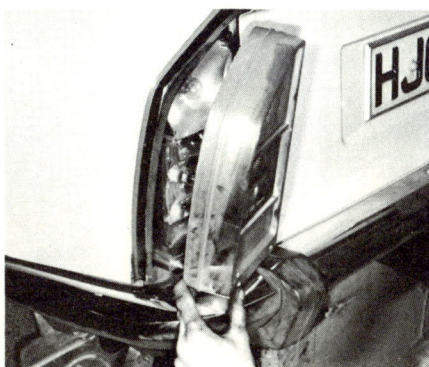

24.4a Removing the transparent cover from a rear light cluster

24.4b Replacing a rear light bulb

24.4c Interior light with cover fitted

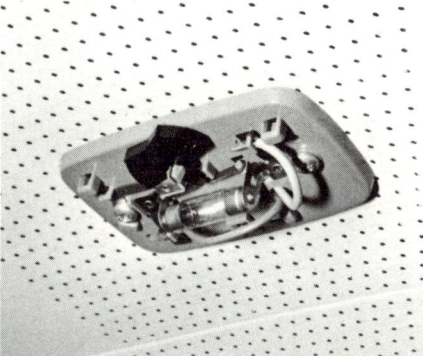

24.4d Replacing an interior light bulb

26 Fault diagnosis - electrical system

Symptom	Reason/s
Starter fails to turn engine	Battery discharged.
	Battery terminal leads loose or earth lead not securely attached to body.
	Loose or broken connections in starter motor circuit.
	Starter motor switch or solenoid faulty.
	Starter motor pinion jammed in mesh with flywheel ring gear.
	Starter brushes badly worn, sticking or brush wire connections loose.
	Commutator dirty or worn.
	Starter motor armature faulty.
	Field coils earthed.
Starter motor turns engine very slowly	Battery in discharged condition.
	Starter brushes worn, sticking or brush wires loose.
	Loose wires in starter motor circuit.
Starter spins but does not turn engine	Starter motor pinion sticking on the screwed sleeve.
	Pinion or flywheel gear teeth broken or badly worn.
Starter motor noisy or excessively rough engagement	Pinion or flywheel gear teeth broken or badly worn.
	Starter motor retaining bolts loose.
Battery will not hold charge for more than a few days	Battery defective internally.
	Electrolyte level too low or electrolyte too weak due to leakage.
	Battery terminal connections loose or corroded.
	Alternator drivebelt slipping.
	Alternator not charging.
	Regulator defective.
Ignition light fails to go out	Alternator drivebelt loose or broken.
	Regulator faulty.
	No output from alternator.
Lights do not come on	Engine not running, battery discharged.
	Loose, disconnected or broken connections.
	Light switch faulty.
	Bulb filament burnt out or blown fuse.
Lights work erratically	Battery terminal or earth connections loose.
	Lights not earthed properly.
	Lights switch faulty.
Horn operates all the time	Horn cable to horn switch earthed.
	Horn switch faulty.
Horn fails to operate	Cable connections loose, broken or disconnected.
	Blown fuse.
	Horn faulty.
Horn operates intermittently	Loose connections.
Windscreen wipers fail to work	Blown fuse.
	Wiring connections loose, disconnected or broken.
	Wiper motor faulty.
	Wiper mechanism jammed or seized.
Wiper arms move sluggishly	Wiper motor faulty.
	Wiper mechanism sticking or worn.

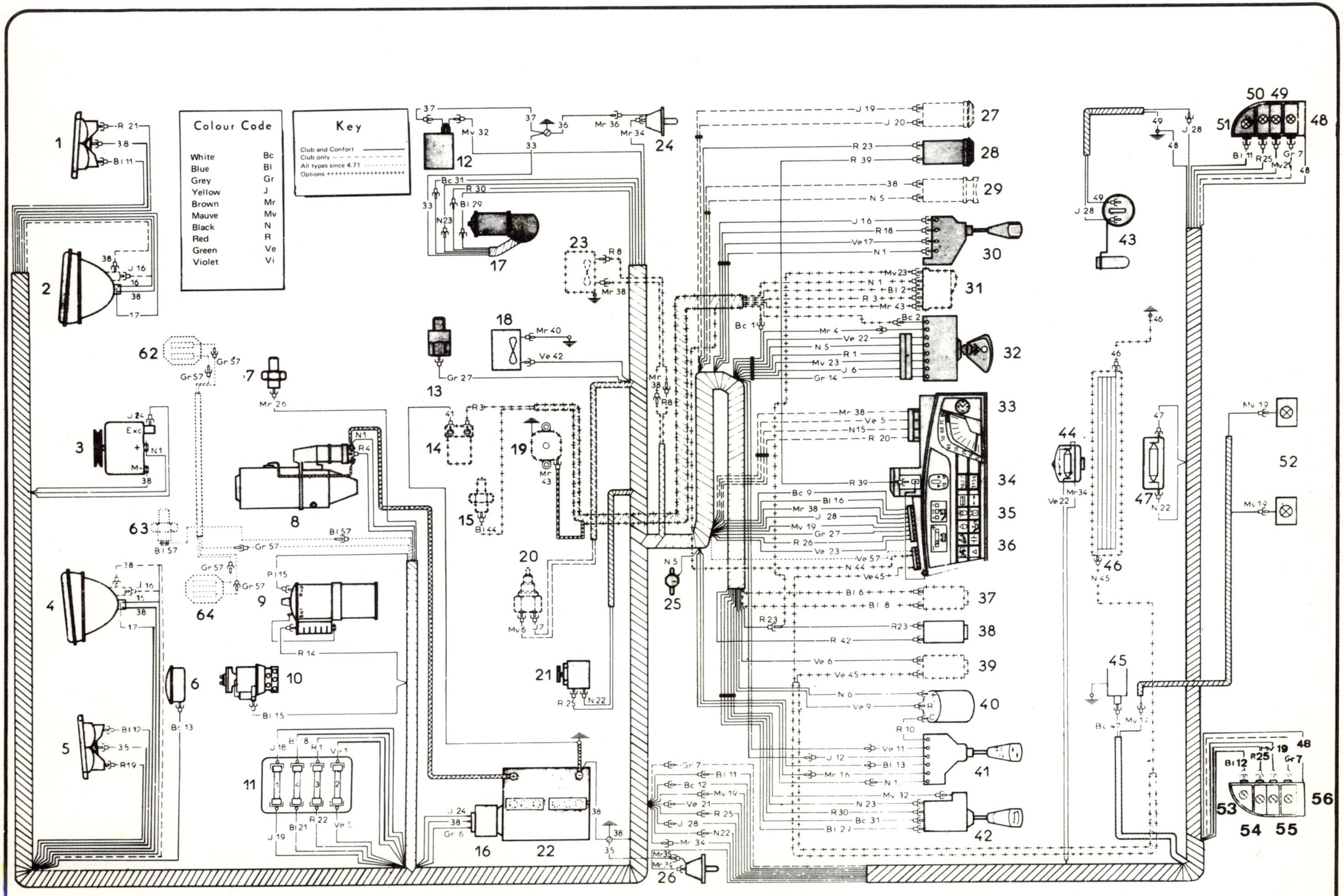

Key

Club and Comfort
Club only
All types since 4.71
Options

Colour Code

White	Bc
Blue	Bl
Grey	Gr
Yellow	J
Brown	Mr
Mauve	Mv
Black	N
Red	R
Green	Ve
Violet	Vi

Fig. 10.14. Wiring diagram - LH drive models

Fig. 10.14. Wiring diagram - LH drive models

1 Direction indicator and sidelamp right-hand
2 Headlamp, right-hand
3 Alternator
4 Headlamp, left-hand
5 Direction indicator and side lamp, left-hand
6 Horn
7 Engine oil pressure switch
8 Starter with solenoid
9 Ignition coil
10 Distributor
11 Fuse box
12 Windscreen washer
13 Brake system pressure switch
14 Electro-valve (torque converter option)
15 Oil temperature switch
16 Voltage regulator
17 Windscreen wiper motor
18 Warm air blower
19 Switch on gearbox (torque converter option)
20 Reversing lamp switch (Club)

21 Stoplamp switch
22 Battery
23 Fresh air blower (option)
24 Door pillar switch, right-hand
25 Terminal for accessories
26 Door pillar switch, left-hand
27 Lighting rheostat for tachometer, clock and battery meter (Club)
28 Speedometer light rheostat
29 Cigar lighter (Club)
30 Lighting switch
31 Relay (torque converter option)
32 Ignition and starter switch
33 Printed circuit connector for tachometer and clock unit (Club)
34 Speedometer light
35 Printed circuit connector for instrument and warning lamp unit
36 Printed circuit connector for warning lamps
37 Fresh air blower switch (option)
38 Warm air blower switch
39 Heated rear window switch (option)
40 Flasher unit

41 Direction indicator switch
42 Windscreen wiper and washer switch
43 Fuel gauge tank unit
44 Interior lamp
45 Boot lamp switch
46 Rear heated window
47 Boot lamp
48 Reversing lamp, right-hand (Club)
49 Tail lamp, right-hand
50 Stoplamp, right-hand
51 Rear direction indicator, right-hand
52 Number plate lamp
53 Rear direction indicator, left-hand
54 Stop lamp, left-hand
55 Tail lamp, left-hand
56 Reversing lamp, left-hand (Club)
62 Front brake unit, right-hand
63 Engine oil temperature thermal switch
64 Front brake unit, left-hand

Fig. 10.15. Wiring diagram - RH drive models

1 Front RH lamp cluster
2 Front RH headlamp
3 Front LH headlamp
4 Front LH lamp cluster
5 Alternator
6 Horn
7 RH brake unit
8 Oil temperature warning switch
9 LH brake unit
10 Fluid temperature warning switch (torque converter)
11 Starter motor
12 Oil pressure warning switch
13 Ignition coil
14 Front fusebox
15 Windscreen washer motor
16 Windscreen wiper motor
17 Hydraulic pressure warning switch
18 Solenoid valve (semi-automatic transmission)
19 Warm air blower
20 Control switch (semi-automatic transmission)
21 Distributor

22 Reversing light switch
23 Battery
24 Regulator
25 Rear fusebox
26 RH door switch
27 Fresh air blower motor
28 Accessory terminal
29 Brake warning light switch
30 LH door switch
31 Torque converter relay
32 Fresh air blower motor switch
33 Rear window heater switch
34 Warm air blower motor switch
35 Fluid temperature warning light (torque converter)
36 Rear window heater warning light
37 Fuel gauge
38 Warning light (brake pads and engine oil temperature)
39 Direction indicator warning light
40 Speedometer light
41 Hydraulic pressure warning light
42 Side and tail lamps warning light

43 Clock and light
44 Panel lighting rheostat
45 Headlamp main beam warning light
46 Engine oil pressure warning light
47 Tachometer and light
48 Charging rate indicator and light
49 Ignition switch
50 Windscreen wiper and washer switch
51 Direction indicator, horns and headlamp flasher switch
52 Direction indicator flasher unit
53 Lighting switch
54 Cigar lighter
55 Fuel gauge transmitter
56 Rear window heater
57 Interior light
58 Luggage compartment light
59 Luggage compartment light switch
60 Rear RH lamp cluster
61 Number plate light
62 Rear LH lamp cluster
63 Second horn

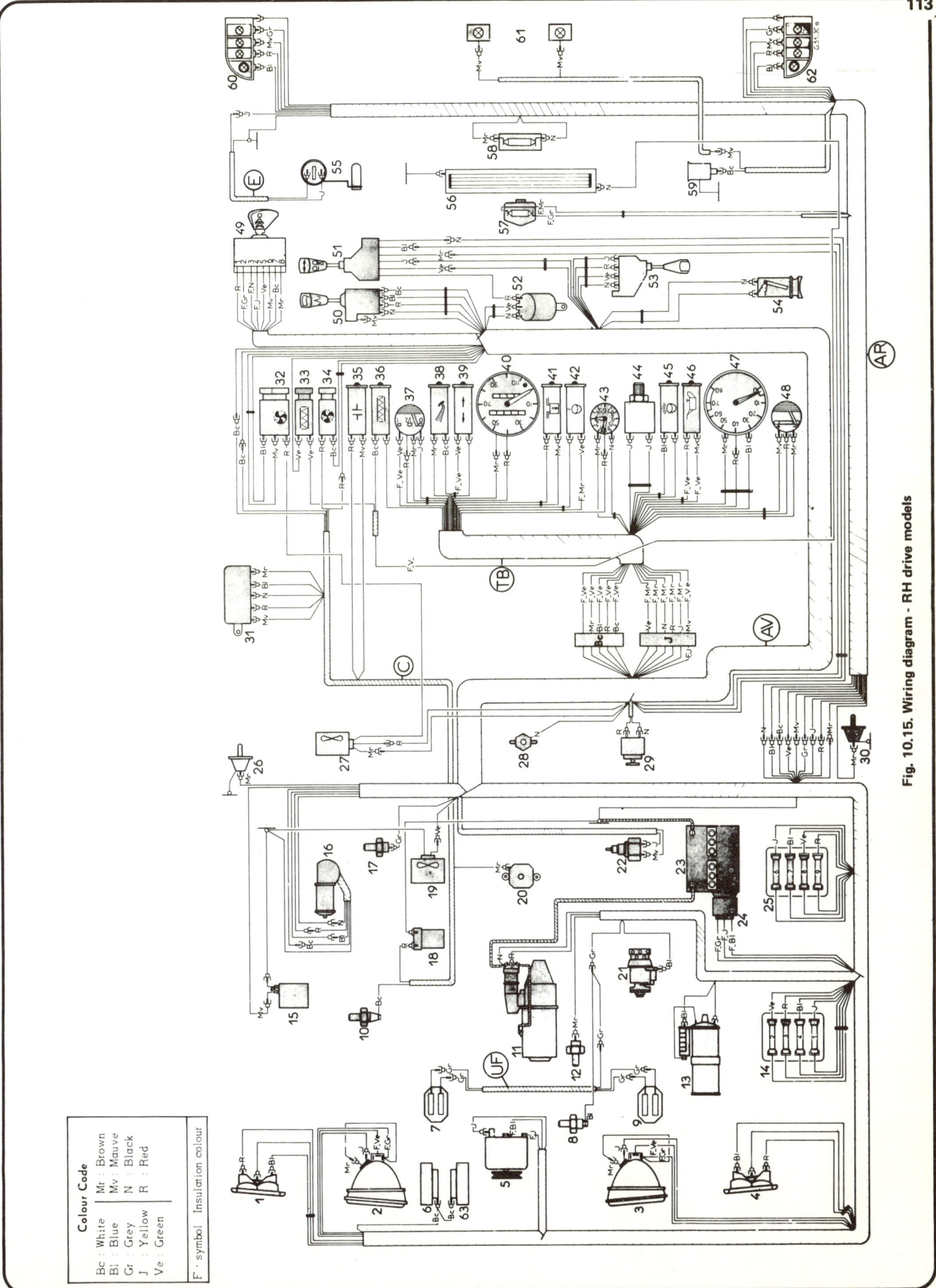

113

Fig. 10.15. Wiring diagram - RH drive models

Colour Code

Bc : White	Mr : Brown
Bl : Blue	Mv : Mauve
Gr : Grey	N : Black
J : Yellow	R : Red
Ve : Green	

F · symbol Insulation colour

Chapter 11 Rear axle and suspension

Contents

Specifications

Suspension

Type	Independent, trailing arms
Springing	Hydropneumatic cylinders
Damping	Integral with suspension cylinders
Anti-roll bar	18mm diameter
Suspension height (normal)	272 ± 10mm (10.71 ± 0.4in)
Suspension cylinder spheres:	
Inflation pressure	$35 \pm {}^{5}_{10}$ bar ($500 \pm {}^{70}_{140}$ psi)

Rear wheel alignment (not adjustable)

Cars until September 1973	4mm (0.16in) toe-in to 4mm toe-out
Cars from September 1973	0 to 2mm (0 to 0.08in) toe-in
Camber angle (not adjustable)	$0^o \pm 40'$

1 General description

1 The rear axle unit is attached to the bodyframe by four flexible mountings. The suspension and damping effect is through the hydro-pneumatic cylinder units acting on each end of the trailing suspension arms which pivot on needle bearings. As on the front suspension three different heights can be selected manually.

2 The stub axles are integral with the ends of the suspension arms and carry the wheel hubs which run on ball bearings. The brake discs are part of the hub assembly and the brake calipers are mounted on the suspension arms.

2 Rear suspension balls - lubrication

The procedure for lubricating the suspension balls is the same as described in Chapter 7, for the front suspension balls, except that on cars from November 1972 the dust shields contain 25cc (1.52cu in) of LHM fluid.

3 Suspension arm - removal

1 Jack-up and support the rear of the car. Release the pressure from the hydraulic system. Remove the rear wheels. Refer to Fig. 11.2. Remove the pin and push back the piston rod of the suspension cylinder. Should there still be pressure in the suspension circuit, operate the manual control several times until the piston rod is free.

2 Slacken the collar and disconnect the union. Bend back the tab of the lockplate and remove the retaining bolt, the lockplate and, if fitted, the shims from behind the lockplate.

3 Using an extractor (Citroen tool 2068-T) in place of the bolt, screw in the extractor bolt to release the suspension arm from the anti-roll bar. Remove the extractor and the arm.

4 Suspension arm - replacement

1 The suspension arms are attached to each end of the anti-roll bar and the distance between them determines their lateral play. This play is adjusted by fitting shims behind the retaining bolt lockplate on only one of the two arms. The adjustment must always be reset whichever arm is removed (the one with or without shims).

2 If the bearing face 'c' (Fig. 11.3) of the support tube shows signs of binding, clean it up with a fine grade stone. Carefully clean the support tube, the bearing surface 'b' of the anti-roll bar and the suspension arm. Using a multi-purpose grease lubricate the face 'c' and the bearing surfaces of the support tube, and the bearings of the arm hub.

3 When fitting an arm without shims proceed as follows:

a) *Engage the hub of the arm on the support tube and connect it to the anti-roll bar with the mark 'a' on the face of the anti-roll bar in line with the gap of a missing spline in the arm hub. Check that the arms are fitted in the same plane without twisting the bar.*

b) *Remove the retaining bolt from the other arm.*

c) *Using Citroen tool 2069-T as shown in Fig. 11.4 fit the arm by screwing the rod A into the anti-roll bar then tightening nut B until the arm is in place, with the face of the support tube bearing on the friction washer in the arm hub. Remove the tool 2069-T.*

d) *Fit the lockplate, smear the threads of the bolt with CURTLYON, fit and tighten the bolt to 1.8 to 2 kg f m (13 to 14 lb f ft). Lock the bolt by bending over a tab of the lockplate.*

e) *Set the lateral play of the arms by adjustment of the shimming at the other suspension arm as described in Section 5.*

4   Fitting an arm with shims is the same procedure as described in paragraph 3 above. Adjust the lateral play, as described in Section 5.

5   Suspension arms - lateral play adjustment

1   Position the tool 2069-T as shown in Fig. 11.4, screw the central bolt 'A' into the anti-roll bar. Tighten the nut 'B' while moving the arm, when the arm falls slowly under its own weight, stop tightening the nut. This indicates that the support tube is bearing on the friction washer in the hub of the arm causing slight friction. Remove the tool 2069-T.

2   Using a straightedge and a depth gauge measure the distance between the face of the anti-roll bar and the face of the arm hub. This dimension plus 0.05mm (0.002in) indicates the thickness of shimming required on the end of the anti-roll bar.

3   Using tool 2068-T bring the anti-roll bar out by 2 to 3mm (0.08 to 0.12in). Remove the tool 2068-T.

4   Place the required thickness of shims on the end of the anti-roll bar and fit the tool 2069-T. Tighten the nut 'B' moderately until the shims are in contact with the end face of the anti-roll bar. Never use the retaining bolt for this operation as the splines are a very close fit and the bolt would be subjected to abnormal stress. Remove the tool 2069-T taking care that the shims remain in place. Smear the threads of the retaining bolt and the faces of the lockplate with CURTLYON sealing paste. Fit the lockplate and retaining bolt and tighten to 1.8 to 2 kg f m (13 to 14 lb f ft). Bend over a tab of the lockplate to lock the bolt.

5   Position the rod of the suspension cylinder and fit the lock pin. Connect the pipe to the union (use a new seal) and tighten it to 0.8 to 0.9 kg f m (6 to 6.5 lb f ft). Tighten the collar.

6   Start the engine. Tighten the pressure regulator bleed screw. Bleed the rear brakes, as described in Chapter 8. Fit the rear wheels and lower the car to the ground.

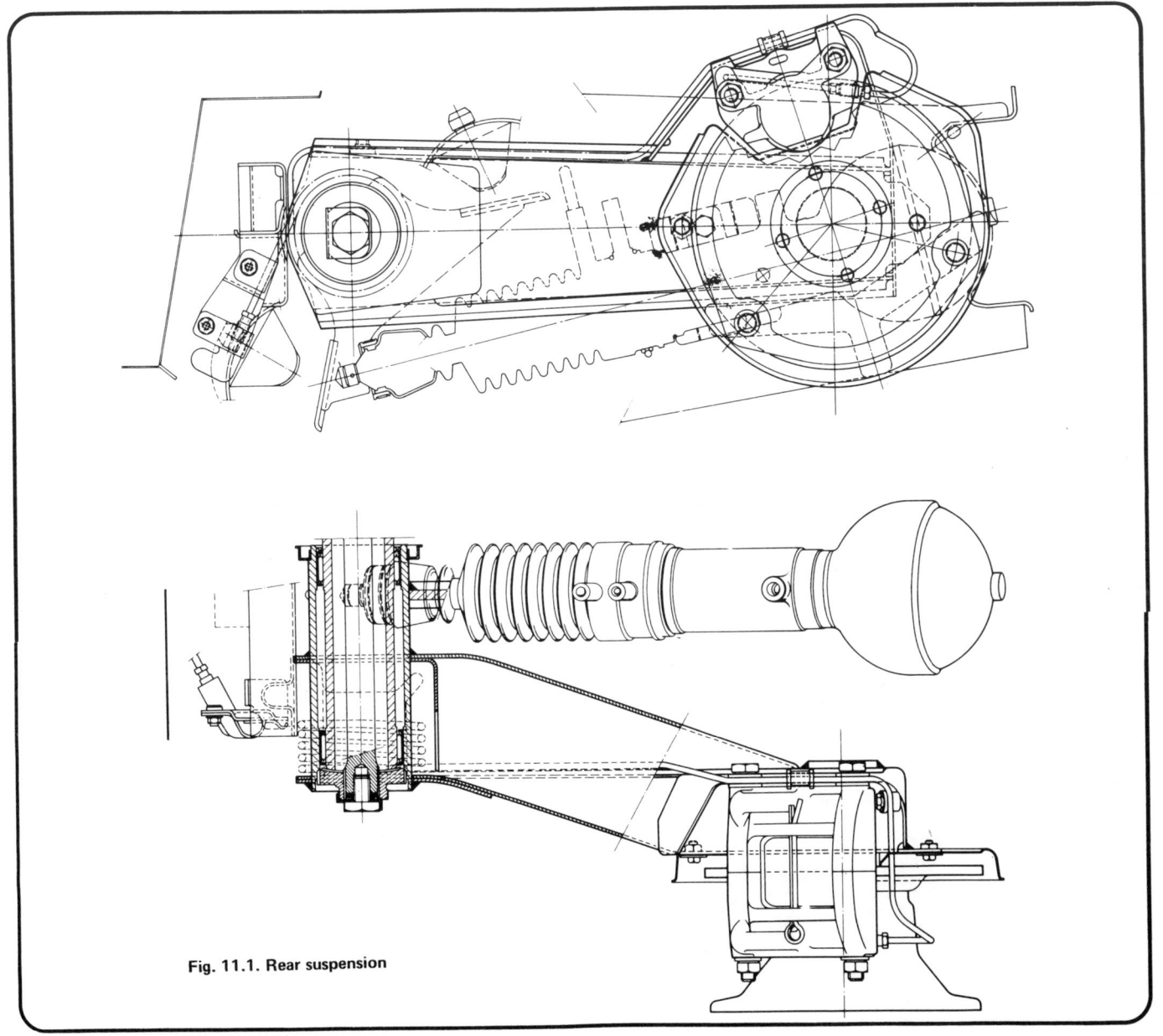

Fig. 11.1. Rear suspension

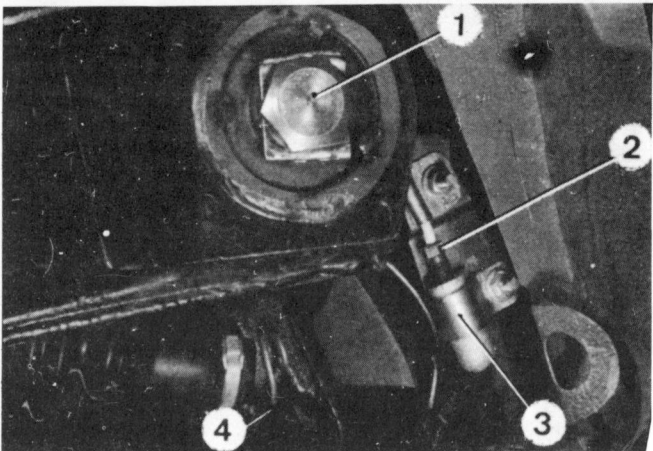

Fig. 11.2. Removing a suspension arm

1	Bolt	3	Collar
2	Union	4	Pin

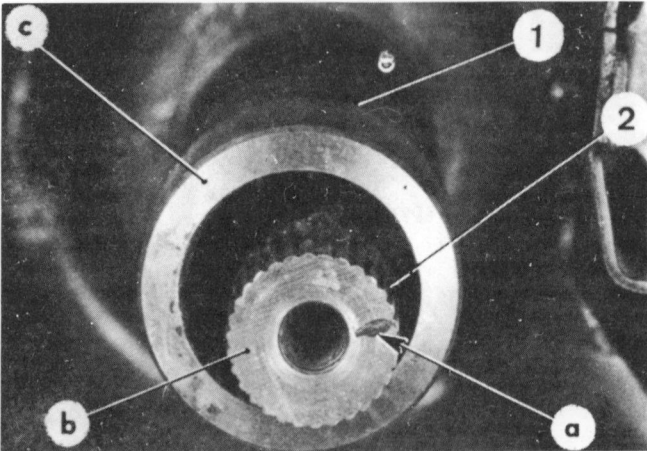

Fig. 11.3. Support tube and anti-roll bar

1 Support tube   2 Anti-roll bar

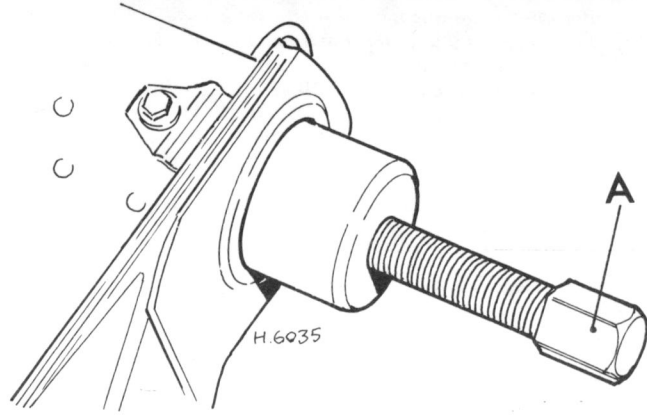

Fig. 11.5. Suspension arm extractor (A) - tool 2068-T

6 Suspension arm hub - replacing bearings, seal and friction washer

1   Remove the suspension arm as described in Section 3. Refer to
Fig. 11.6. If necessary, remove the arm hub deflector. Remove the
seal. Using an extractor remove the bearing. (The Citroen extractor is
tool 1671-T fitted with an end piece 2070-T). Remove the friction
washer.
2   Carefully clean the inside of the suspension arm hub and the
support tube. Grease the bearing areas of the support tube. Smear
both faces of the friction washer with grease and fit it in the hub.
Always fit a new friction washer at each dismantling.
3   The needle bearings are fitted with seals 'a' in Fig. 11.6. These
must be fitted the right way round, the edge with the seal must be
positioned in the direction of the arrow 'F1' for the bearing '5' and
in the direction of the arrow 'F2' for the bearing '4'. To ensure
correct positioning of the bearings use Citroen mandrel 2071-T 'A' with
sockets 'B' and 'C'. Place the mandrel 2071-T 'A' inside the suspension
arm hub, fit the bearing '5' on the mandrel, and using the socket 'B',
push on the bearing until the socket comes in contact with the end
of the mandrel. The length of the socket determines the correct
position of the bearing. Bearing '4' is fitted in the same way using
socket 'C'.
4   Remove the assembly tool and smear the needle bearings with
multi-purpose grease. Fit the seal with the face having the inscription
on it, towards the outside of the hub (direction of arrow 'F2') and
in contact with the bearing. If necessary, fit the deflector, this must
be set in from the edge of the hub by 2 to 3mm (0.08 to 0.12in).
5   Replace the suspension arm, as described in Section 4.

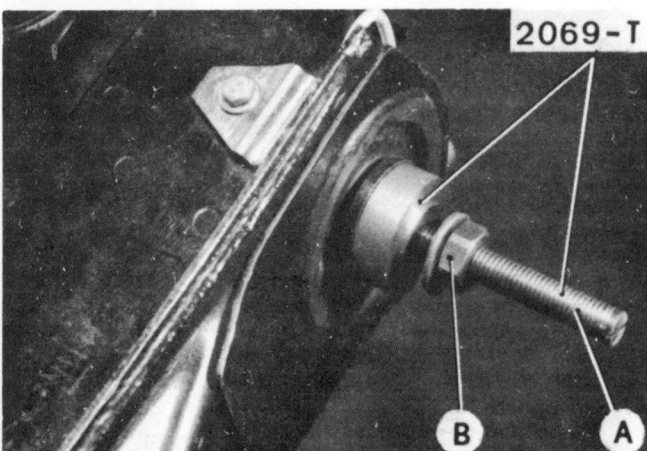

Fig. 11.4. Replacing a suspension arm

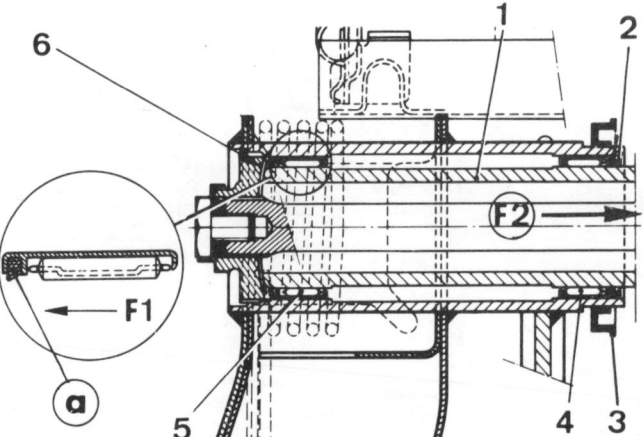

Fig. 11.6. Suspension arm hub

1	Support tube	4	Inner bearing
2	Seal	5	Outer bearing
3	Deflector	6	Friction washer

7 Hub, bearing and brake disc - removal

1   Remove the brake caliper, as described in Chapter 8, Section 9.
2   Using a 4mm drill remove the peening locking the ring nut. Remove the ring nut using Citroen tools 3321-T and 3304-T. Remove the locking on the retaining nut and remove the nut. Using tool 3321-T remove the hub. Remove the disc securing bolts and collect the disc and the bearing plate. Remove the hub bearing.

8 Hub, bearing and brake disc - replacement

1   Fit the disc with the bearing plate between the disc and the hub, fit the securing bolts and tighten to 4.5 to 5 kg f m (33 to 36 lb f ft).
2   Position the new bearing with the sealed side facing the brake disc and press it into the hub.
3   Offer up the hub assembly to the stub axle (without the inner race) and start to position it by tightening the hub nut. Remove the nut, fit a spacer with an inside diameter of 37mm, and of 7mm thickness. Refit the nut and finally fit the bearing. Fit the inner race with the face 'b' of the nylon race to the inside. The faces 'b' Fig. 11.7 of the two races should face each other. Fit a new retaining nut with the threads greased and tighten to 35 to 40 kg f m (250 to 290 lb f ft). Bend the tab of the nut into the slot of the stub axle.
4   Grease both faces and thread of the ring nut and fit it using tool assembly 3321-T and key 3304-T. Tighten to 35 to 40 kg f m (250 to 290 lb f ft) and lock by peening in two places.
5   Fit the brake caliper and complete the assembly as described in Chapter 8, Section 10.

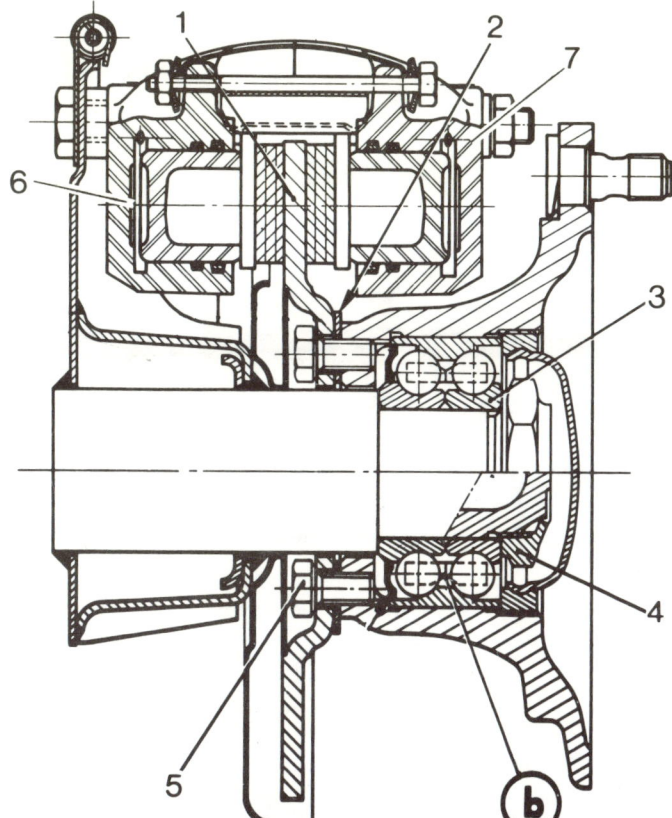

Fig. 11.7. Rear hub, brake caliper and disc

1 Brake disc	5 Disc retaining bolt
2 Shim	6 Caliper inner half
3 Bearing	7 Caliper outer half
4 Nut	

9 Anti-roll bar - removal and replacement

Removal of the anti-roll bar necessitates the removal of both suspension arms, as described in Section 3, and the uncoupling of the height corrector from the bar. The anti-roll bar has a different number of splines at each end and can only be fitted the right way round.

10 Rear axle unit - removal

1   Position the rear of the car as described for the removal of the suspension arms, Section 3. Remove the battery earth strap from the negative terminal of the battery.
2   Remove the exhaust bracket and flexible supports. Remove the exhaust pipe and silencer. Empty the fuel tank, if necessary, and disconnect the filler pipe. Disconnect the manual control rods and remove the bolts securing the protective plate and the bolt holding the pipe bracket. Disconnect the union.
3   Slide the embellishers, on the rear shelf towards the rear to uncover the upper mounting bolts and remove the bolts. In the boot, lift the carpet at each side to give access to the suspension unit flexible mountings. Remove the inspection plate in the floor of the boot.
4   Place a jack with a cross beam under the suspension unit equidistant between the suspension cylinder spheres and the suspension arm swivels. Remove the nuts from the flexible mountings and with the jack lower the unit by no more than 100mm (4in) so that the pipes can be disconnected through the inspection plate aperture.
5   Remove the bolt securing the collar holding the pipes and disconnect the pipes from the corrector, the flexible pipe from the overflow return union, the flexible pipe from the tank gauge unit, the tank vent pipe, the pipe from the four-way union and the lead from the fuel gauge unit. Identify and note each pipe as it is disconnected.
6   Make a check that all pipes have been disconnected and lower the unit, ensuring that it does not foul any of the pipes, and remove it from under the car.

11 Rear axle unit - dismantling and reassembly

1   For removal and replacement of the component parts of the axle unit refer to the relevant Chapters and Sections of the manual describing the different procedures. Do not remove more than is necessary to rectify the fault which required the removal of the unit.
2   Make sure the flexible mountings are in good condition. If new travel stops are being fitted use soapy water on their pegs (do not use oil or grease).
3   Preset the automatic height control and set the position of the manual height control rod as described in Chapter 6, Sections 24 and 27.

12 Rear axle unit - replacement

1   Replacement of the axle unit is the reverse of the removal sequence. Fit new seals in the pipe connections and tighten the unions to 0.8 to 0.9 kg f m (6 to 6.5 lb f ft). Tighten the flexible mounting nuts to 3.4 kg f m (25 lb f ft).
2   Start the engine, tighten the pressure regulator bleed screw and check that there are no leaks at the pipe connections. Bleed the brakes as described in Chapter 8, Section 19. Adjust the suspension heights as described in Chapter 6, Section 26.

13 Suspension arm support tube - removal and replacement

A Citroen tool set 2072-T is required for the removal and replacement of the support tube.
1   Remove the suspension arm, as described in Section 3. Remove the inspection plate on the floor of the boot. Slacken by two or three turns the automatic height control bolt on the anti-roll bar so that

the bar can slide in the collar. The bolt must remain in place on the collar.

2   Measure the amount the support tube protrudes from the suspension unit for comparison with the new support tube. Push the anti-roll bar into the tube to allow the tool 2072-T to be fitted in the tube. Position the tool sleeve over the support tube and push the assembly into the support tube until the dogs of the tool can be heard to engage. Tighten on the extractor nut and remove the support tube from the housing.

3   Clean the support tube housing of the suspension unit. Fit the support tube in the suspension unit using the appropriate parts of tool 2072-T. The tightening torque of tool nut remains fairly high during the whole operation of fitting the support tube and becomes very high when the tube is in position.

4   Check that the tube protrudes approximately the same distance from the suspension unit as the one that was removed. Re-position the anti-roll bar. Fit the suspension arm and adjust the lateral play, as described in Sections 4 and 5.

5   Preset the automatic height control as described in Chapter 6, Section 24. Bleed the rear brakes. Fit the road wheels and lower the car. Check the rear height. Fit the inspection plate on the boot floor.

14 Wheel alignment check

1   Excessive tyre wear or vibration can be caused by incorrect wheel alignment, especially if the car has been involved in an accident or the rear suspension has been subjected to abnormal stress.

2   The wheel alignment is not adjustable and if it is found to be incorrect, consult your Citroen agent.

3   Position the car on level ground and set the suspension to the 'normal' road position. Check the tyre pressures. Using a suitable track gauge, of which there are various types available, check that the rear wheels are parallel to within 4mm (0.16in) toe-in to 4mm toe-out for cars produced until September 1973. For cars produced after that date the toe-in must be 0 to 2mm (0 to 0.08in).

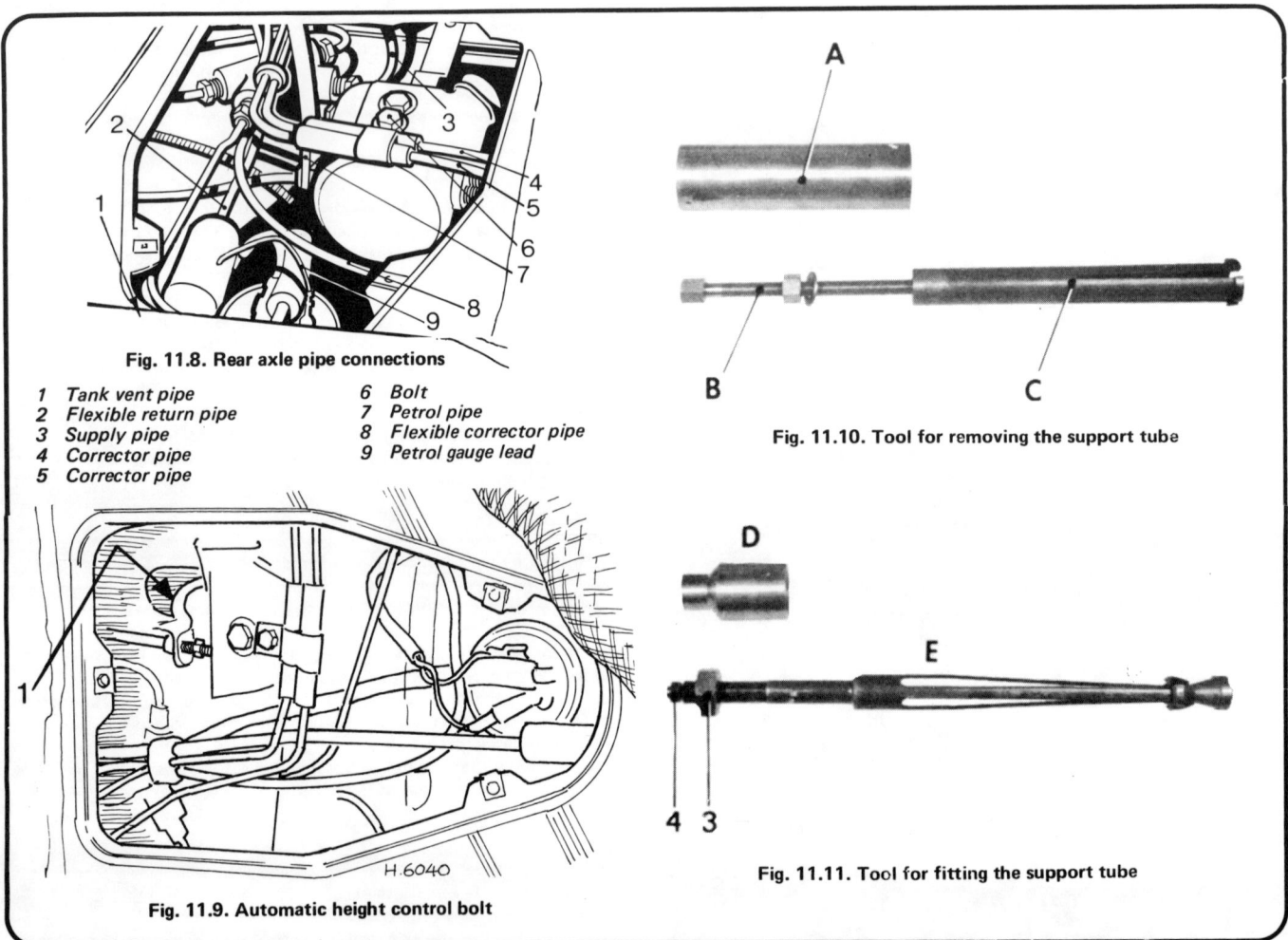

Fig. 11.8. Rear axle pipe connections

1   Tank vent pipe
2   Flexible return pipe
3   Supply pipe
4   Corrector pipe
5   Corrector pipe
6   Bolt
7   Petrol pipe
8   Flexible corrector pipe
9   Petrol gauge lead

Fig. 11.9. Automatic height control bolt

Fig. 11.10. Tool for removing the support tube

Fig. 11.11. Tool for fitting the support tube

15 Fault diagnosis - rear axle and suspension

Before diagnosing faults from the following chart, check that any irregularities are not caused by:

1 - Incorrect tyre pressures, 2 - Incorrect 'mix' of tyres, 3 - Defects in the braking system.

Symptom	Reason/s	Remedy
Vibration and rattles	Loose suspension cylinder	Tighten the cylinder retaining collar.
	Suspension cylinder ball and socket worn	Replace the cylinder.
	Suspension arm hub bearing worn	Renew the bearing.
	Worn hub bearing	Renew the bearing.
	Axle unit flexible mountings loose or defective	Tighten or renew as necessary.
	Pipe clips and brackets loose	Tighten as necessary.
	Wheel alignment incorrect	Check alignment, if confirmed consult your Citroen agent.
Suspension bottoming	Fault in the hydraulic system	Check through the hydraulic system.
	Defective suspension cylinder/s	Replace as necessary.
	Suspension heights set incorrectly	Readjust the suspension height.
Excessive tyre wear	Incorrect wheel alignment	Check wheel alignment.

Chapter 12 Bodywork and fittings

Contents

1 General description

The Citroen GS is of monocoque construction. The front and rear axle units being bolted directly to the rigid, sheet metal bodyshell. All the front panels are readily detachable for economy of replacement in the event of accident damage. Each one is rustproofed and dip-primed before being sprayed and stored.

The bumpers and all exterior bright parts are made of stainless steel.

The passenger rear doors are locked from the inside. The front doors are locked by key. The front doors can be locked by key, the key placed inside and the doors slam locked!

Protection of the body is by electropheric priming to ensure an even coat and penetration of the paint into every cavity and potential rust-trap.

2 Maintenance - bodywork exterior

1   The general condition of a car's bodywork is the one thing that significantly affects its value. Maintenance is easy but needs to be regular and particular. Neglect, particularly after minor damage, can lead quickly to further deterioration and costly repair bills. It is important also to keep watch on those parts of the car not immediately visible, for instance the underside, inside all the wheel arches and the lower part of the engine compartment.

2   The basic maintenance routine for the bodywork is washing - preferably with a lot of water, from a hose. This will remove all the loose solids which may have stuck to the car. It is important to flush these off in such a way as to prevent grit from scratching the finish.

The wheel arches and underbody need washing in the same way to remove any accumulated mud which will retain moisture and tend to encourage rust. Paradoxically enough, the best time to clean the underbody and wheel arches is in wet weather when the mud is thoroughly wet and soft. In very wet weather the underbody is usually cleaned of large accumulations automatically and this is a good time for inspection.

3   Periodically it is a good idea to have the whole of the underside of the car steam cleaned, engine compartment included, so that a thorough inspection can be carried out to see what minor repairs and renovations are necessary. Steam cleaning is available at many garages and is necessary for removal of accumulation of oily grime which sometimes is allowed to cake thick in certain areas near the engine, gearbox and back axle. If steam facilities are not available, there are one or two excellent grease solvents available which can be brush applied. The dirt can then be simply hosed off.

4   After washing paintwork, wipe off with a chamois leather to give an unspotted clear finish. A coat of clear protective wax polish will give added protection against chemical pollutants in the air. If the paintwork sheen has dulled or oxidised, use a cleaner/polish combination to restore the brilliance of the shine. This requires a little effort, but is usually caused because regular washing has been neglected. Always check that the door and ventilator opening drain holes and pipes are completely clear so that water can drain out. Bright work should be treated the same way as paintwork. Windscreens and windows can be kept clear of the smeary film which often appears if a little ammonia is added to the water. If they are scratched, a good rub with a proprietary metal polish will often clear them. Never use any form of wax or other body or chromium polish on glass.

3 Maintenance - upholstery and carpets

1   Mats and carpets should be brushed or vacuum cleaned regularly to keep them free of grit. If they are badly stained removed them from the car for scrubbing or sponging and make quite sure they are dry before replacement. Seats and interior trim panels can be kept clean by a wipe over with a damp cloth. If they do become stained (which can be more apparent on light coloured upholstery) use a little liquid detergent and a soft nail brush to scour the grime out of the grain of the material. Do not forget to keep the head lining clean in the same way as the upholstery. When using liquid cleaners inside the car do not over-wet the surfaces being cleaned. Excessive damp could get into the seams and padded interior causing stains, offensive odours or even rot. If the inside of the car gets wet accidentally it is worthwhile taking some trouble to dry it out properly, particularly where carpets are involved. **Do not** leave oil or electrical heaters inside the car for this purpose.

4 Minor body repairs

Repair of minor scratches in the car's bodywork

If the scratch is very superficial, and does not penetrate to the metal of the bodywork, repair is very simple. Lightly rub the area of the scratch with a paintwork renovator (eg; T-Cut), or a very fine cutting paste, to remove loose paint from the scratch and to clear the surrounding bodywork of wax polish. Rinse the area with clean water.

Apply touch-up paint to the scratch using a thin paint brush, continue to apply thin layers of paint until the surface of the paint in the scratch is level with the surrounding paintwork. Allow the new paint at least two weeks to harden; then, blend it into the surrounding paintwork by rubbing the paintwork, in the scratch area with a paint-work renovator (eg; T-Cut), or a very fine cutting paste. Finally apply wax polish.

An alternative to painting over the scratch is to use a paint transfer. Use the same preparation for the affected area; then simply pick a transfer of a suitable size to cover the scratch completely. Hold the transfer against the scratch and burnish its backing paper; the transfer will adhere to the paintwork, freeing itself from the backing paper at the same time. Polish the affected area to blend the transfer into the surrounding paintwork. Where the scratch has penetrated right through to the metal of the bodywork, causing the metal to rust, a different repair technique is required. Remove any loose rust from the bottom of the scratch with a penknife, then apply rust inhibiting paint (eg; Kurust) to prevent the formation of rust in the future. Using a rubber or nylon applicator fill the scratch with bodystopper paste. If required, this paste can be mixed with cellulose thinners to provide a very thin paste which is ideal for filling narrow scratches. Before the stopper-paste in the scratch hardens, wrap a piece of smooth cotton rag around the top of a finger. Dip the finger in cellulose thinners and then quickly sweep it across the surface of the stopper-paste in the scratch; this will ensure that the surface of the stopper-paste is slightly hollowed. The scratch can now be painted over as described earlier in this Section.

Repair of dents in the car's bodywork

When deep denting of the car's bodywork has taken place, the first task is to pull the dent out, until the affected bodywork almost attains its original shape. There is little point in trying to restore the original shape completely, as the metal in the damaged area will have stretched on impact and cannot be reshaped fully to its original contour. It is better to bring the level of the dent up to a point which is about 1/8 inch (3mm) below the level of the surrounding bodywork. In cases where the dent is very shallow anyway, it is not worth trying to pull it out at all.

If the underside of the dent is accessible, it can be hammered out gently from behind, using a mallet with a wooden or plastic head. Whilst doing this, hold a suitable block of wood firmly against the impact from the hammer blows and thus prevent a large area of bodywork from being 'belled-out'.

Should the dent be in a section of the bodywork which has a double skin or some other factor making it inaccessible from behind, a different technique is called for. Drill several small holes through the metal inside the dent area - particularly in the deeper sections. Then screw long self-tapping screws into the holes just sufficiently for them to gain a good purchase in the metal. Now the dent can be pulled out by pulling on the protruding heads of the screws with a pair of pliers.

The next stage of the repair is the removal of the paint from the damaged area, and from an inch or so of the surrounding 'sound' bodywork. This is accomplished most easily by using a wire brush or abrasive pad on a power drill, although it can be done just as effectively by hand using sheets of abrasive paper. To complete the preparations for filling, score the surface of the bare metal with a screwdriver or the tang of a file, or alternatively, drill small holes in the affected area. This will provide a really good 'key' for the filler paste.

To complete the repair see the Section on filling and respraying.

Repair of rust holes or gashes in the car's bodywork

Remove all paint from the affected area and from an inch or so of the surrounding 'sound' bodywork, using an abrasive pad or a wire brush on a power drill. If these are not available a few sheets of abrasive paper will do the job just as effectively. With the paint removed you will be able to gauge the severity of the corrosion and therefore decide whether to replace the whole panel (if this is possible) or to repair the affected area. Replacement body panels are not as expensive as most people think and it is often quicker and more satisfactory to fit a new panel than to attempt to repair large areas of corrosion.

Remove all fittings from the affected area except those which will act as a guide to the original shape of the damaged bodywork (eg; headlamp shells etc.,). Then, using tin snips or a hacksaw blade, remove all loose metal and any other metal badly affected by corrosion. Hammer the edges of the hole inwards in order to create a slight depression for the filler paste.

Wire brush the affected area to remove the powdery rust from the surface of the remaining metal. Paint the affected area with rust inhibiting paint (eg; Kurust); if the back of the rusted area is accessible treat this also.

Before filling can take place it will be necessary to block the hole

in some way. This can be achieved by the use of one of the following materials: Zinc gauze, Aluminium tape or Polyurethane foam.

Zinc gauze is probably the best material to use for a large hole. Cut a piece to the approximate size and shape of the hole to be filled, then position it in the hole so that its edges are below the level of the surrounding bodywork. It can be retained in position by several blobs of filler paste around its periphery.

Aluminium tape should be used for small or very narrow holes. Pull a piece off the roll and trim it to the approximate size and shape required, then pull off the backing paper (if used) and stick the tape over the hole; it can be overlapped if the thickness of one piece is insufficient. Burnish down the edges of the tape with the handle of a screwdriver or similar, to ensure that the tape is securely attached to the metal underneath.

Polyurethane foam is best used where the hole is situated in a section of bodywork of complex shape, backed by a small box section (eg; where the sill panel meets the rear wheel arch - most cars). The unusual mixing procedure for this foam is as follows: Put equal amounts of fluid from each of the two cans provided in the kit, into one container. Stir until the mixture begins to thicken, then quickly pour this mixture into the hole, and hold a piece of cardboard over the larger apertures. Almost immediately the polyurethane will begin to expand, gushing out of any small holes left unblocked. When the foam hardens it can be cut back to just below the level of the surrounding bodywork with a hacksaw blade.

Bodywork repairs - filling and respraying

Before using this Section, see the Sections on dent, deep scratch, rust hole, and gash repairs.

Many types of bodyfiller are available, but generally speaking those proprietary kits which contain a tin of filler paste and a tube of resin hardener (eg; Holts Cataloy) are best for this type of repair. A wide, flexible plastic or nylon applicator will be found invaluable for imparting a smooth and well contoured finish to the surface of the filler.

Mix up a little filler on a clean piece of card or board - use the hardener sparingly (follow the maker's instructions on the packet) otherwise the filler will set very rapidly.

Using the applicator, apply the filler paste to the prepared area; draw the applicator across the surface of the filler to achieve the correct contour and to level the filler surface. As soon as a contour that approximates the correct one is achieved, stop working the paste - if you carry on too long the paste will become sticky and begin to 'pick-up' on the applicator. Continue to add thin layers of filler paste at twenty-minute intervals until the level of the filler is just 'proud' of the surrounding bodywork.

Once the filler has hardened, excess can be removed using a Surform plane or Dreadnought file. From then on, progressively finer grades of abrasive paper should be used, starting with a 40 grade production paper and finishing with 400 grade 'wet or dry' paper. Always wrap the abrasive paper around a flat rubber, cork, or wooden block - otherwise the surface of the filler will not be completely flat. During the smoothing of the filler surface the 'wet-or-dry' paper should be periodically rinsed in water. This will ensure that a very smooth finish is imparted to the filler at the final stage.

At this stage the 'dent' should be surrounded by a ring of bare metal, which in turn should be encircled by the finely 'feathered' edge of the good paintwork. Rinse the repair area with clean water, until all of the dust produced by the rubbing-down operation is gone.

Spray the whole repair area with a light coat of grey primer - this will show up any imperfections in the surface of the filler. Repair these imperfections with fresh filler paste or bodystopper, and once more smooth the surface with abrasive paper. If bodystopper is used, it can be mixed with cellulose thinners to form a really thin paste which is ideal for filling small holes. Repeat this spray and repair procedure until you are satisfied that the surface of the filler, and the feathered edge of the paintwork are perfect. Clean the repair area with clean water and allow to dry fully.

The repair area is now ready for spraying. Paint spraying must be carried out in a warm, dry, windless and dust free atmosphere. This condition can be created artificially if you have access to a large indoor working area, but if you are forced to work in the open, you will have to pick your day very carefully. If you are working indoors, dousing the floor in the work area with water will 'lay' the dust which would otherwise be in the atmosphere. If the repair area is confined to one

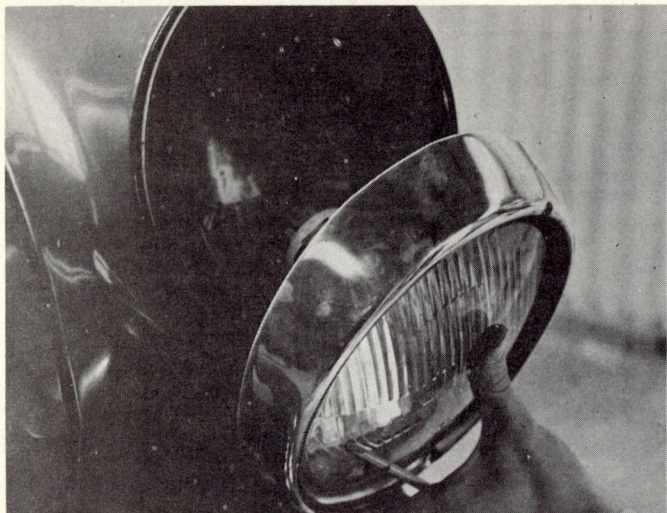

Typical example of rust damage to a body panel. Before starting ensure that you have all of the materials required to hand. The first task is to ...

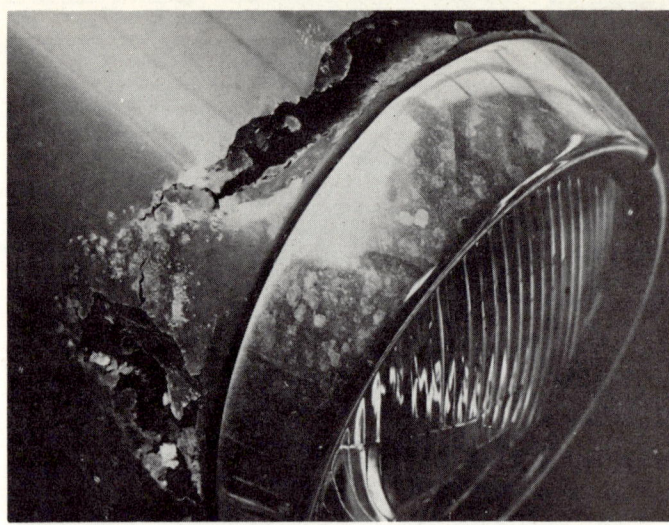

... remove body fittings from effected area, except those which can act as a guide to the original shape of the damaged bodywork - the headlamp shell in this case.

Remove all paint from the rusted area and from an inch or so of the adjoining 'sound' bodywork - use coarse abrasive paper or a power drill fitted with a wire brush or abrasive pad. Gently hammer in the edges of the hole to provide a hollow for the filler.

Before filling, the larger holes must be blocked off. Adhesive aluminium tape is one method; cut the tape to the required shape and size, peel off the backing strip (where used), position the tape over the hole and burnish to ensure adhesion.

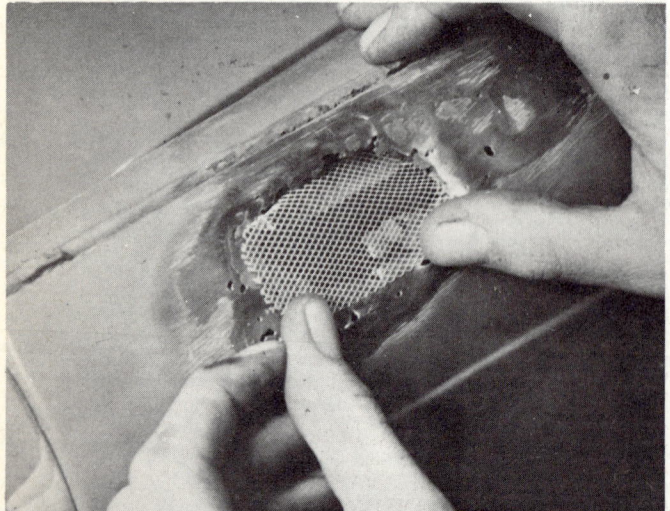

Alternatively, zinc gauze can be used. Cut a piece of the gauze to the required shape and size; position it in the hole below the level of the surrounding bodywork; then ...

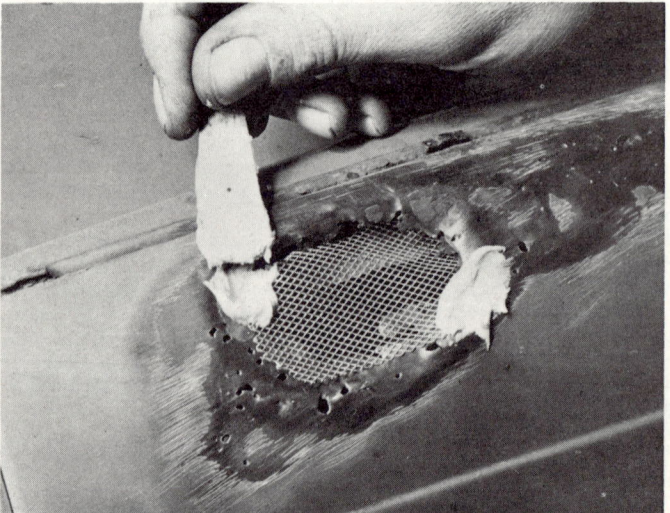

... secure in position by placing a few blobs of filler paste around its periphery. Alternatively, pop rivets or self-tapping screws can be used. Preparation for filling is now complete.

Mix filler and hardener according to manufacturer's instructions - avoid using too much hardener otherwise the filler will harden before you have a chance to work it.

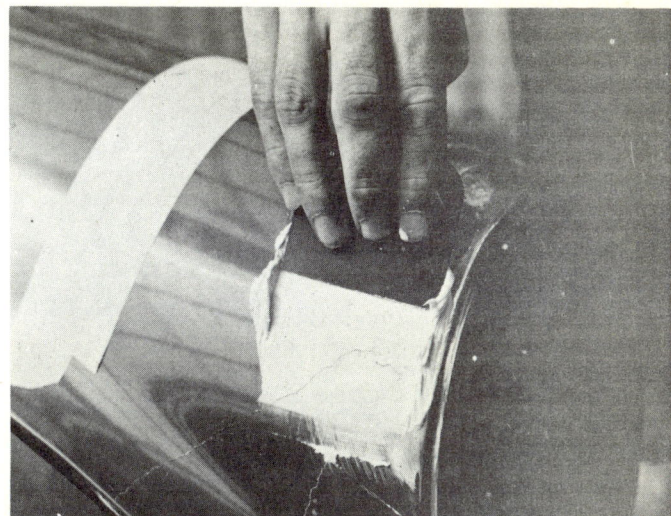

Apply the filler to the affected area with a flexible applicator - this will ensure a smooth finish. Apply thin layers of filler at 20 minute intervals, until the surface of the filler is just 'proud' of the surrounding bodywork. Then ...

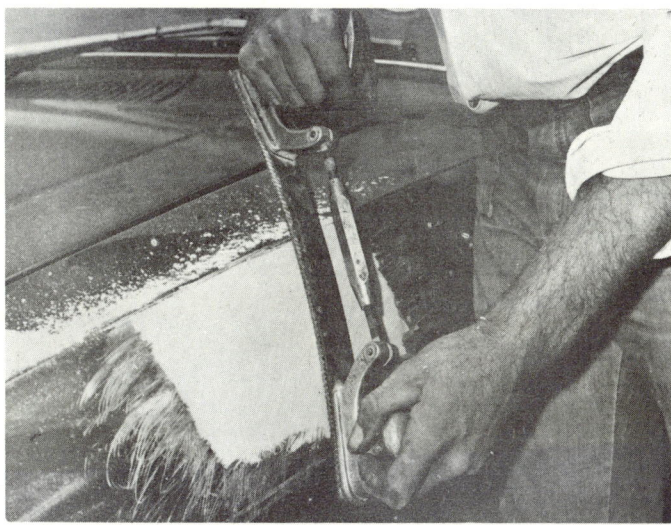

... remove excess filler and start shaping with a Surform plane or a Dreadnought file. Once an approximate contour has been obtained and the surface is relatively smooth, start using ...

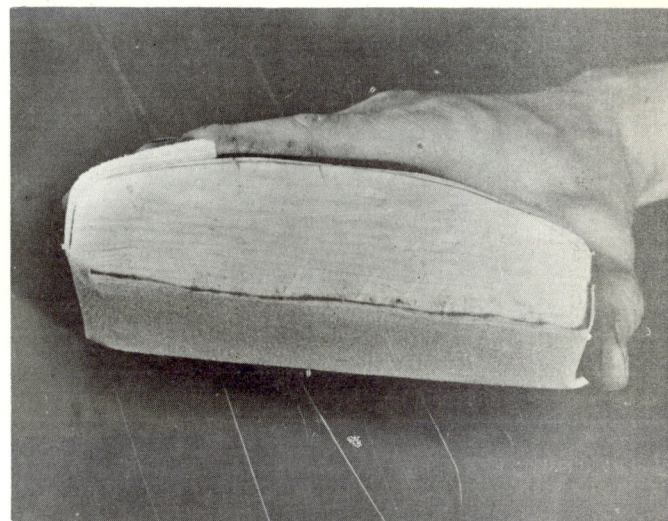

... abrasive paper. The paper should be wrapped around a flat wood, cork or rubber block - this will ensure that it imparts a smooth surface to the filler.

40 grit production paper is best to start with, then use progressively finer abrasive paper, finishing with 400 grade 'wet-or-dry'. When using 'wet-or-dry' paper, periodically rinse it in water ensuring also, that the work area is kept wet continuously.

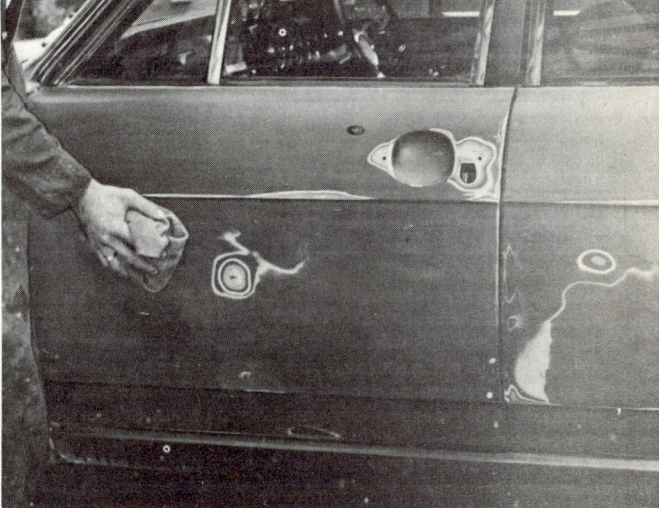

Rubbing-down is complete when the surface of the filler is really smooth and flat, and the edges of the surrounding paintwork are finely 'feathered'. Wash the area thoroughly with clean water and allow to dry before commencing re-spray.

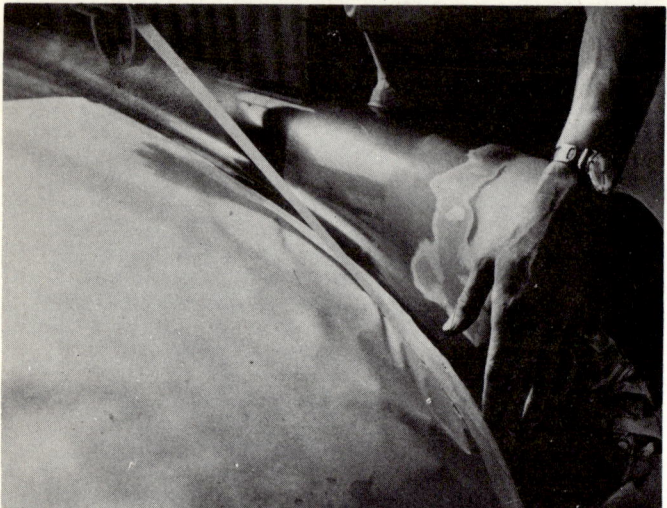

Firstly, mask off all adjoining panels and the fittings in the spray area. Ensure that the area to be sprayed is completely free of dust. Practice using an aerosol on a piece of waste metal sheet until the technique is mastered.

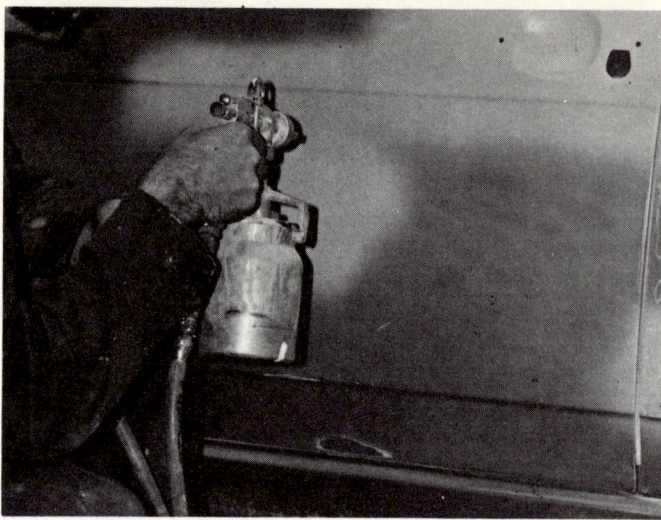

Spray the affected area with primer - apply several thin coats rather than one thick one. Start spraying in the centre of the repair area and then work outwards using a circular motion - in this way the paint will be evenly distributed.

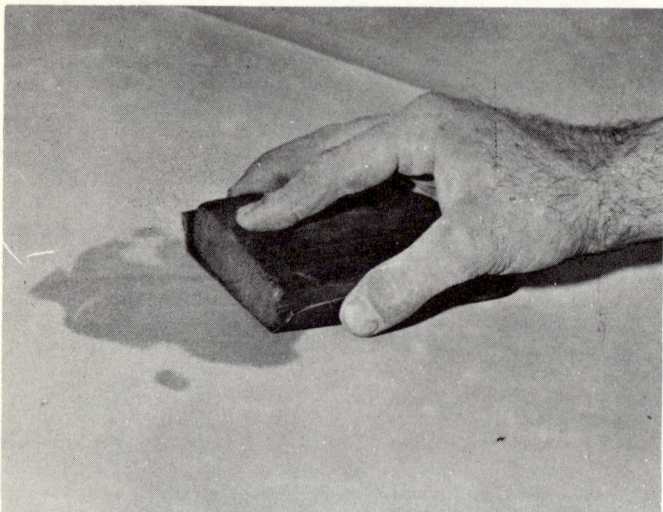

When the primer has dried inspect its surface for imperfections. Holes can be filled with filler paste or body-stopper, and lumps can be sanded smooth. Apply a further coat of primer, then 'flat' its surface with 400 grade 'wet-or-dry' paper.

Spray on the top coat, again building up the thickness with several thin coats of paint. Overspray onto the surrounding original paintwork to a depth of about five inches, applying a very thin coat at the outer edges.

Allow the paint two weeks, at least, to harden fully, then blend it into the surrounding original paintwork with a paint restorative compound or very fine cutting paste. Use wax polish to finish off.

The finished job should look like this. Remember, the quality of the completed work is directly proportional to the amount of time and effort expended at each stage of the preparation.

body panel, mask off the surrounding panels; this will help to minimise the effects of a slight mis-match in paint colours. Bodywork fittings (eg; chrome strips, door handles etc.,) will also need to be masked off. Use genuine masking tape and several thicknesses of newspaper for the masking operation.

Before commencing to spray, agitate the aerosol can thoroughly, then spray a test area (an old tin, or similar) until the technique is mastered. Cover the repair area with a thick coat of primer; the thickness should be built up using several thin layers of paint rather than one thick one. Using 400 grade 'wet or dry' paper, rub down the surface of the primer until it is really smooth. While doing this the work area should be thoroughly doused with water, and the 'wet or dry' paper periodically rinsed in water. Allow to dry before spraying on more paint.

Spray on the top coat, again building up the thickness by using several thin layers of paint. Start spraying in the centre of the repair area and then, using a circular motion, work outwards until the whole repair area and about 2 inches of the surrounding original paintwork is covered. Remove all masking material 10 to 15 minutes after spraying on the final coat of paint.

Allow the new paint at least 2 weeks to harden fully; then, using a paintwork renovator (eg; T-Cut) or a very fine cutting paste, blend the edges of the new paint into the existing paintwork. Finally, apply wax polish.

5 Major body repairs

Where serious damage has occurred or large areas need renewal due to neglect, it means certainly that completely new sections or panels will need welding in and this is best left to professionals. If the damage is due to impact it will also be necessary to completely check the alignment of the bodyshell structure. Due to the principle of construction the strength and shape of the whole car can be affected by damage to a part. In such instances the services of a Citroen agent with specialist checking jigs are essential. If a body is left misaligned it is first of all dangerous as the car will not handle properly and secondly uneven stresses will be imposed on the steering, engine and transmission, causing abnormal wear or complete failure. Tyre wear may also be excessive.

6 Maintenance - hinges and locks

1 Oil the hinges of the bonnet, boot and doors with a drop or two of light oil periodically. A good time is after the car has been washed.
2 Oil the bonnet release catch mechanism and striker pin periodically.
3 Do not over lubricate door latches and strikers. Normally a little oil on the rotary cam spindle is sufficient.

7 Door rattles - tracing and rectification

Door rattles are due either to loose hinges, worn or maladjusted catches or loose components of the locking mechanism or window winding assembly inside the door. Loose hinges can be detected by opening the door and trying to lift. Any play will be felt. Worn or badly adjusted catches can be found by pushing and pulling on the outside handle when the door is closed. Once again any play will be felt. Readjust or replace the striker plate as necessary. To check the window winding mechanism open the door and shake it with the window open and then closed. If rattles are heard the mechanism is loose or worn, rectify as necessary.

8 Front wing - removal and replacement

1 Jack-up the car and remove the relevant roadwheel.
2 With the front door open to give access to the upper and lower rear bracket attachment screws, loosen these screws by a few turns. Remove the lower screw from the cover at the rear of the wheel arch. Remove the screw, available through the circular aperture on the inner panel and

the two screws through the aperture at the front.
3 Remove the screws securing the wing to the upper edge of the inner panel and remove the front wing.
4 Replacement is the reverse of the removal sequence.

9 Bonnet catch - adjustment

1 Slacken the screw securing the safety catch to adjust the clearance; this must be between 0.5 and 2mm (0.02 and 0.08in).
2 Adjust the locking peg of the bonnet so that no play is present when attempting to lift the bonnet. Tighten the locking peg locknut.
3 Should the bonnet catch release cable break with the bonnet closed or should the bonnet be closed accidentally while the cable is disconnected, the catch can be released by inserting a wire hook into the gap existing between the headlamp, the front grille and the bonnet. Hook the end of the wire into the bonnet release and pull to operate the unlocking action. A light directed through the front grille will assist when hooking the wire on to the bonnet release.

10 Boot lid and tail door - removal and replacement

1 Disconnect the earth strap from the negative terminal of the battery. Disconnect the wiring from the number plate light and the interior light switch. Undo the wiring from the left-hand stay. Disconnect the lead from the heated rear window on the tail door.
2 Slacken the left-hand screw of each hinge by a few turns. Remove the right-hand screws. With the lid held firmly open, disconnect the bottom end of the stays and uncouple them by pushing them towards the centre of the car. Remove the screw from each hinge and lift off the lid. Collect any shims fitted and note to which hinge they are fitted.
3 Replacement is the reverse of the removal sequence. If necessary, adjust the thickness of shims behind the hinges. Adjust the lid lock by slackening the screws of the striker plate and positioning the striker plate so that when the boot lid is closed, there is no gap between the lid and its sealing strip. Tighten the securing screws.
4 The boot lid locks are fitted with two locking positions: 1st click is the safety catch; 2nd click is the locked position. Close the lid a few times to ensure that both these positions operate.

11 Windscreen glass - removal and replacement

1 When working on a windscreen or other glass fittings never use metal tools such as screwdrivers, hooks, etc., as these will scratch the glass and damage the rubber sealing strip and trimmings. Use the tapered down end of a piece of hard wood to replace these tools, 'A' in Fig. 12.3.
2 After taking off the windscreen wiper arms, loosen the rubber sealing strip by running a hard wood tool round the aperture to break the seal between the moulding and the body aperture. If the windscreen has been shattered cover the facia air vents and stick adhesive sheeting on the windscreen then pull sections away. If the glass is intact press on the glass from inside the car and remove it complete with the moulding. Remove the embellisher strips, if fitted.
3 Before fitting a windscreen ensure that the rubber surround is completely free from old sealant, glass fragments and has not hardened or cracked. Clean the opening in the body in contact with the moulding, ensuring that there are no burrs or unevenness as these could lead to breakage of the new glass.
4 Fit the cleaned moulding to the replacement glass. Refit the embellisher strips. Cut a piece of cord greater in length than the periphery of the glass and insert it into the body flange locating channel of the rubber moulding.
5 Apply a thin bead of sealant to the face of the rubber channel which will eventually mate with the body. With the help of an assistant offer the windscreen to the body aperture and pass the ends of the cord, previously fitted and located at the bottom centre, into the vehicle interior.
6 From outside the vehicle press the windscreen into place and at the same time have an assistant pulling the cords to engage the lip of the rubber moulding over the body flange.
7 Check that the moulding fits snugly inside and outside all the way round. Remove any excess sealant with a cloth soaked in white spirit.

12 Side window and rear window - removal and replacement

The procedure for removing and replacing side windows and rear windows is the same as described for the windscreen in Section 11. When removing a heated rear window disconnect the wiring.

13 Door - removal and replacement

1   Remove the two screws securing the door check to the door. Support the door in the open position and remove the screw securing the hinges to the pillar. Collect the shims, if fitted, from behind the hinge.
2   Replacement is the reverse of the removal sequence. The clearance between the door and the pillar is adjusted by the fitment of shims between the door hinge and the pillar. This clearance should be 6 ± 1 mm for the front door and $6 \pm \frac{2}{0.5}$ mm for the rear door.

14 Door windows and winding mechanism - removal and replacement

1   Although the shape of the windows in the front and rear doors are different, the winding mechanism is the same and the removal and replacement procedure is the same for all the doors.
2   Removal of the winding mechanism and window necessitates the removal of the door trim. Remove the door lock release by removing the two securing screws and unhooking them from the door lock release mechanism. Remove the window winding arm by pressing back the spring loaded retaining escutcheon and carefully levering the handle off the spindle. Remove the arm rest.
3   Remove the door trim panel by levering its spring retaining clips out of their holes with a thin-bladed screwdriver or similar tool.
4   Remove the four retaining screws of the winding gear and disengage the two locators from the guide at the lower edge of the glass. The winding gear can be withdrawn through the aperture in the door panel.
5   Lower the glass by hand as far as possible and remove the inner and outer embellishers. Remove the screw retaining the glass guide and remove the glass upwards and out through the top. Because of the shape of the front door glass it has to be tilted forward to get it up and out.
6   Replacement of the window, the winding mechanism and the door trim is the reverse of the removal sequence. The window winding handle should be fitted on its splines in the two o'clock position with the window closed.

15 Door lock - removal, replacement and adjustment

1   To remove the door lock mechanism it is necessary to remove the door trim as described in Section 14. Remove the lock assembly retaining screws, disconnect the remote control rods and withdraw the clock.
2   Replacement is the reverse of the removal sequence.
3   The door striker is secured by three screws to the pillar. Adjustment is made by fitting the required thickness of shims between the striker and the pillar to ensure correct engagement of the catch and adequate compression of the sealing strips. The rear edge of the front door and of the rear door must not stand proud by more than 2mm (0.08in).

16 Bumpers - removal and replacement

1   Remove the front grille by opening the bonnet and slackening the two bolts retaining the grille brackets. Pull the grille forward and lift out by pulling upwards.
2   Remove the screws retaining the bumper side pieces, two screws and one nut to each side piece. Remove the five screws from the top and the five screws from underneath which secure the bumper to the lower panel assembly.
3   The end pieces of the rear bumper are separate from the central part of the bumper, which is attached to the boot lid.
4   Open the boot lid and remove the three screws securing the rear of the side piece, the screw from underneath and the screw securing the front end from inside the car.
5   Remove the two screws at each end of the central bumper. Remove the two rubber joint sections and the two screws securing the bumper to the boot lid. Remove the bumper.
6   Replacement is the reverse of the removal sequence.

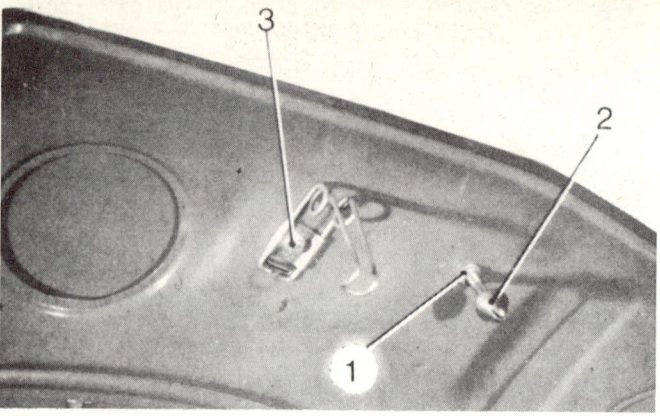

Fig. 12.1. Bonnet catch adjustment

1   Locknut   3   Safety catch
2   Locking peg

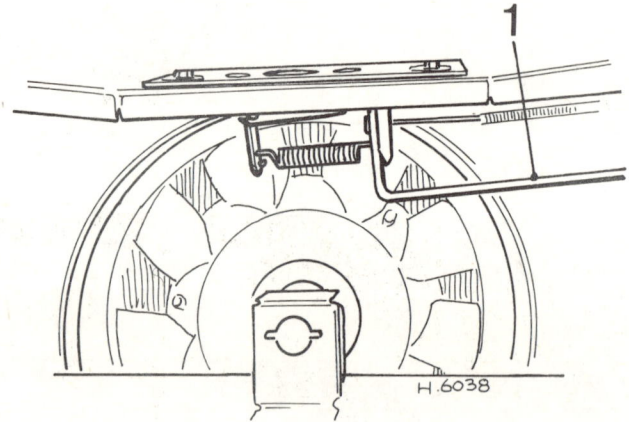

Fig. 12.2. Releasing the bonnet catch

1   Wire hook

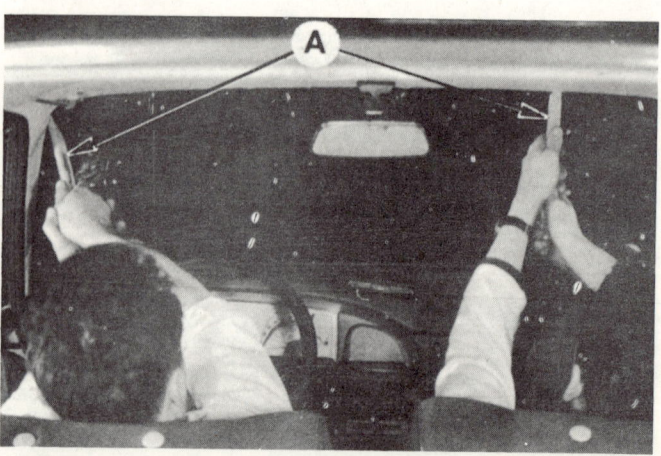

Fig. 12.3. Removing the windscreen

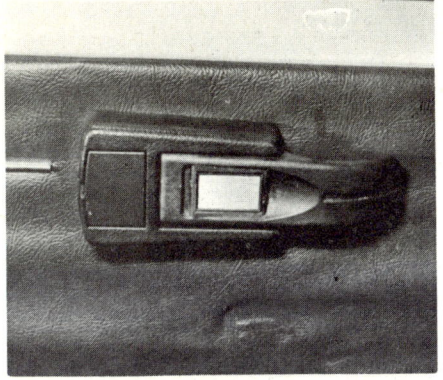

14.2 Door lock release lever

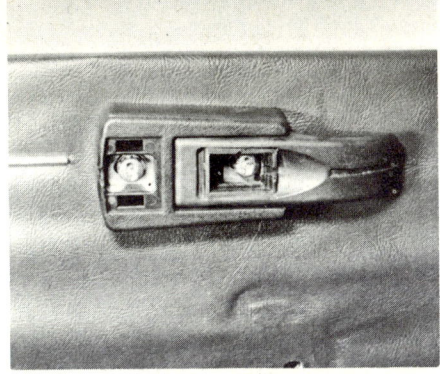

14.2a Door lock release retaining screws

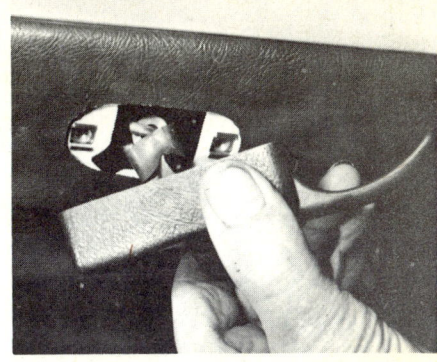

14.2b Unhooking the lock release from the lock control

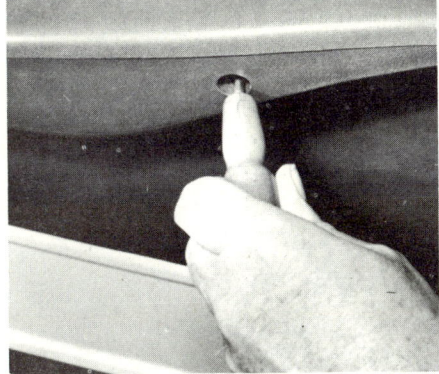

14.2c Removing the armrest retaining screws

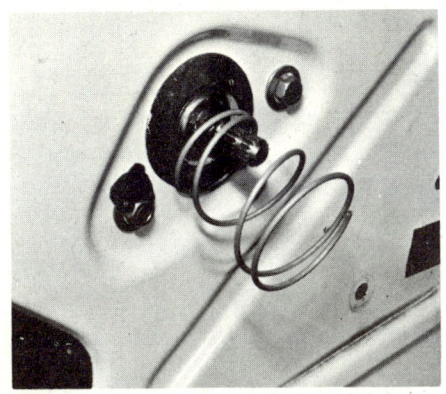

14.2d Window winding spindle and spring

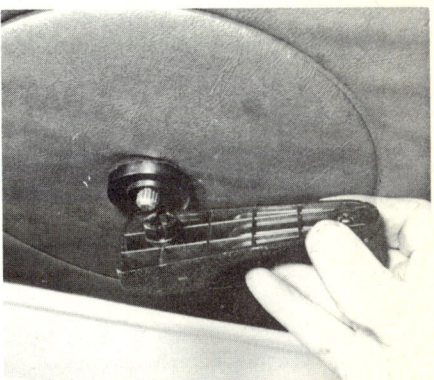

14.2e Fitting the window winding handle

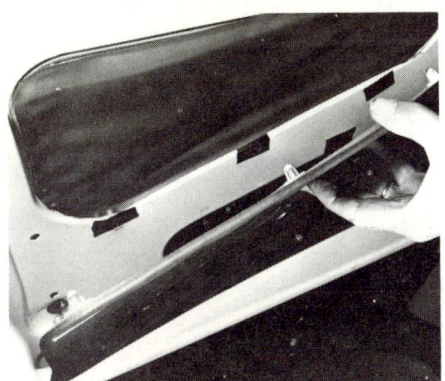

14.3 Removing the door trim panel

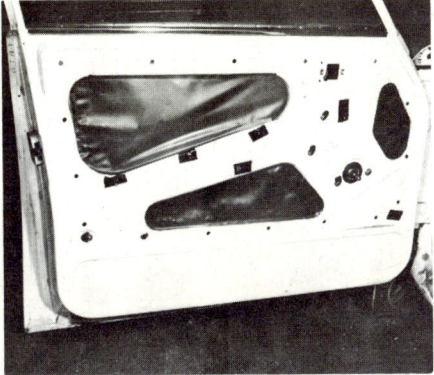

14.3a Door with trim removed

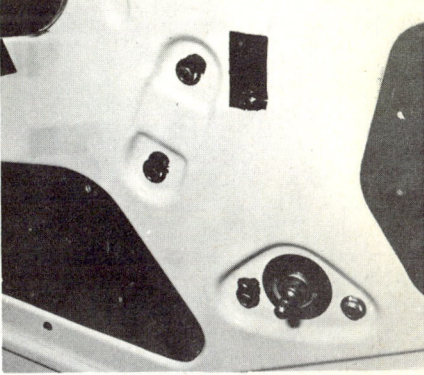

14.4 Window winding mechanism retaining screws

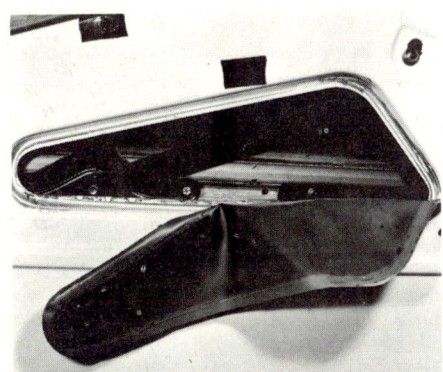

14.5 Door window lifting channel

Metric conversion tables

Inches	Decimals	Millimetres	Millimetres to Inches mm	Inches	Inches to Millimetres Inches	mm
1/64	0.015625	0.3969	0.01	0.00039	0.001	0.0254
1/32	0.03125	0.7937	0.02	0.00079	0.002	0.0508
3/64	0.046875	1.1906	0.03	0.00118	0.003	0.0762
1/16	0.0625	1.5875	0.04	0.00157	0.004	0.1016
5/64	0.078125	1.9844	0.05	0.00197	0.005	0.1270
3/32	0.09375	2.3812	0.06	0.00236	0.006	0.1524
7/64	0.109375	2.7781	0.07	0.00276	0.007	0.1778
1/8	0.125	3.1750	0.08	0.00315	0.008	0.2032
9/64	0.140625	3.5719	0.09	0.00354	0.009	0.2286
5/32	0.15625	3.9687	0.1	0.00394	0.01	0.254
11/64	0.171875	4.3656	0.2	0.00787	0.02	0.508
3/16	0.1875	4.7625	0.3	0.1181	0.03	0.762
13/64	0.203125	5.1594	0.4	0.01575	0.04	1.016
7/32	0.21875	5.5562	0.5	0.01969	0.05	1.270
15/64	0.234275	5.9531	0.6	0.02362	0.06	1.524
1/4	0.25	6.3500	0.7	0.02756	0.07	1.778
17/64	0.265625	6.7469	0.8	0.3150	0.08	2.032
9/32	0.28125	7.1437	0.9	0.03543	0.09	2.286
19/64	0.296875	7.5406	1	0.03937	0.1	2.54
5/16	0.3125	7.9375	2	0.07874	0.2	5.08
21/64	0.328125	8.3344	3	0.11811	0.3	7.62
11/32	0.34375	8.7312	4	0.15748	0.4	10.16
23/64	0.359375	9.1281	5	0.19685	0.5	12.70
3/8	0.375	9.5250	6	0.23622	0.6	15.24
25/64	0.390625	9.9219	7	0.27559	0.7	17.78
13/32	0.40625	10.3187	8	0.31496	0.8	20.32
27/64	0.421875	10.7156	9	0.35433	0.9	22.86
7/16	0.4375	11.1125	10	0.39270	1	25.4
29/64	0.453125	11.5094	11	0.43307	2	50.8
15/32	0.46875	11.9062	12	0.47244	3	76.2
31/64	0.484375	12.3031	13	0.51187	4	101.6
1/2	0.5	12.7000	14	0.55118	5	127.0
33/64	0.515625	13.0969	15	0.59055	6	152.4
17/32	0.53125	13.4937	16	0.62992	7	177.8
35/64	0.546875	13.8906	17	0.66929	8	203.2
9/16	0.5625	14.2875	18	0.70866	9	228.6
37/64	0.578125	14.6844	19	0.74803	10	254.0
19/32	0.59375	15.0812	20	0.78740	11	279.4
39/64	0.609375	15.4781	21	0.82677	12	304.8
5/8	0.625	15.8750	22	0.86614	13	330.2
41/64	0.640625	16.2719	23	0.90551	14	355.6
21/32	0.65625	16.6687	24	0.94488	15	381.0
43/64	0.671875	17.0656	25	0.98425	16	406.4
11/16	0.6875	17.4625	26	1.02362	17	431.8
45/64	0.703125	17.8594	27	1.06299	18	457.2
23/32	0.71875	18.2562	28	1.10236	19	482.6
47/64	0.734375	18.6531	29	1.14173	20	508.0
3/4	0.75	19.0500	30	1.18110	21	533.4
49/64	0.765625	19.4469	31	1.22047	22	558.8
25/32	0.78125	19.8437	32	1.25984	23	584.2
51/64	0.796875	20.2406	33	1.29921	24	609.6
13/16	0.8125	20.6375	34	1.33858	25	635.0
53/64	0.828125	21.0344	35	1.37795	26	660.4
27/32	0.84375	21.4312	36	1.41732	27	685.8
55/64	0.859375	21.8281	37	1.4567	28	711.2
7/8	0.875	22.2250	38	1.4961	29	736.6
57/64	0.890625	22.6219	39	1.5354	30	762.0
29/32	0.90625	23.0187	40	1.5748	31	787.4
59/64	0.921875	23.4156	41	1.6142	32	812.8
15/16	0.9375	23.8125	42	1.6535	33	838.2
61/64	0.953125	24.2094	43	1.6929	34	863.6
31/32	0.96875	24.6062	44	1.7323	35	889.0
63/64	0.984375	25.0031	45	1.7717	46	914.4

1   Imperial gallon = 8 Imp pints = 1.16 US gallons = 277.42 cu in = 4.5459 litres

1   US gallon = 4 US quarts = 0.862 Imp gallon = 231 cu in = 3.785 litres

1   Litre = 0.2199 Imp gallon = 0.2642 US gallon = 61.0253 cu in = 1000 cc

Miles to Kilometres		Kilometres to Miles	
1	1.61	1	0.62
2	3.22	2	1.24
3	4.83	3	1.86
4	6.44	4	2.49
5	8.05	5	3.11
6	9.66	6	3.73
7	11.27	7	4.35
8	12.88	8	4.97
9	14.48	9	5.59
10	16.09	10	6.21
20	32.19	20	12.43
30	48.28	30	18.64
40	64.37	40	24.85
50	80.47	50	31.07
60	96.56	60	37.28
70	112.65	70	43.50
80	128.75	80	49.71
90	144.84	90	55.92
100	160.93	100	62.14

lb f ft to Kg f m		Kg f m to lb f ft		lb f/in^2 : Kg f/cm^2		Kg f/cm^2 : lb f/in^2	
1	0.138	1	7.233	1	0.07	1	14.22
2	0.276	2	14.466	2	0.14	2	28.50
3	0.414	3	21.699	3	0.21	3	42.67
4	0.553	4	28.932	4	0.28	4	56.89
5	0.691	5	36.165	5	0.35	5	71.12
6	0.829	6	43.398	6	0.42	6	85.34
7	0.967	7	50.631	7	0.49	7	99.56
8	1.106	8	57.864	8	0.56	8	113.79
9	1.244	9	65.097	9	0.63	9	128.00
10	1.382	10	62.330	10	0.70	10	142.23
20	2.765	20	144.660	20	1.41	20	284.47
30	4.147	30	216.990	30	2.11	30	426.70

Index

Printed by
Haynes Publishing Group
Sparkford Yeovil Somerset
England